THE LIVES OF K̶E̶N̶ ̶W̶A̶L̶L̶I̶S̶

Engineer And Aviator *Extraordinaire*

To Ken Mulford

****

with Best Wishes

An informal biography of
WING COMMANDER KEN WALLIS
MBE, DEng(hc), PhD(hc), CEng, FRAeS, FSETP, FInsTA(hc),
RAF (Ret'd)

from Ken Wallis

by
Ian Hancock

Published by Ian Hancock
Norfolk & Suffolk Aviation Museum
The Street
Flixton, Nr. Bungay
Suffolk. NR35 1NZ

© Ian Hancock 2001 - 2008
ISBN 978-0-9541239-4-9

First published 2001
Revised second edition 2002
Revised third edition 2004
Revised fourth edition 2007
Reprinted with amendments 2008

All photographs copyright Ken Wallis
or author unless otherwise credited.
Cover photographs:
Top: Ken in his Austin 7 "Special" of 1938
Middle: Ken flying "Little Nellie"
Bottom: Ken on "Per Ardua III" in 1933

Printed by:
The Bidnall Press Ltd
37 Ellough Industrial Estate
Beccles, Suffolk.
NR34 7TD

Contents:

A debonair Ken Wallis in Royal Air Force uniform - 1941

Foreword

I first met Ken Wallis in the early 1990s through our mutual support of the Norfolk & Suffolk Aviation Museum at Flixton, near Bungay in Suffolk. This collection was formed in 1972, as one of the earliest volunteer, civilian bodies devoted to preserving aviation artefacts in the UK. Ken has been President of the Museum since June 1977 and is a regular attendee. He is present on many of the special event days held during the year and usually brings along an autogyro for visitors to inspect. On these occasions, he spends much of the day answering the many questions the raised about these exceptional and fairly rare aircraft. Ken is very popular with visitors and more often than not he is asked to pose for photographs and sign autograph books. All of which he does with customary good humour.

Ken is acknowledged internationally for his considerable expertise and innovation in the development of the modern autogyro but he describes himself simply as *'a self-taught aero-dynamist and engineer'*. This does not adequately describe him in my view but a suitably short description is hard to find to embrace the skills of inventor, engineer and aviator. His interests have been exceptionally varied over his adult years but his love of speedy transportation of one sort or another has ruled supreme, and for each type of conveyance tackled he has been almost consumed by the challenges encountered. His engineering skills and inventiveness, coupled with a single-mindedness to succeed, have been exercised in many ways as a result.

He is often invited to address interested audiences around the country and one day it can be a large gathering of learned members of a professional body, the next a small group of people in informal surroundings who have little or no knowledge of aviation matters, let alone the very special qualities of his aircraft. He is entirely at home with both assemblies, however, and can switch from making highly technical deliveries to telling humorous anecdotes without changing gear. Any income from these events he generously shares between the Norfolk & Suffolk Aviation Museum and the Wymondham branch of the Royal Air Forces' Association, being the President of both, along with the contents of the donation tins strategically placed in his hangar next to his beautiful Georgian home, Reymerston Hall, near Shipdham in Norfolk. Ken feels that this is a positive way he can do his bit for the museum he admires so much. Museum members would say, however, that simply having Ken "on board" is more than enough.

When I decided to write something about Ken, I had in mind a simple article of a few hundred words for the Museum's newsletter *The Flixton Flier* but my notes very quickly grew in volume and complexity to something well beyond the capacity of that vehicle. With so much material and fascinating stories emerging every time I asked Ken what I thought was a simple question, begging a short answer, it was obvious that something much more substantial was called for.

Having long been surprised that a professional biographer had failed to spot Ken as a worthy subject, I was grateful for the opportunity to be the first to be invited in 2001 to write something substantial about his life. Subsequent editions of this book are as a result of our regular chats and this fourth one (approaching 90,000 words!) embraces the fruits of many such occasions in the months up to April 2007. This may appear a strange way of producing a biography but Ken is a complex subject to study and there are many avenues ("lives") to explore so I would defy anyone capturing the whole story in a set period. Whilst enjoying a dry sherry with him in his study, he often produces the leading remark *"Did I ever mention ....?"* and I have found that such a comment by Ken can very easily produce several paragraphs or even another chapter!

Despite all of this, I hesitate to offer these pages as a definitive biography because I believe a lot of untapped material is still with Ken, and certainly a considerable amount would be of a very technical nature. To achieve something approaching a full biography would probably require me to be a house-guest for a very long time. I tend to feel, therefore, that I am offering the reader merely a collection of selected reflections! In recording them, however, I am particularly grateful to Ken for his invaluable help, supreme patience and the flowing explanations of technical detail that sometimes I can only just about grasp - not being a professional aviator or engineer. I have also been conscious of the need to balance the content so that it is interesting to both technical and non-technical readers. I sincerely hope this has been achieved.

In addition to being technically gifted, he is a warm and engaging person so it has not been hard work for me in any way - I hope that something of these qualities comes over in what I have written. Being in close contact with Ken on so many occasions has been a truly fascinating time for me but the most surprising discovery is the very small amount of personal time he has. A typical week can find him going to several different locations around the country to give talks and demonstrations, attending ceremonies, or entertaining an almost non-stop flow of visitors to his hangar at Reymerston. He certainly possesses unbelievable stamina and energy. Sadly for Ken, a little of the joy of life has now gone for he lost his very supportive and understanding wife Peggy in November 2003. A lovely lady in every way and very down-to-earth; I greatly miss chatting with her over lunch at the local country club on my visits to Reymerston.

In keeping with our mutual support for the Norfolk & Suffolk Aviation Museum, all profit from the sale of this book is donated to the museum - a Registered Charity with a policy of providing free admission. I very much hope that when you have read it you will want to spend a few hours viewing the vast collection of over 50 aircraft and 22,000 artefacts displayed on its large site at Flixton, near Bungay, with perhaps lunch at the adjacent and popular Buck Inn. Donation tins can be found in the hangars!

The Buck Inn has aviation links too, as it was the "watering-hole" of the 446th Bomb Group, USAAF - *"The Bungay Buckaroos"*- when based on the airfield opposite during World War II. Post-war, units of the Fleet Air Arm and then the Royal Air Force were stationed there so they also sampled its delights. It was once owned by Alan Breeze, the popular singer in the Billy Cotton Band Show on BBC radio (was that the Light programme?) but you will have to be of a certain age to remember the name. Sadly, his son was killed in a tractor accident on what is now part of the Museum grounds.

Sales of this book, both here and overseas, have exceeded my expectations, despite the modest amount of publicity I have managed to create. One of the most rewarding parts of the exercise has been to read the unsolicited remarks and tributes made about Ken by the many purchasers. It is very clear that those who have met him take away a treasured memory. One avid supporter is Edwin Shackleton of Bristol who, at 76, went into the Guinness Book of Records for having flown in more types of aircraft than anyone else. He had achieved 789 by the end of 2003, the 60th anniversary year of his first flight as an ATC cadet, and has even enjoyed the rare privilege of being taken aloft in Ken's two-seat G-BGGW. Those who have not actually met Ken still speak of him with great affection and considerable respect for "our local hero and national treasure".

When I produced the First Edition of this book I also offered a special Limited Edition run of 100 copies and, in doing so, may have logged a "first". Flown and signed philatelic covers are extremely popular, and quite valuable, but I have never come across the term *"flown & signed"* in connection with a

3

book. Ken willingly took the unbound covers aloft for me and copies of the completed book were later snapped up at great speed. We repeated the exercise with Edition 4 and copies are selling steadily.

Ken has had more than a fair share of experiences as you will go on to read but I shall not be surprised if yet another interesting chapter opens up in the near future. But that - as they say - is another story and perhaps will guarantee an enlarged Edition 5 sometime in the future!

Ian Hancock
Braintree, Essex
April 2007

With stocks of the ordinary edition very low by late summer, I decided to go for a reprint with some amendments rather than expand into Edition 5 at this point. The last eighteen months have been very busy for Ken as usual - he would rather not disappoint people by reducing his working pace, personal appearances or availability. During April 2008, he delivered "Little Nellie" to the Imperial War Museum in Lambeth to feature in the Ian Fleming Exhibition for a year. This left the problem, however, of maintaining fundraising activities for various organisations by appearing with James Bond's very famous autogyro so Ken set about restoring G-AVDH - this is the studio example where Sean Connery was "ruffled but not stirred" by a large fan during filming. The aircraft had been used for spares in past years but wears "G-ARZB" of course. The only difference between the two, to the untrained eye, is the lack of stickers on the nacelle, placed on the "flier" by enthusiastic "zappers" at airshows.

My own activities with the museum have also made it difficult to allocate time on a new edition. Our current project is to erect a new display building - The Ken Wallis Hall - at Flixton and I have been pursuing grants and donations; income from this book goes in that direction too. At a future date - a long time to come we hope - Ken's lifetime collection of aircraft, engines, other inventions, and achievements will come to Flixton for permanent display. In the meantime, we have plenty of things to occupy the space.

Ian Hancock
Braintree, Essex
September 2008

Introduction

Ken's dogged determination to succeed in everything he attempts was quite likely honed at an early age, for he developed a keen interest in his father's work building motor cycles when at school and, by eleven years of age, he had built his own machine. His early fascination for road vehicles led him to apply his growing skills in several directions during his teens but he could not have foreseen that his adult life would be dominated by the design and construction of machines for travel on land, sea and in the air, with many excursions into other fields.

The contents of the following pages flow with some difficulty, therefore, as I set out to record the main events in Ken's life, broadly in chronological order. Owing to his often simultaneous and quite varied interests, I decided to devote a number of separate chapters to specific areas of his research and interests, pursuing each of these subjects across the years of activity. The subjects were too important to be left out because they contributed to the overall picture and helped to shape Ken's life, but I felt it made easier reading to be covered in one place. In adopting this approach, though, I hope that it does not spoil the flow for the reader.

One noticeable thing about Ken is his motivation. Interests and skills would seem to have evolved either through the influence of, or contact with, members of his family, or were self-driven and developed often through experimentation to find solutions. He certainly has been attracted to engineering problems producing difficult challenges for him to solve. Finding a technical inefficiency within a mechanical operation has also given him the challenge to design and build an efficient replacement.

His impressive range of inventions and modifications has come about following often the route of: inspection and analysis to fully understand the task, or the purpose and application of a product; the competent design of a solution or modification, followed by uncomplicated manufacture for practical usage. Ken advocates that the application of common sense will often play a major part in producing simple solutions.

In the closing stages of writing this book, I scanned Ken's archive for photographs of his motorcars and was surprised to discover that there were several designs he had not mentioned. The most impressive find, however, was the collection of superb drawings featuring these vehicles from which he would have based construction. Not all his creations achieved life but the more I looked into his records the greater the find! At this point I was tempted to reconsider what I was doing in producing a single volume spanning his life to date. With so much material available it was almost possible to contemplate a series of books, one for each of his interests. Common sense prevailed, however, and I decided that I must resist the temptation for fear of never publishing anything at all. Clearly, Ken's talents include a considerable skill for sketching intricate and artistic designs that deserve to be reproduced in detail to illustrate the "breadth of his inventor's canvas." Being with Ken is simply a never-ending journey of discovery!

Outside of his many inventions and modifications employed during his service with the Royal Air Force, much of his other pioneering work seems not to have been pursued with any urgent view to mass manufacture and profit. Although he may not have vigorously pursued commercial exploitation, nor dwelt much upon the prospect of any great wealth from his inventions, he has achieved a comfortable journey and is very much at peace with the world.

Despite the different setbacks and disappointments over the years, Ken has also managed to lead an exciting life by most standards but, even with a long line of achievements behind him, he is certainly not resting upon his laurels. His conversation is always optimistic for the future and the part he can still play in it. Ken's credentials are impeccable and his mind still razor-sharp so I am confident that opportunities will occur in order that he may continue to make important contributions to the science of aviation in the years to come.

Ken is frequently in the news. Hardly a week goes by without him being heard on radio or appearing on television, particularly in the Anglia region, for one reason or another. This is in addition to making many personal appearances - often fundraising in support of a good cause. Articles also regularly appear in respected journals, usually reviewing his work on the development of the modern autogyro. Other times, it is to recount some of his flying experiences during World War II and into the jet age.

I do not think it is an over-statement to suggest that Ken has become something of a legend in his own lifetime but I leave you to make up your own mind.

His aviation ancestry

Aeronautical engineering has been Ken's main calling, of course, but he was not the first member of his family to develop an interest in this direction. The story really begins, therefore, over a decade before his birth, with his father (Horace Samuel Wallis) and his uncle (Percival Valentine Wallis) who worked for their father. He was born on Rangles Farm, March, Isle of Ely on the 22nd September 1855 and set up his wholesale grocery, and tea importing and blending business, at 12 St. Barnabas Road, Cambridge.

This particular trade unwittingly provided the brothers with the first nudge towards an interest in road transport. The Sunlight Soap Company introduced an exciting promotion for their product by offering a Rex motorcycle in exchange for a quantity of the coupons that accompanied bars of their soap. The number of coupons required would have been high, and the company may well have thought it unlikely to be achieved, but the challenge was not beyond the determined efforts of the brothers because, in 1902, they took delivery of the valuable machine.

An interest in motorcycle racing quickly developed and they began building their own machines around J.A.P. engines. They went on to race them with considerable success but purely as amateurs. Building such machines was relatively simple in those days; construction was by means of brazing frames made of steel tube and Chater Lea lugs, and assembling the wheels and belt rims from available spokes, hubs, etc.

Although the age was dominated by road transport developments it was obvious that the mechanically-minded brothers would take an interest in the growing number of reports on the feats achieved by the early "flying machines" and their fearless aviators. It went beyond a passing interest. In fact, their imagination was clearly seized by this new challenge for they approached their father seeking a loan of £300 and, with his support, set about the construction of their own flying machine late in 1908.

It is interesting to note that the American Wright brothers also ran a bicycle shop *(The Wright Cycle Co.)* in Dayton, Ohio, so perhaps the practical knowledge they gained made some small contribution to their design of the Wright Flyer. Their aircraft was made mostly from wood of course and Ken is sure that his father and uncle would have commented *"Who'd make a motorcycle of wood!"* The 17th Century ancestors of the Wright family came from Kelvedon in Essex.

Identifying a suitable engine was a priority and they were attracted to one displayed in The Paris Salon. This was a V-4 cylinder J.A.P. air-cooled petrol engine manufactured by J. A. Prestwich & Co. (Tottenham) in North London. It weighed 130lb and developed 25hp at 1,500 revolutions but could reach 2,000. An additional loan of £300 was negotiated with their father in order to purchase the motive power.

Their plan was quite simple: win the £1,000 prize offered by *The Daily Mail* newspaper for the first powered flight from England to France and thus make a nice profit. Being fiercely patriotic they had vowed that the machine would be of entirely British construction but, on discovering that their magneto was of German manufacture, they converted to coil ignition. Unfortunately, 37 year-old Louis Bleriot of France beat them to their goal when he made an uneventful crossing of the Channel on 25th July 1909.

Bleriot's achievement followed closely on the heels of the near successful attempt on the 19th July by 26 year-old Oxford graduate Hubert Latham; the non-stop flight had failed when his Antoinette IV monoplane suffered engine failure six miles from the French coast. Latham had been waiting for a calm morning to make a second attempt in a more powerful machine but, on the 25th, a friend conducted a pre-dawn inspection and judged that the weather was unsuitable for the epic flight so did not disturb Latham. The unexpected sound of Bleriot's engine rudely awoke members of Latham's camp at 4.40a.m. Frantic preparations followed but, by then, the earlier calm had been disrupted by a gusty breeze so Latham could only retire in tears.

If Latham had been the first to cross the Channel it would not have been heralded as a British triumph, however, as he was born in Paris of French and English parents. He had already made one aerial crossing by this time of course - in a balloon in 1905. It is interesting to note that the crossing of the Channel was not greeted universally as a triumph. The renowned writer H. G. Wells for one bemoaned the loss of England's *'invulnerability'*. He deplored the nation's lack of initiative and summed up the event as *'unpalatable to our national pride for this thing* (the aircraft) *was made abroad'*.

Another race at this time, to fly the first all-British aeroplane, was won by Alliot Verdon Roe on the 23rd July 1909 with his Roe 1 Triplane. He made three flights of 900 feet at a height of between 10 and 20 feet near his workshop within a railway arch on Lea Marshes, East London. The aircraft was powered by a 9 hp J.A.P. air-cooled engine. The flights could have been longer but he had not mastered a turn and was soon obstructed by trees.

Despite the disappointment, the two brothers continued their work and by May 1910 their *"Wallbro"* Monoplane was completed in its shed at the bottom of their garden. (The spelling with two "l"s denoted the involvement of two brothers). It was no ordinary machine by any means. In general appearance it resembled the Bleriot XI but was much more advanced for the time. The fuselage frame and wings were made from steel tubing - a construction method employed in their motorcycles; the ribs, plus leading and trailing edges, were made of spruce and ash; it also had conventional "ailerons" to give the pilot lateral stability. This was at a time when primitive wing warping was customarily employed so, in several ways, the design was revolutionary.

The monoplane was 25 feet long and had a wingspan of 30 feet - aerofoil surfaces being covered in cream-coloured "Pegamoid" aero cloth. An advert placed by this company in the July 1911 edition of *The Aero*, claimed the material was waterproof and contained no rubber. The company proudly referred to the fact that The Michelin Prize for the longest flight had been won by Mr. F. S. Cody, flying a biplane machine entirely covered with this material. The wooden, two-bladed adjustable tractor (propeller) for the *"Wallbro"* had been manufactured and patented by A.V. Roe of London and Manchester; the special tyres also came from them.

Neither brother had any pilot training but they embraced the challenge together with true Edwardian confidence. Early flights were therefore not without mishap. The local newspaper reported upon one incident on the 8th July as follows:

'A peculiar accident occurred to the new "Wallbro" all-British aeroplane, built by Messrs. P.V. and H.S. Wallis of Cambridge, on Monday during the course of a trial run, the machine turned a complete somersault and, although Mr. P.V. Wallis who was driving jumped to the ground unhurt, the aeroplane suffered considerable damage. The machine which is housed in a field near Abington, landed upside down. Messrs. Wallis Bros. are by no means disheartened through the accident'. Another account in the local press reported: 'It rose a few feet from the ground and sailed along for three or four yards and then came down nose first and turned a somersault, fortunately without injuring Mr. Wallis.'

9

We do not know what Wallis senior was thinking of all this activity at the time but Ken recalls his father telling him about a bill received requiring payment of £30 for damaged telephone wires. This would seem to indicate that the brothers had several hair-raising experiences, plus a very tolerant father. Despite these mishaps, their confidence was obviously high because a business card survives from the time that grandly introduced:

The "Wallbro" Aeroplane Co.,
Offices & Works: 12, St. Barnabas Rd., Cambridge.

An original poster from the time also survives (more of this later) and it proclaims that public viewing was provided at their home on the 16th and 17th May 1910, between the hours of 11 and 7.30. The text goes on, rather invitingly:

'All who have not seen a real full-sized Flying Machine should avail themselves of this opportunity.....the machine will be Staked Down and the Motor and Tractor SET RUNNING at 12 and 4 o'clock each day'.

Admission was 6d per person (under 3p today). The sum was not inconsiderable in those days of course so it would have been interesting to discover just how much was raised by the event.

With the aircraft and its shed, moved from the garden to a test field close to the Fulbourn/Teversham crossroads near Cambridge, the *"Wallbro"* was flown successfully on several occasions in 1910. It is not known if a complete circuit of the field was ever achieved but the area was not really ideal for flying. The high embankment running along the southwest side, upon which sat a disused railway line, was not ideally placed in view of the normal prevailing wind. The brothers "dossed down" in a tent within the shed, and there was a well nearby from which they drew water. They were quite disturbed one day to find a dead cat in the pail when hauling it up for another drink.

Sadly, the aircraft was wrecked beyond repair later that year but its demise did not come about through a flying mishap. The shed was blown down by a freak storm and this collapsed upon the aircraft.

Horace and Percy Wallis did not continue with their interest in aviation; the loss of the aircraft and the impatience of their father at their expensive deviation from the family business were no doubt compelling reasons. Two

10

NOTICE.

Messrs. WALLIS BROS., Builders of the

"*WALLBRO*" (ALL BRITISH)

AEROPLANE

(THE FIRST ONE BUILT IN CAMBRIDGE)

Having had numerous requests from friends and the Public to
see their New Monoplane, they have decided to place it

ON VIEW

To the Public on

WHIT-MONDAY & TUESDAY

May 16th and 17th, 1910, from 11 to 7.30 each day, at

12, ST. BARNABAS' ROAD,

CAMBRIDGE (Three Minutes from Station).

The Machine will be Staked Down and the Motor and Tractor
SET RUNNING at 12 and 4 o'clock each day.

All who have not seen a real full-sized Flying Machine should avail
themselves of this opportunity.

Admission = = 6d. each.

The original poster inviting spectators to view *"The Wallbro"*.

other brothers and two sisters made up the family but it is not recorded if they took any great interest in their brothers' exploits. A photograph does survive which shows brother Victor seated in the cockpit and handling the control wheel whilst smoking a large pipe but this was possibly a rare visit.

This particular record was very useful to Ken in later years when building the replica because it depicts the final arrangement of the control wheel mounted on a lever above a pitch axis, similar to most of the larger, modern aeroplanes. In some pictures of the *"Wallbro"* there is a wheel on either side of the cockpit and Ken had no knowledge of how these worked but was glad that he did not have to fly the replica in this format. In some photographs taken at the early stages of the build, a more usual control wheel can be seen but it was not mounted on a conventional pitch lever.

Ken has a good collection of photographs of the aircraft taken at different times and a selection now follows, charting the birth and demise of *"The Wallbro"* from 1909 to 1910.

The "aerodrome" site in the middle of a recent photograph.

Top: Taken from the first floor "office" (bedroom) window. It shows the general construction, with the "tractor" resting on the ground beside it.
Bottom: Taken at ground level. Horace Wallis is seen holding the "tractor" and youngest brother Garnet sits in the cockpit.

Top: "Flying machine delivery team" - Horace Wallis "piloting" the horse.
Bottom: The hangar/shed, originally at St. Barnabas Road, re-erected on the "aerodrome" with sleeping tent on the right.

14

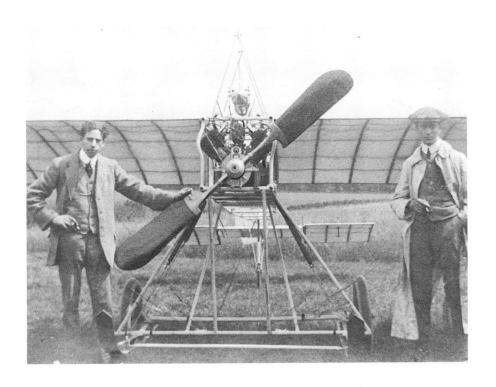

Top: Horace and Percival Wallis stand proudly with *"The Wallbro"*.
Bottom: With other members of the family and their tricar motorcycles.
Both taken at the "aerodrome".

The last views of the *"Wallbro"* late in 1910, with Wallis senior inspecting the wrecked aeroplane and shed. The site has been pinpointed and it is planned to scan the area with a metal detector in the hope of finding a few small components

Fresh excitement was soon to loom for the brothers when large-scale military manoeuvres took place in East Anglia in 1911. The Army did not have any skilled motorcyclists to act as despatch riders in this "modern" form of warfare so called for civilians in the role. Horace and Percival jumped at the opportunity to escape the family business and volunteered. Being patriotic their father agreed to their absence from the business.

The experience obviously had a profound affect upon them because at the end of these exercises they both went into the motor, or motorcycle and cycle business; Percival with motors in Cambridge (later to run the Central and Tivoli cinemas there) and Horace to Ely (Walbro Cycle & Motorcycle) with brother Garnet, although the latter was soon to be "bought out". Percival and Horace were involved in the International Speed Trials of 1912 in Holland, with Horace driving one of the quite new Morgan three-wheelers.

When World War I arrived Horace was found to be medically unfit to serve owing to a heart condition but still made an important contribution to the war effort by making welded steel fittings as a sub-contractor of Boulton & Paul, a local aircraft manufacturer. Ken can recall seeing a cabinet containing examples or patterns of metal wing boxes for fitting around the wing spars of biplanes, and some spars on the beams of the converted barn where the welding was undertaken, using acetylene gas made from carbide and water. It would appear that this was the last contact Ken's ancestors had with flying machines and suchlike. I close this chapter with a wonderful "action shot" of the *"Wallbro"*, sometime in 1910, being restrained whilst the engine is "run up". The Union Jack flies proudly from the roof of the "hangar".

From school days to the 1930s

Kenneth Horatio Wallis was born in Ely on the 26th April 1916. He was educated at The King's School, Ely, which traces its origins back for more than 1,000 years. Boys have been educated there since 970 AD, boasting Edward the Confessor, King and Saint (1003-1066) as a former pupil.

Ken can remember being asked to write an essay under the title "My Ambition In Life". His response was somewhat prophetic for he wrote *'I want to break a World Record with a speed boat'!* During his pupil years he was content to think that he would one day join the family business in motorcycles and cycles, and also have the opportunity to explore the new phenomenon of radio which was then in its early days. The latter interest had developed after his father erected a mast, sixty feet high, in the back garden in 1923. His father still had some involvement with motorcycle racing so Ken was often taken to see these popular events.

His earliest aviation treat took place in the mid to late 1920s with a visit to the RNAS Cardington in Bedfordshire to view the R101 airship being built. He remembers going there on a number of occasions and climbing the mooring mast with his father on the last visit for a closer look. Within a few months, early in October 1930, it would crash at Beauvais in France with 48 of the 54 crew and passengers on board losing their lives. He was also taken to see some of the early air shows when aviation was still very much in the "barnstorming" age, and was enthralled to see people bravely walking along the wings of aircraft in flight.

Around 1927, Ken built his first motorcycle with the fuel tank and general design coming from one of his father's racers. It had direct belt drive and he describes the start up procedure as having been fairly basic: *"run and jump on"*! He recalls having fallen from it on many occasions before he went on the roads as an experienced motorcyclist when aged fourteen.

When Ken was quite young his father gave him a powerful German air rifle. This was a good idea, as it taught him the necessary discipline in safe shooting. Target practice soon led to some reduction in the local sparrow and starling population but, as usual, he was interested in the technicalities of the weapon: a powerful spring, driving a piston compressing air until it broke free the pellet in the breech, accelerating it down the barrel and achieving a velocity sufficient to bury it quite deeply in a plank of wood.

18

Ken wondered what would happen if, without the pellet in the breech, sufficient pressure of a thumb at the end of the barrel would hold the piston back against the pressure of the spring when the trigger was pulled. There was only one way to find out! He duly prepared the airgun for firing without the pellet. Then, pressing very hard on the opening of the barrel, with the butt pushed into the ground, he released the trigger. The piston moved forward under pressure from the spring but soon came to rest against the pressure of the air compressed by it. He then slightly reduced the pressure of his right thumb against the end of the barrel, allowing the air to escape under control, and the piston then move gently to the end of the barrel.

After trying this successfully a few times, the next logical step would be to do the same experiment with a pellet in the breech. Obviously, it could be held back if the piston providing the compressed air to propel it could be prevented from accelerating. Ken duly loaded the air rifle and again pressed his right thumb against the end of the barrel with the butt hard into the ground. The rifle did not propel the pellet into his thumb and as he continuously released the pressure it did indeed gently progress up the barrel until it came in contact with his thumb, then dropped to the ground.

He saw this as a good trick to impress his friends and was soon demonstrating first the loading of the rifle with a pellet and firing it deeply into a piece of wood. Then, when reloaded, following the rehearsed procedure and even inviting a spectator to pull the trigger. Some were reluctant to oblige so then he had to do it himself. He recalls that he must have become a little complacent, for the next time he did not concentrate sufficiently upon pressing his thumb to the barrel. It fired as normal but the pellet buried itself deeply into his thumb and he still has a scar to show for it. He did not try that particular trick again.

Undeterred by the injury, he thought up another trick and this one he considered to be potentially less dangerous. It entailed firing pellets that would explode on hitting a hard surface! A small drilling was made in the solid lead nose of the pellet and explosive centres from toy caps were placed inside. The nose was then burred over to retain them in position. When fired against a hard object they made an impressive explosion but Ken suspected that it would only improve lethality against a starling or rook if the pellet hit bone and initiated the caps. He also adapted a bicycle valve to be a tiny gun that was able to fire metal gramophone needles through a glass jam jar. These experiments were obviously an early sign of things to come!

19

Ken's father was always interested in the latest technology and was quickly into the radio business when 2LO (Ken thinks this was the name of the station) was set up around 1923. A 60 feet tall steel mast, in three parts telescoping together, was erected at the end of the garden, with a long aerial extending to the house. He recalls that much of the "works" of the early radios were visible on the big black "ebonite" board, being the days of thermionic valves, with "accumulators" for the filaments and high tension and grid batteries. The black "ebonite" board, a form of very early plastic, was wonderful stuff and Ken used this material much later in many ways.

Ken's father had also been interested in the very early stages of television, which started transmitting successfully from Alexandra Palace somewhere around 1936; Ken recalls that reception was quite good in Ely. Some years prior to this, his father had tried an electro-mechanical television system - possibly known as *The Baird* after John Logie Baird the pioneer of television - but without any success. He also had a recording system for early radio-transmitted, still pictures. Paper was wrapped around a clockwork-driven cylinder, which turned slowly - much like the old cylinder gramophones. A needle moved slowly along the cylinder and electrical impulses in it caused short and longer black marks on the specially-treated paper – thus gradually making up a picture from the "dots and dashes". Ken still has this curious apparatus, which must represent the earliest way to send pictures by radio.

In the late twenties, Ken also became interested in radio and started to build his own crystal sets, winding the coils and rubbing off the insulation for a slider to move along the windings to select frequency. In view of the quality of reception, he said it was usual to feel that there must be a slightly better place on the crystal that the "cat's whisker" had not found. He made several sets, including one inside a walnut shell.

Inquisitiveness led him to acquire a primitive spark transmitter radio around 1931, which he describes as *"all very bitty"* and thinks it may have been of World War I vintage. He rigged up a coil and trembler that gave a big spark between two large steel balls, and remembers going up to the loft in his house at 45a Cambridge Road, Ely, to rig up some wire, hanging from the rafters, to act as an aerial. He then made up the spark-gap arrangement for the coil and hooked on an "accumulator", as wet batteries were called in those days.

His friends, the Runciman brothers with whom he attended the King's School, lived on a farm in West End, Ely, about half a mile away. He told them to turn their "wireless set" on and listen while he went back home. Not knowing Morse Code, he sent a string of mixed-up dots and dashes on the button. Not only was this transmission picked up by the brothers, it caused some alarm in official quarters being received by, or reported to, The General Post Office. Apparently, the illicit transmissions covered about all the wavelengths then in use. The source was soon traced and officers of the G.P.O. called at his home but no doubt there was some relief that they were found not to have been sent by a spy using a secret code. Needless to say, Ken did not experiment further. Much later, when joining his father's business, he was required to attend courses in radio at Pye in Cambridge and E. K. Cole at Southend.

It did not stop him being *'particularly naughty'* though (Ken's description), around the same time, in taking a package containing an old alarm clock to the Ely Post Office and posting it to himself. At this time there was a scare over bombs being posted by the IRA, or whatever, employing clockwork devices to detonate at a prescribed time. Young Ken was somewhat surprised that his package, ticking loudly, was accepted by the clerk. It was still ticking healthily on delivery to his home by an unsuspecting postman!

School was also a good place to make a name for himself. Around the age of 13 he recalls sitting in the back row of the "Remove" classroom in the very old school. He was always interested in chemistry and physics and had somehow "acquired" a piece of (he thinks) sodium from the school laboratory during a chemistry class. The pupils were sat at individual desks and these had internal inkwells. Ken's inkwell happened to be dry so he put the lump of sodium inside it.

As the lesson progressed, and his mind wandered from the subject, he started to "tease" the sodium by dipping his pen-nib into a full inkwell and then shaking a drop of ink onto it within the well. Only a little "fizz" resulted, much to the amusement of a fellow pupil, Billy Friend, on his right. (Billy was to become one of the first to serve in the Long Range Desert Group in North Africa during World War II. They met again when Billy was in the scrap business at Watton, not far from Reymerston. Some of Ken's equipment, such as the engine-lifting rig used for installing engines into his autogyros, owes something to Billy. The large vertical tubes were in fact rocket motor tubes from 64lb Rockets, as fired by Typhoon aircraft).

Ken kept shaking the drops of ink onto the sodium without the master noticing the fizzing noise this produced but he reckons the sodium must then have become irritated by the "teasing", for there was a sudden explosion that shattered the inkwell and caused lasting damage to the desk. Needless to say, Ken was in serious trouble and required to attend the "Court" held by the Headmaster - the Reverend Canon T J Kirkland - on three days a week. Ken was sentenced to, and duly received, "six of the best" with a strong cane. The force of the cane across the open palm left blue marks and a line of blood. Another pupil survivor of the incident recalls that the explosion left young Wallis somewhat blackened; so too several of his classmates. The master was very angry, having probably received quite a shock, and had dragged Ken from the wreckage of the desk by his ear. In Ken's own words *"I must have been a menace in those days"*.

Having grown up with the smell of castor oil from racing engines (a liquid most young boys of that era avoided at all cost owing to its unpopular use as a laxative), and been thrilled by rides in "Aero Morgan" three-wheelers, he felt it was entirely natural that he would one day work alongside his father at the Walbro Cycle & Motor Works, at Lynn Road in Ely. (The spelling here deliberately uses only one "l" in the name to denote the one brother.) Another smell, however, produced a lifetime aversion to fish! Lunch at King's School on a Friday was always fish and its preparation pervaded the corridors and classrooms from dawn. Whilst he had little choice when at school, he has refused to consume it by choice throughout adulthood.

On leaving school in 1932, he was already quite knowledgeable about cycles and motorcycles; he could make wheels from hubs, rims and spokes, and strip and assemble engines. These skills were gained "hands on" because of his genuine interest in all things mechanical, rather than through any family pressures. Ken happily settled down in the family's motorcycle and cycle business and steadily gained a lot of practical knowledge.

Although his engineering skills are no doubt due to his father's early guidance, his ability and patience to pay close attention to detail very likely came from his ex-schoolteacher mother. He recalls that she was meticulous in everything she did and very accomplished with the intricacies of needlework and tapestry, plus portrait photography to a very high standard - this is touched upon later in the book.

The Walbro Cycle and Motor Works.

The Firm for QUALITY and SERVICE.

Top: A proud Ken, around 11 years of age, with his first motorcycle.
Bottom: A sketch of the Works at Ely by Ken's father.

The *"Town And Country News"* publication for 22 August 1930 included a detailed write-up on the family business (Walbro Cycle and Motor Co.), being described as *"an extremely flourishing cycle and motor works at Ely"*. It had been set up by Ken's father Horace and his brother Garnet in 1912/1913. (Garnet later sold his share to Horace. Garnet and the eldest brother Victor had not been involved in the *Wallbro* monoplane venture). Annual production levels according to the article were running at around 175-200 motorcycles and 300-400 bicycles, although Ken thinks this might be a bit over-the-top. They were made up from "bought-in" parts and Ken had become very adept at making up wheels from their separate components. Frames were made up from steel tube and brazed lug joints. It further reported that, through steady expansion, a special section had been created for the sale of electrical, wireless and gramophone requisites.

Horace Wallis attributed this success to personal attention to the needs of customers, and also advertising. The article went on to call for *'special attention to the window-dressing'*, as it had attracted prizes in a number of competitions. As the business was based in Ely the choice of the cathedral as a trademark was obvious and Ken managed to find an old transfer of it, as applied to all their cycles. Although the *"Walbro"* bicycles were quite well finished, Ken is surprised that their manufacturing business did so well, considering that they were also agents for all the major companies such as Raleigh; also Morgan and B.S.A three-wheeled motorcars. Ken loved the "Aero" Morgan as these were *"very lively"* in his words.

The company trademark as a transfer.

Raleigh three-wheelers were also popular around this time - they were quite sporty-looking, with long bonnets and one wheel at the front. Ken received his first fine for speeding in one around 1934 - it cost him 30 shillings (£1.50 today). On one occasion, he had to collect a broken-down motorcycle in a three-wheel van and found it too long to fit inside. He loaded it but had to leave a fair amount protruding out of the rear doors. He set off and all was fine until he went over a bump in the road - the front wheel left the road and rose straight up into the air. Managing to stop, Ken pushed the nose of the vehicle to the ground again and proceeded but with great caution.

The Walbro business also provided a very useful little booklet in the form of the "Motorists Route Guide". It gave distances between locations, lighting up variations around the country (no longer practiced of course), licensing information, and other helpful items. It included some adverts, reproduced on the next page.

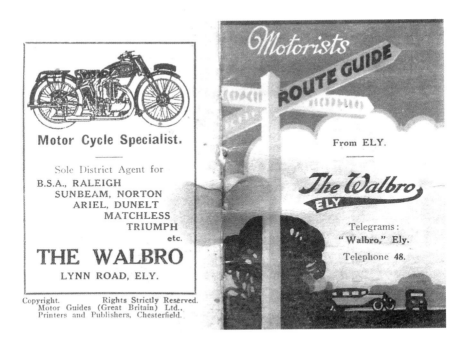

The cover of the booklet

Over

200 BICYCLES

in stock at

THE WALBRO

ELY.

Call and Inspect them.

You can Pay as you Ride.

OFFICIAL

LUCAS

C·A·V-ROTAX

GENUINE SPARES

STOCKIST

BATTERIES

for any makes of cars in stock.

Battery Repair Service

All Types of Electrical and Radio Goods in Stock.

THE WALBRO

LYNN ROAD, ELY.

LIGHTING-UP VARIATIONS from London time in minutes.
ADD to London Time if in Light Type; SUBTRACT if Heavy.

DISTRICT.	Jan.	Feb.	Mr.	Apl.	May	Jn.	July	Aug.	Spt.	Oct.	Nov.	Dec.
Bedford ...	1	1	2	3	5	6	6	4	2	1	0	2
Bradford ...	3	2	6	12	18	22	19	14	8	3	2	6
Birmingham	4	6	8	10	12	14	13	11	8	6	4	2
Brighton ...	4	3	1	0	2	3	3	1	1	2	4	5
Bristol ...	10	10	10	10	10	10	10	10	10	10	10	10
Cambridge ...	3	1	0	1	3	4	4	2	0	1	2	4
Canterbury ...	3	4	4	4	5	5	5	5	4	4	3	3
Carlisle ...	4	4	11	20	28	34	30	23	14	5	2	8
Chester ...	5	8	12	16	20	23	21	17	13	9	5	2
Colchester ...	6	5	4	3	2	1	·1	3	4	5	6	7
Coventry ...	2	4	6	8	10	12	11	9	6	4	2	0
Darlington ...	8	1	5	13	20	25	22	16	8	1	6	11
Derby ...	0	3	6	9	12	15	14	10	7	4	1	2
Dorchester ...	13	12	10	8	6	5	6	8	10	12	13	14
Exeter ...	17	16	14	12	10	9	10	12	14	16	17	18
Falmouth ...	25	23	20	17	14	12	14	16	20	23	25	27
Gloucester ...	8	8	9	10	10	11	11	10	9	8	8	7
Hereford ...	9	10	11	12	13	14	14	12	11	10	9	8
Hull ...	9	4	0	6	12	16	13	8	2	3	8	12
Kendal ...	1	5	10	17	25	29	25	19	13	6	1	5
Keswick ...	2	6	12	20	27	33	30	23	15	8	0	5
Lincoln ...	5	2	2	6	10	13	11	7	3	1	5	8
Liverpool ...	3	8	12	16	21	25	22	18	13	8	4	1

Corrections are made out for middle of month and give approximate time, but vary only slightly.

ROUTES AND DISTANCES.

Note—Items in Brackets, thus ( ), indicate that place given is on a branch road. Gradients are given in Forward Direction: R. denotes "rise at"; D. "descent at."

1 Ely to King's Lynn, &c.

Ely — Gradients—Easy.

5 Littleport
17½ 12½ Downham
29 24 11½ King's Lynn
33¾ 28¾ 16¼ 4¾ Castle Rising
45¼ 40¼ 27¾ 16¼ 11½ Hunstanton
62¼ 57¼ 44¾ 33¼ 28½ 17 Wells
82¾ 77¾ 65¼ 53¾ 49 37½ 20½ Cromer

2 Swaffham and Cromer.

Ely — Gradients—Easy.

5 Littleport
17½ 12½ Downham
31½ 26½ 14 Swaffham
47 42 29½ 15½ Fakenham
59 54 41½ 27½ 12 Holt
68¾ 63¾ 51¼ 37¼ 21¾ 9¾ Cromer

3 Norwich, Yarmouth, &c.

Ely — Gradients—Easy.

17½ Downham
31½ 14 Swaffham
43½ 26 12 East Dereham
51¼ 33¾ 19¾ 7¾ Horningham
59½ 42 28 16 8¼ Norwich
(70¾ 53¼ 39¼ 27¼ 19½ 11¼ Acle)
(79 61½ 47½ 35½ 27¾ 19½ 8¼ Yarmouth)
71½ 54 40 28 20¼ 12 Aylsham
82 64½ 50½ 38½ 30¾ 22½ 10½ Cromer

MOTOR INDEX MARKS.

Index Mark	Registering County or Boro' Council.
A	London (C.C.) see also GC to GY, LA to LY, QQ, UC to UW, XA to XY and YE to YY
A A	Southampton(C.C.)
A B	Worcestershire
A C	Warwickshire
A D	Gloucestershire
A E	Bristol
A F	Cornwall
A G	Ayrshire
A H	Norfolk
A I	Co. Meath
A J	Yorkshire N.R.
A K	Bradford, Yks.
A L	Nottinghamshire
A M	Wiltshire
A N	West Ham
A O	Cumberland
A P	Sussex, East
A R	Hertfordshire
A S	Nairnshire
A T	Kingston-on-Hull
A U	Nottingham
A V	Aberdeenshire
AW	Shropshire
A X	Monmouthshire
A Y	Leicestershire
A Z	Belfast (C.B.)
B	Lancashire
B A	Salford
B B	Newcastle-on-Tyne

Index Mark	Registering County or Boro' Council.
B C	Leicester
B D	Northamptonshire
B E	Lindsey, Lincs.
B G	Birkenhead
B H	Buckinghamshire
B I	Co. Monaghan
B J	Suffolk, East
B K	Portsmouth
B L	Berkshire
B M	Bedfordshire
B N	Bolton
B O	Cardiff
B P	Sussex, West
B R	Sunderland
B S	Orkney
B T	Yorkshire, E.R.
B U	Oldham
B V	Blackburn
BW	Oxfordshire
B X	Carmarthenshire
B Y	Croydon
C	Yorkshire, W.R.
C A	Denbighshire
C B	Blackburn
C C	Carnarvonshire
C D	Brighton
C E	Cambridgeshire
C F	Suffolk, West
C H	Derby
C I	Queen's County
C J	Herefordshire
C K	Preston
C L	Norwich

A selection of adverts within the publication.

A small diversion: I received an interesting letter in February 2005 from Mrs Sue Aldridge of Ely in which she explained that her father (Henry Haythorn Harmston) had been the Manager of the Ely shop between 1946 and 1969, and lived in 53 Cambridge Road; Horace Wallis lived at number 45a. Her father suffered a very serious eye injury and it was necessary later to have it removed. Horace drove him to the Evelyn Nursing Home in Cambridge for private treatment and she believes Horace was instrumental in getting him admitted, as private care was unheard of for the "working class".

Sue provided photographs from the late 1950s/early 1960s of the window displays entered in several of the annual Chamber of Trades Window Dressing competitions - only one window entry was permitted each year. They featured: a range of *"Ever Ready"* battery products; a Matchstick Man pedalling a cycle to the tune of *"Daisy, Daisy"* from a record, playing at the back of the display; *"Ever Ready"* products again. Finally, a good selection of bicycle makes for the time, priced between £22 and £27: including Rudge, Raleigh, Triumph, Royal Enfield, Hercules and Claud Butler - see below.

Another photograph shows Mr. Harmston being presented with the Chamber of Commerce winner's cup for the year of the bicycle display. Also appearing in the presentation line-up is a Miss Trent who worked in the office, and a Mr Michael Brown who worked in the shop until it closed.

An impressive and cup-winning display of bicycles.

Although he knew of his father's pioneering pre-war aviation work, Ken's interest next turned to high-speed marine craft. He mostly built his own craft and experimented with above-water airscrew propulsion because he could not afford an outboard engine. At this time, exciting high-speed boats were being raced, on Lake Garda in Italy for example, with aero engines driving airscrews. Ken conducted some experiments with under-water propulsion and made his own propellers to suit the engines used.

In 1934, he managed to acquire a racing outboard engine plus hull from a man who was so frightened of it the price was very low - at around £5! It had a simple automatic inlet valve to each crank chamber and fuel was freed the moment the valve was lifted from its seat. There were no throttle butterflies in the fuel/oil inlet system - it was fully open all the time. The speed of the engine depended entirely upon the ignition timing, with an advance/retard lever mounted beneath the flywheel. A remote control was mounted on the port side of the hydroplane hull, and the ignition of the engine was by the "Atwater Kent" coil ignition "uni-spark" system. The recommended fuel/oil mixture for this two-stroke was 4:1; a quart of oil for every gallon! It was promptly christened *"Per Ardua IV"* - all Ken's powerboats were named *"Per Ardua"* and they went up to number XIV. Later that year he won his first speed boat race with *"Per Ardua IV"* at Denver Sluice, on the Ouse near Downham Market. He was "scratch man" in the handicap race but won comfortably - he was then 18 years of age.

Ken recalls that the lively engine was very temperamental and it sometimes started backwards at full throttle! He had the bright idea of including a switch in the engine mounting, which would switch off the ignition the moment the engine hinged back after starting in reverse. All went well until he was racing again about 10 days after his success at Denver Sluice - this was at Clayhithe, near Cambridge. He was the last to start but was soon catching up and decided to overtake some stragglers. He moved closer to the bank on his right-hand side to do this but the skeg and propeller of his 820 cc, four-cylinder "Elto Super Quad" engine then struck the bottom, causing the engine to hinge back and thus switching off the engine. Completely out of control, the boat left the water and climbed to the top of the bank, which was about 7 feet high, from where he watched the remainder of the race! Ken felt that the switch was still a good idea but it needed another to short it out once the engine had started in the correct direction and was behaving.

Around this time he "flipped" one of his boats, and the engine and his glasses went to the bottom of the River Great Ouse, between the Ely High Bridge and the railway bridge. Ken admits that this was his own fault for ignoring his father's advice when he had arrived at the boathouse where Ken was working on the engine and hull. The engine was turned for steering by cables on either side and controlled by a steering wheel. He had rigged a steel tube across the engine and the cable ends were attached by steel clips around the tube (from a bicycle that had once held the pump on the frame). His father looked at this arrangement and advised that Ken ought to drill through each end of the tube across the end and put a bolt in it. This would ensure that the clip did not slide off if they were inadequately tightened. Ken ignored this.

Once on the water, Ken moved the lever to full advance and as usual the boat leapt out of the water at a high angle, followed by two or three flattening bumps, before assuming its considerable level speed. It had reached a high speed by the time it was passing under the railway bridge but, suddenly, he was flying through the air with the boat tumbling and bouncing off the water behind him. His lower body hit the water, causing rapid deceleration, whilst the rest of him above water continued at speed. He was quickly submerged but his life-jacket soon brought him back to the surface.

From a very early age, until that day, he had been compelled to wear glasses in the hope that his defective right eye, from birth, might be corrected or compensated for. Vowing never to wear the glasses again, he borrowed a set of special hooks from a boatyard - the type used to drag the bottom for bodies of persons who had drowned - and, unbelievably, the first thing to come up were his glasses. The engine took a day to locate and retrieve. The cause of the problem was that one of the bicycle pump clips had slid off the steering tube on the engine causing it to be pulled by the other cable to about 90 degrees to the direction of travel. He suspected that in his haste to get started he had omitted even to tighten the bolt in the clip, after slipping the clips on as he fitted the engine. Once repaired, *"Per Ardua IV"* was as lively as ever, and the event had been part of his learning process.

The design of the earlier *"Per Ardua III"*- an airscrew propelled hydroplane (see front cover) - had provided for a passenger to sit in the bow, and a frame made of electrical conduit tubing was positioned in front of the propeller. It is interesting to note Ken's philanthropic phraseology when he explains that: *"the purpose of the frame was to stop the passenger being drawn into the propeller and damaging it!"* With *"Per Ardua VI"*, he employed a V-Twin J.A.P. motorcycle engine driving an airscrew.

Ken still has *"Per Ardua X"*, an inboard hydroplane, at his home and this

29

design is powered by his popular use of a World War II "Riedel" starter engine from a German jet, which he water-cooled. It was intended for World Records in its Class but he never actually got around to achieving this schoolboy ambition. His very last race was the 56-mile speedboat U.S. *Missouri Marathon* in 1957 but more of this later.

Top: Winning his first speedboat race at Denver Sluice (*"Per Ardua IV"*).
Bottom: Ken with *"Per Ardua X"*.

30

By 1936, he was in charge of a branch of the Walbro empire in Soham, some six miles from Ely. Occasionally people would call in and ask if he had enjoyed time on the river at Ely the previous evening. The reason for their knowledge of his whereabouts was that the boat in which Ken had his first racing successes made such a noise that it could be heard six miles away so everybody knew when he was "in action"!

He was now having fun designing and building motorcars and the neighbouring store (Waddington's) had a drapery section, happy to provide material to order. Mrs Jean Linghorn, now living in Braintree, worked there in the late 1930s and can still recall Ken arriving in one of his sports cars to outline his needs. One order was for a tonneau cover in a black canvas, rubberised material upon which he had chalked the shape to be cut and stitched. It required a second person to feed the heavy material to the girl operating the Singer sewing machine, and a special cotton thread was called for. She recalls that he was very tall, well-spoken and always smartly dressed so no doubt turned the heads of the young female employees. Apparently, he sometimes shaved off his moustache. Jean recalled that Ken's family business also sold and repaired radio sets. A Mr & Mrs Gwen/Reg Martin lived over the business and Reg did this work. She remembers that on one November 11th Remembrance Day, Ken brought in a radio set trailing a long aerial so that the girls could listen to the Service.

By now Ken felt he had "conquered" both land and water so turned to the remaining frontier still to be mastered - the air. In 1936 he applied to join the newly-formed Royal Air Force Volunteer Reserve but was turned down owing to a defective right eye. Ken was very disappointed at this lost opportunity to learn to fly but having seen a demonstration in Cambridge by the Frenchman Henri Mignet, flying his unusual aeroplane the 'Pou de Ciel' (*"The Flying Flea"*, as the type was later to be named in the UK), he decided to build one for himself. There was a choice of power-plants but he decided to use a V-Twin J.A.P. motorcycle engine from one of his airscrew-propelled boats.

Owing to a number of fatalities in several countries, the aircraft type was banned in the UK before he could complete its construction. Ken claims that the resultant adverse attitude by the authorities to aircraft of amateur design and construction was to last well into the 1950s when he was to build his first light autogyro in the UK. The decision may well have saved lives but, knowing Ken, it is very likely that he could have improved upon the design for successful flight - as was done later by others.

31

Although his interests led him to work on most forms of transport, Ken's love for the motorcar was ever present. Powerful vehicles had always attracted him but he was also very fussy about their looks. In 1937 he decided to sell his Bentley 3-Litre "Special" - this was a scrap motorcar he had purchased in 1936 for £25 and rebuilt into a racy, two-seater. He had made it from the chassis that had been fitted with a wood-framed, four-seat fabric body. The sale was probably greeted with relief by his girl friends because the design featured a large exhaust pipe, high on the outside of the body, and this had been the cause of a nasty leg burn for at least one of them.

The sale was intended to raise funds to purchase a desirable 61/2 litre "Speed Six" Bentley but he found that he still needed to borrow the £15 balance so approached his father. Wallis senior briefly considered the request and then announced that a 3 litre motorcar was powerful enough for a 21-year old, no doubt in the interests of preserving his heir. Although disappointed, in disposing of the "Special" the deal had involved a degree of part exchange and Ken had gained an Alvis 12/70 so he was still mobile. With the Bentley "off-limits" he decided to spend some of his money on flying lessons.

At this point it should be mentioned that Ken's birth, apparently was a difficult one and he still bears the marks of the forceps on the right side of his forehead. At the same time there was some damage to his right eye, described as being "lazy". When very young he had to wear a black patch over his good eye in the hope that this would enliven the other one but it never happened. It was also very uncomfortable not to be able to use his "good" eye. From the age of four he had to wear glasses but they did no good, nor did he take kindly to being referred to as "four-eyes" by other boys at school.

Ken's G.P. was happy to sign him up as a potential pilot as he knew he was generally healthy and didn't bother to check his eyesight. Ken then went to a small field owned by the Cambridge University Aero Club where he received tuition on a de Havilland Gypsy Moth. He qualified for his pilot's 'A' Licence in a total of 12 hours 10 minutes on the 11th April 1937 for the grand sum of £14 - this included the flying helmet, goggles and speaking tubes, plus membership of the Royal Aero Club.

After learning to fly on the DH-60 "Moths" with the upright engine ahead, a useful indicator of fuselage attitude, Ken went to a field at Caxton Gibbet where he flew solo in a BAC "Drone", a motorised glider with a converted Douglas motorcycle engine above the wing. Ken said that he missed the

32

"attitude indicator" provided by the upright engine so had to look back, to see where the tail was pointing! At 7/6d per hour (approximately 36p today) it was good value and he clocked up valuable hours.

As the twelve months since qualifying was almost up, the Cambridge Aero Club reminded him of the need to do some further flying to keep his licence extant. He pleaded poverty and they replied that if he would be willing to fly at a time suited to them there would be no charge. He duly met at Cambridge another pilot with whom he could achieve the required time and they flew to the old airfield at Mousehold Heath, Norwich, returning after a "liquid lunch". At the time, the Aero Club was receiving a subsidy on pilot qualifications, hence the two of them getting in the required hours for free.

Ken's interest in motorcars was maintained during this time in the air and the *"Wallis Special"* built in 1938 was the last of his three Austin 7 *"Specials"*. This was a waist-high, roadster with a very long bonnet - his idea of the perfect sports car for the time - but, typically, the construction was somewhat unorthodox. It featured two overlapping Austin 7 chassis with the end of the front one turned upwards to facilitate better steering, and an Austin 7 engine. He made the entire body himself from aluminium so that nothing would spoil its lines and the special French Marchal headlights were hidden behind a curved grill set low between the front wheels.

Ken sold this back in 1945 so was very surprised to be telephoned by Kenneth Cotterell of Bristol mid-2006. It transpired that he had owned the vehicle around the 1950s and had achieved quite a bit of success racing it. He had recently read about it in a book titled "Cars That Time Forgot"; he then came across this book and another mention of it.

Ken's first Austin 7 "*Special*" had been completed in 1934 and for this he used the chassis of a little open two-seater "*Chummy*" that he had managed to overturn. He had left a fair at Lakenheath with a friend and, after enjoying a few beers, decided to race another friend in an Alvis 12/50 along nearby roads. Unfortunately, he failed to negotiate a bend. Somehow Ken stayed in the vehicle whilst his passenger was ejected but, fortunately, without too much damage to the machine or passenger. They were both lucky to escape without injury considering that the vehicle body was simply fabric on wood. Ken also built a two-seat 4½ litre Invicta, and a 7½ litre Rolls-Royce Silver Ghost "*Special*" followed in 1948. The latter he purchased in rather poor condition for £60 as the chassis had been used for a breakdown truck, complete with a crane on the back. When rebuilt, it sported a 7 feet 6 inch bonnet from windscreen to radiator, and *"The Long Dog"* was (in Ken's words) "very dramatic". Soon after this he acquired a Rolls-Royce Phantom III (12 cylinders) that had been an insurance "write off" and rebuilt it to original form. This was his last effort with motorcars.

With flying still very much on his mind in 1938, Ken applied with confidence for a Short Service Commission in the Royal Air Force, omitting mention of his rejection by the RAFVR in 1936 because of the eyesight defect. He got as far as the eyesight test whereupon the doctor declared that he would never be able to land an aeroplane owing to the defective right eye. Ken protested at this and proudly announced he had gained his "A" licence flying Gypsy Moths. The doctor was not impressed and grandly countered that the modern RAF flew high-speed fighters such as the Hawker Hart (at around 150 miles per hour). With this put down, the session ended abruptly.

Ken's disappointment was short lived, however, as the Civil Air Guard was instituted in the July of that year by the Air Minister, Sir Kingsley Wood. This body was intended to provide inexpensive flying tuition for "air-minded persons" between the ages of 18 and 50, for possible RAF aircrew. Ken was at the front of the queue and able to hire a Gypsy Moth or Moth Minor for as little as 2/6d (just over 12p today) per hour for extra experience. As a C.A.G. pilot (or Pilot U/T) his name would be automatically put forward for consideration as a potential RAFVR pilot if the expected war materialised. The C.A.G. was very popular so many applicants were disappointed because there were too few instructors and machines.

With the disappointing experience of the medical and the doctor's comments still fresh in his mind Ken decided on some added insurance and acquired a copy of the official book "Medical Fitness For Flying". From this he learned enough about the "Bishop Harman Binocular Test", etc., in order to (in his words) *"distort the facts somewhat"* at the medical test. Not surprisingly, a "pass" was achieved on this occasion.

Top: Ken's first Austin 7 "Special" of 1934.
Middle: 3 litre Bentley "Special" in 1936
Bottom: At an early stage with his last Austin 7 "Special"

Three views taken at different times of the final Austin 7 "Special" of 1938. See also the front cover.

Preparing for war

Ken was duly sworn in at RAF Uxbridge in October 1939 but had to wait whilst on "Deferred Service" until a training place became available. He recalls that just about all of those in his intake to Initial Training, and then to Flying Training, were from the Civil Air Guard.

Possibly Ken's first taste of fame came when he was at Woodley, with No.8 Elementary Flying Training School. He was photographed with three others in flying suits and carrying parachutes as they walked out to their Magister aircraft. This then appeared on the cover of Noel Monks' book *"Taking Off! - Our Airmen In The Making"*, published by Raphael Tuck & Sons. The book ended with the words *'Every morn brought forth a noble chance and every chance brought forth a noble knight'*. Ken was clearly in possession of all the necessary requirements of the day being tall, dark and handsome!

During 1939 Ken purchased a two-seat glider for leisure time use, which he thinks may have been built at Ingworth near North Walsham in Norfolk. It cost 30 shillings (£1.50 today) and this included the towing cable. He then paid £2 for a tow-car from a scrapyard on the understanding that they would re-purchase it for 30 shillings when he no longer wanted it!

Ken's glider plus tow vehicle.

Flying the Miles Magister made Ken very aware of the possibility of attack from behind and pilots probably spent more time looking back than the direction of flight. One afternoon in the Summer of 1940, there was a sudden attack on the airfield and bombs were dropped, and two of the parked Magisters were destroyed. After the raid they spent some time inspecting the wreckage and collected one or two souvenirs. The next morning, at about 05.00am, their building shook as a result of a very loud explosion. The spot where they had spent time exploring the wrecked aircraft was now a large crater; an unexploded bomb with a delayed fuze had been buried in the ground under the wreckage.

Off duty moments were spent following the usual pursuits and Ken sometimes carried his Royal Aero Club Certificate with him. It is an important-looking document, similar to a passport with a photograph of the holder, and written in six different languages are the words: *'The Civil, Naval and Military Authorities including the Police are respectfully requested to aid and assist the Holder of this Certificate'*. Ken says that he only found it useful on one occasion. He was with a girl in his little Austin 7 saloon one evening and had parked in a convenient place. A policeman then appeared and told him that he could not park there - *"there is a war on"* - etc., in an officious manner. Ken calmly produced his Certificate and the officer's attitude changed immediately. *"I am sorry Sir. I will tell them at the station and you will not be disturbed!"* He must have thought that they were on a special security mission. Anyway, Ken recalls that the girl was very impressed.

At the conclusion of EFT training on Magister aircraft, Ken was invited by a girlfriend to spend the weekend at her parent's house in Hampstead Heath. The visit started on Saturday the 7th September 1940 and in the afternoon they were able to see and hear the raid on London Docks. They then went, as planned, to the Criterion Theatre in the evening and the show went on in spite of the further heavy bombing of London. When they came out of the theatre, the whole sky was lit up by burning buildings.

Above the head of his bed, at her parent's home, there was a heavy glass chandelier and he remembers being aware that it might drop on him when it shook, as further bombs dropped through the night - he moved the bed. He had other experiences of being in London during the Blitz, and on the receiving end at Moreton-in-the-Marsh when it was attacked and aircraft were damaged.

Whilst with No.15 Flying Training School at Kidlington in 1940, Ken had his first real experience of the dangers that can occur whilst aloft. He was flying solo in a North American Harvard II trainer at 10,000 feet. On returning to level flight after he had *"done a bit of flinging around"* he noticed spots of what looked like water on the windscreen but it was not raining. Further, the spots did not seem to be blown along the screen in quite the same way as water. He slid back the hood, put out a finger to touch one of the droplets and then tasted it. It was quite clearly battery acid!

He commenced a hurried descent but in no time at all battery acid was being sprayed into the cockpit and on to his face via the hot air intake, which rapidly became very painful. On landing, he jumped out of the aeroplane and ran to the nearest water supply instead of taxiing to dispersal. After washing, and with both hands and face still burning, he inspected the aircraft. The ground crew had opened up the engine cowlings whereupon it could be seen that the front bulkhead, upon which the battery was mounted, was "frizzing". The battery had burst - probably due to an electrical spark. Not a happy experience, and his cousin Bob was killed in a Harvard at Brize Norton around this time when its wings came off due to aileron flutter.

One evening he was again parked up in his Austin 7, with a new girl, when an Air Raid Warden, just like "Mr Hodges" in the television series *"Dad's Army"*, appeared. *"You can't park here, there is a blackout"* etc. Ken thought this was odd as his car's lights were not switched on so decided to repeat the previously successful "Certificate routine". On producing it the Warden said *"Don't come the acid with me young man"*. Ken meekly departed and has used the Certificate only in the intended manner ever since.

On another occasion he had gained a girlfriend who was a Sister at the Radcliffe Hospital, and pupils were required to be back in camp by 10.30pm, clocking in through the Guard Room. The Sister, however, had to be back in her quarters (which she described as *"The Virgin's Retreat"*) by 11.00pm and Ken naturally did not like to lose any of their time together. One night, after delivering her back to *"The Virgin's Retreat"* in his little Austin 7 saloon he arrived back at camp after 10.30pm. He was accordingly sentenced to 10 Days "Confined To Camp".

After he had served his time on camp he decided to find a way round the problem. He would deliver the Sister by 11.00pm to her quarters then find a convenient gateway to park the car where he would spend the night in it. In the morning he would drive into camp, unnoticed, when all the civilian workmen and others were arriving for the day. He now suspects that such uncomfortable nights were hardly appropriate preparation for instrument flying practice when having to be enclosed under the hood of a Link Trainer.

After flying training - where he gained *'above average'* rating - Ken was posted to No.1 School of Army Co-operation in December 1940 and flew the Westland Lysander. He recalls with sadness having to attend four funerals of fellow pupils at Old Sarum: two Pilots and two Air Gunners were killed on the Course of twelve Pilots and twelve Air Gunners.

He served very briefly with No. 268 Squadron at Westley on Army Co-operation duties and anti-invasion patrols around the coast of East Anglia. His Log Book shows that between the 10th and 26th March 1941 he undertook thirty-three flights. He would take off early in the morning, in darkness, to be on coastal patrol at first light and if an invasion fleet was spotted he would give first warning to No.2 Corps Headquarters near Newmarket. Ken said that it was always a relief to transmit in Morse "NMS" (No Movement Seen) every ten minutes, then to drop the Message Log that had been written up in the message bag at No.2 Corps HQ and head back to Westley for breakfast.

On the 21st March he flew Lysander III "NM-B" on a photographic mosaic imagery task under A.I.L.O. Demand No. 114 covering all of Norwich in Norfolk. An interesting assignment, very much along the lines of work he would undertake in later life with his autogyros, but the purpose behind the task was not disclosed.

Prior to this, on the 19th February 1941, his Log Book records a flight in Lysander R2010 over Porton Down on S.C.I. Exercise IA and IB. (Smoke Curtain Installation was a euphemism for practice for poison gas spraying from the air.) The "Lizzie" was fitted with a large tank between the undercarriage legs and extended aft, much like a long-range tank used in Special Operations but this tank had a horizontal fishtail spray at the rear and was filled with a water/aniseed mixture. The spread of the coloured fluid was recorded on slips of blotting paper spread over the "target area".

On the 21st February, in Lysander P1698, he undertook Exercise IIB over the Chemical & Biological Warfare Research Establishment, Porton Down and then, on the 23rd February, the S.C.I. flight was over Bournemouth in Lysander P1726.

Much later, on the 21st April 1942 when he was nearing the end of his "tour" of operations with 103 Squadron, Bomber Command, he flew an S.C.I. flight for forty minutes over an area of north Lincolnshire in Wellington Mk.IC Z8832, and the tank occupied the bomb bay. Ken speculates that if the weapon had been employed for real then mustard gas might have been used. At that time, the crews did not know of the development of the nerve gases Tabun and Sarin by Germany.

Ken was sent to serve briefly with No. 241 Squadron, Army Co-operation, at Inverness in Scotland and made twenty-two flights between 5th April and 2nd May. Many were quite long distance down to Barnstaple in Devon, with stops en route, rather than in one "hop" as he would do later in his autogyros. In Lysanders there were no co-pilots and the pilot had to write up his log, navigate, etc., whilst rattling away on the Morse Key, sending messages back to Corps Headquarters. The odd thing was the lack of communication between the pilot and the Gunner in the rear, owing to there being an armour-plate bulkhead between them. Ken recalls that the pilot could pass a written message such as *"3 degrees port on the camera"* - the apparatus being in the Gunner's compartment - through a small door in the bulkhead. The Gunner would likely see it as it fell in. Attempting a message the other way would have failed, as it would have fallen behind the pilot's seat.

A "major breakthrough" occurred when a hole was drilled in the bulkhead and a cord passed through it to the pilot's harness at each shoulder - the other end could be pulled by the Gunner to indicate the side from which an attack was being made if it happened: one pull would indicate an attack on that side and below, two pulls for level, etc. The pilot would respond by a tight turn into the attack - if the aircraft had not already been seriously damaged!

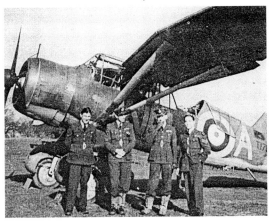

Ken - second from left - with a Lysander III of 268 Squadron.

41

Following short periods on the operational 241 and 268 Army Co-operation squadrons, RAF pilots found themselves "volunteered" for Bomber Command. Some of the Squadron pilots were ex-Army who had transferred and been trained to fly on Army Co-operation work. Thus, they could hardly be expected to "volunteer" for bombers.

Pilot Officers 89388 Ken Wallis (left) and 89387 "Tommy" Westlake with 268 Squadron at Westley in Suffolk, March 1941.

To Bomber Command

Ken transferred to Bomber Command in June 1941 and converted straight onto the twin-engined Vickers Wellington with 20 Operational Conversion Unit at Lossiemouth and not via training on a smaller "twin" such the Oxford or Anson. Following a short course he was given the choice of three stations and chose No. 103 Squadron at Newton, near Nottingham, *"because of the reputation of the Nottingham girls!"* (I wonder if Ken meant they were pretty, witty and good conversationalists?) Ken's friend Tommy Westlake had joined his crew as Second Pilot but on their move to 103 Squadron he went as Second Pilot to a Captain who had finished the required number of bomber "ops", then became a Captain himself. Ken learned only recently he was killed in April 1944 while serving with No. 290 Squadron.

Ken was required to undertake bomber operations as Second Pilot before becoming a Captain and, as such, joined a crew Captained by Pilot Officer David Petrie - he had also served on Lysanders before being "volunteered" as a bomber pilot. They both had a great mutual interest in weapons and target shooting, as well as making joint expeditions into Nottingham, or Brigg when the squadron moved to Elsham Wolds on 11th July, to "sample the night life". Ken had flown three bombing operations (Rotterdam and twice to Cologne) from Newton's grass runway, with a railway embankment invariably on the "up wind" side, so found that Elsham Wolds was much better suited to a bomber squadron with its hard runway. On the debit side, the nearest town for entertainment was Scunthorpe and *"No further comment was needed"* per Ken!

In August 1941, Ken had a bad spell of tonsillitis and was sent to the RAF Hospital at Cranwell, flying back to Elsham Wolds on the 27th in an Oxford. He always feels obliged to qualify his stay there because it was also the local V.D. hospital! Ken also recalls a Mess Meeting around that time with the first mention of WAAF Officers and him jumping up asking *"Does this mean there will be women in the Ante-Room?"* That was something unheard of - until then there had been a Ladies Room. It did happen, however, and the atmosphere in the Mess changed somewhat, although he thinks this may have been the result of increased operations and losses.

On the 11th September, after a few days of transit flying and practice, P/O Petrie said *"Get yourself on the crew list with me tonight, we are going to Turin!"* Ken recalls that he spoke of this as though the invitation was for a lively night out in town. Ken rushed to Wing Commander Ryan, the Squadron Commander, and asked to be put on the crew list with Petrie but the response was *"You'll be a Captain with a crew of your own from now on and you're not going on ops tonight"*. Instead, Ken did some practice night landings with Ryan and those selected to become his crew. That night David Petrie and his crew were lost without trace and their fate was never discovered. Ken had shared a room with Petrie so had the unpleasant task of going through his belongings and writing letters to family and friends.

There were no special navigation instruments on Wellingtons, recalled Ken, just a compass and a watch; they had to rely upon Dead Reckoning. His first operation as Captain was against Cherbourg on the 12th September with Wing Commander Ryan as his Second Pilot. Visibility was very poor and they had a problem with an engine exhaust ring, which was very bright. They returned with a full bomb load as crews had to be sure of precise bombing of a target in France. The raids that followed were rarely uneventful and always life-threatening but some were more so than others.

Enemy anti-aircraft fire (*"Flak"*) was a constant problem. Sometimes the damage was severe but "it was not done" per Ken to write much more in Log Books than "hit by flak." A couple of examples of this understatement can be gathered by the raid on Hamburg on August 2nd when the aircraft was hit three times and the Log recorded simply that. Then there was the night of the 7th August, when the target was the Krupps Works at Essen. On the approach over Duisburg, Ken happened to check the fuel gauges. He was surprised to see the needle on one of the gauges, for a tank in the starboard wing, moving rapidly to the empty position. It was only on landing back in England that the cause could be determined. The aircraft had been subject to the usual *"flak"* in the Ruhr area and there were many holes but a shell had passed straight through the wing and fuel tank without detonating. It was probably on a time-fuze, set for a greater altitude and there was no doubt as to its 88mm calibre. Fluke situations like this were not uncommon.

On another occasion the aircraft was approaching the target and the Navigator had advanced forward to stand beside Ken. He was looking ahead before taking up his position for the bomb aiming and there was plenty of *"flak"* with thumps and flashes all around. Suddenly, there was a very loud thump followed by a vertical and twisting spiral of smoke appearing from just forward of where the Navigator was standing. The cause of this was a lethal fragment from a shell, passing through the Bomb Aimer's position and exiting via the top of the nose of the Wellington. Had he been at his station a few seconds earlier he would have been struck and most likely killed. The Navigator then calmly got down and gave the usual directions on the run-in to the target. The crew was pleased to hear him call *"Bombs Gone"*.

The Wellington could take a great deal of punishment from enemy *"flak"* and many of the shell fragments simply passed straight through the fabric with only some doped patches being required for repair. Ken recalls that in the darkness of the waist of the aircraft, when carrying out the regular topping-up of oil to the engines, a lot of light in the night sky came from searchlights and gunfire. It was not unusual, therefore, to see spots of light suddenly appear in the dark fabric as fragments of shells passed through it.

On a successful return to base, and following a healthy breakfast (sometimes enhanced by the rations that had been cooked for comrades who did not return), crew members would go to their billets and try to get some sleep but Ken found he could not overcome the buzzing induced in his ears by the noise of the engines. It was then quite usual for him and the crew to go back up to the dispersal and look over the *"Wimpy"* that had shared their previous night. The ground crew would be locating damage, patching holes and preparing her for the next "op" so they would help them locate pieces of *"flak"* trapped in the cooling fins of the Pegasus engine cylinders, etc. On one occasion, Ken recalls picking up 115 pieces but he never saved any piece as a souvenir. Although in no way superstitious he thinks that, at the time, he must have felt it might have adversely prejudiced his luck to retain any fragments. In wartime, luck was clearly a very important factor.

Flying wartime bomber operations constantly produced life-threatening situations for aircrew and very often at night, but Ken found that not all such experiences occurred when over enemy territory. For example, his Log Book entry for the night of the 13/14th October 1941 is necessarily brief and records *'OPERATIONS, DUSSELDORF. VERY ACCURATE, MOD. FLAK. STARB'D ENG. HIT. INTERCOM.TURRETS W/T, R/T, 'VERY' PISTOL u/s. LANDED AT COLTISHALL'*. In full, Ken was limping back with Wellington Mk.1C T2999 on one engine and steadily losing height. There was no way he could reach his home station of Elsham Wolds in North Lincolnshire and a landing was called for as soon as possible. With all communications gone, he commenced flashing the squadron letters in Morse Code on the Downward Identification Light, together with a "Q" to request an emergency landing.

Landing lights suddenly appeared in front of him and a Green Very Light was fired from the control tower of an airfield he took to be Coltishall in Norfolk.

Ken's Second Pilot, Johnny Ward, was standing in the cockpit beside him and they gestured to each other their satisfaction that "the boys below were on the ball". Ken commenced a circuit, lowered the wheels and then flaps on the final approach to an emergency landing on the grass airfield. With full concentration upon the task ahead, and having reached the very late stages of the difficult approach, he recalls being a little irritated by Johnny Ward. Ward was peering through the bomb-aiming panel and seemed to be trying to attract his attention. Ken signalled back that he did not want to be distracted but this only caused Ward to become more agitated so he took a very quick glance for himself.

To his horror, beneath him he could clearly see the close-up interior of a cockpit and an instrument panel! There was another aircraft immediately below and possibly a distance of no more than a foot or two separated them. The aircraft had passed the point of no return so far as the landing was concerned but somehow Ken managed to pull up the nose of the Wellington, kick on starboard rudder to slew the aircraft to the right, holding her up long enough to clear the other aircraft landing on the flare-path. The Wellington dropped heavily, damaging the tail-wheel, and the two aircraft bounced alongside each other to a halt. The other aircraft turned out to be a Boulton Paul Defiant stationed at Coltishall. The Defiant's armament was contained in the rear-facing dorsal turret so the gunner trapped within had endured the terror of watching the bomber steadily descend to within a foot or two of his exposed position, unable to warn his pilot to take evasive action.

The later explanation given for this near-fatal incident was that the Defiant had also suffered radio failure and the flare-path lights had been switched on for its return; the Green Very Light had been fired to give permission for the Defiant to land but this could be seen by all approaching aircraft. Had an Aldis Lamp been used to give a "Green" for permission to land it would have been directed at the one aircraft concerned. The Wellington was deemed "u/s" on inspection so Ken and his crew stayed at the station the following night before returning to Elsham Wolds by train. Ken recalls that they had a great party in Norwich with the pilot and gunner of the Defiant.

There was something of a repeat performance but in reverse when Ken was a Staff Officer at Central Gunnery School, Catfoss, in August 1944. He was flying a Wellington III for cine-gun recording of fighter attacks, etc., when he received the "Green" for take-off from the Control Caravan. The aircraft was just about to lift off when Ken noticed that the sunlight ahead and above seemed to be "strobing". He looked up and saw the airscrew of a Spitfire with its wheels down about to land. He kicked right rudder and the Wellington ran over the lights at the edge of the runway, taking off beside the landing Spitfire. He never found out the cause of the mix-up or got to know the other pilot.

The Defiant episode was Ken's last flight with Pilot Officer Ward for he soon had his own crew. Shortly afterwards, Ken thought Ward had "bought it" for, on returning from "ops", he saw the burning remains of a Wellington and recognised it as his old T2999. On landing Ken ascertained from the ground crew that it was *"Mr. Ward's aircraft"* but his concerns were soon to be dispelled. On entering the de-briefing room Ward was present, having just consumed the traditional rum issue. Fortunately, he and his crew had escaped on landing and before the aircraft was destroyed.

Later, on the 29th March 1942 and in the Saracen's Head in Lincoln when returning from some home leave in Ely, Ken met Peggy who very soon would become his wife. He was shocked to be told that Johnny Ward had been lost on the return leg from a raid on Lubeck. She explained that they had picked up Ward's message saying that the aircraft had been attacked by a German night-fighter and was on fire. The next message reported that the fighter was attacking again ……….. then all contact had been lost.

An interesting flight had occurred earlier on the 7th November 1941 when the target was Mannheim. The Met. Office had predicted a headwind on the way to the target and, from the time they left the coast of East Anglia, cloud obscured all sight of the sea and ground. They flew to their E.T.A. for Mannheim, and beyond, and eventually saw a few lights on the ground so dropped their bombs and set course for home. (After the earlier losses, caused by crews being required to bring bombs back if the military target could not be positively identified, some common sense was now prevailing.)

They flew for so long without seeing anything that they decided they must have crossed a cloud-covered North Sea and were now over England. Flying this way meant that they ran the risk of encountering their own night-fighters, with the prospect of being shot down, so it was necessary to descend below 4,000 feet and switch on "RESIN" (Recognition & Identification) lights. This they did and occasionally spotted patches of land through the cloud.

Suddenly, they were shot at by an anti-aircraft battery. As there was nothing unusual in this over the U.K., Ken told the Navigator to fire *"The Colours of the Day"* with the Very Pistol fixed in the top of his cabin. The barrage promptly intensified. Then, way ahead, Ken saw the unique type of *"hosepipe flak"* that was typical of the Ostende-Dunkirk coastal defences and wondered if they were over Belgium or Holland. He descended to just above the ground, the cloud no longer prevailing, and flew through the light "flak" …… and out over the North Sea, leaving the Belgian coast at the Northern end behind them! By now they were very short of fuel and he was uncertain about attempting to reach land in the U.K. All the same, they managed it and, with 20 gallons on the gauges, Swanton Morley's flarepath lights were switched on and they landed on the large, grass Norfolk airfield.

They were taken to the Briefing Room and the Intelligence Officer, a Squadron Leader Rose, was summoned from his bed, on this essentially daylight operational station. The usual quite large tots of rum were handed out and the crew laughed about firing the Very Pistol over the enemy guns, inciting them to fire rather than have them stop as would have been the case in U.K. airspace. After de-briefing, they were offered a "doss-down" on chairs in the Mess whilst the Wellington was refuelled to get them back to Elsham Wolds.

By about 7.30am, 180 gallons of fuel had been pumped into the tanks and they took off, landing at their home station around thirty minutes later. As Ken walked into the crew area, passing the Squadron Commanding Officer's office, he heard his name called loudly by Wing Commander Ryan. Ken entered the office and a cable was placed before him. It was from Squadron Leader Rose of Swanton Morley and said something to the effect that: *"the crew was a menace to themselves and to others, having flown for nearly nine hours without a positive pinpoint after leaving the English coast, and having fired The Colours of the Day over enemy territory thus revealing the code"*. Wing Commander Ryan then asked *"What do you think of that Wallis?"* Ken replied that he thought they were *"Bloody lucky to be back at all"*. Ryan agreed and added that thirty-seven aircraft had been lost that night, more than twice the highest percentage of losses on any previous operation.

It transpired that Ken's aircraft actually had a <u>tail</u>wind over Germany and flew way beyond Mannheim before setting out for a slow return journey against the wind. Squadron Leader Rose had no idea of the problems Ken had faced and the whole crew had been relieved and light hearted at the de-briefing after a good rum ration, so he did not appreciate the remarks made. Ken hoped that on learning of the grave losses that night, Rose would have seen the error of his perfectionist attitude on this occasion.

According to the book *"Bomber Command War Diaries"*, Ken's 103 Squadron had the highest loss rate of Bomber Command. 1941/2 was a particularly bad period and the location of the airfield at Elsham Wolds in North Lincolnshire would have meant that their aircraft incurred rather longer flights than from most other Bomber Command stations.

Ken recalled several other very demanding flights and became surprisingly animated, rather than sombre, when recounting these potentially fatal experiences. One was the return flight in Wellington Mk.1C L7886 from an abortive raid on Frankfurt on 20/21 September 1941. The target had been obscured by cloud and, because bombing was not (then) permitted if a military target could not be identified, he had proceeded to the secondary target and dropped his bomb load in the vicinity of the invasion barges along the Dutch Coast. The diversion with a full bomb load had made the aircraft low on fuel but this would not normally have been a problem.

On crossing the coast, however, he discovered that his home airfield and all others in the vicinity were closed owing to fog. Later, he found out that a recall signal had gone out to all bombers owing to home weather conditions as they were crossing the sea on the outward leg but few received it.

Eventually, his "Darkie" emergency radio signal was picked up by Binbrook as he flew over but the unhelpful response advised him that the station was fog-bound and directed he fly further north. The fuel gauges now registered no fuel in the tanks so he called for the "Chance Light" to be switched on and off in order to locate its position, something rarely used in wartime, and a glow appeared beneath the cloud. After making numerous, near suicidal passes in an attempt to land, and wondering just how much longer the engines would run as there could be little more than vapour left, he decided to climb away and radioed for permission for the crew to bail out. Instead, he was ordered to attempt a landing at Linton-on-Ouse! At that very moment, however, the decision was made for him because both the engines cut out. He was very thankful to have gained some height instead of having gone around again to attempt another landing. Ken gave the order to bail out. Sgt. Walker the Navigator wrote *"Bail Out"* on a note and passed it to Sgt. Rouse the Wireless Operator who was listening on the W/T and not the intercom. Always the joker, he promptly scribbled *"I daren't"* and handed it back! Walker grabbed his parachute and started quickly to the rear Escape Hatch but Rouse, realising it was "for real", flashed past him.

For the pilot of a Wellington, escape was a little complicated. The pilot's parachute then used in bomber aircraft was normally carried separate from the harness so that movement around the aircraft was more easily achieved. When flying the aircraft, the pilot would sit on the parachute with its attached cushion in the usual way. To use the parachute, it had to be attached to the two large hooks low on the harness/Mae West, and the rip- cord release handle had to be fitted on press fasteners on the chest. When carrying the parachute separately, however, the pilot normally stowed the rip-cord and release handle between the parachute pack and its attached cushion to prevent them from dragging on the floor.

As the crew baled out, Ken started to put his parachute onto the harness/Mae West by first attaching the two important hooks on the hips. With the parachute attached to the harness, and on raising himself from the seat, he found he could not retrieve the rip-cord and release handle from their location between the parachute and the cushion. Whilst trying to control the bomber in its dying moments he struggled to recover the situation. This required him to undo the two important hooks attaching the parachute to his body, locate the handle and cable, fasten them to his chest by turn-buttons and then do up the two hooks again. Having managed to achieve all this, he looked back down the cathedral-like fuselage to check that the crew had safely escaped. An interior light had been left on and he was pleased to see the aircraft was empty. With the altimeter indicating 700 feet, he lowered himself from the seat to the cockpit floor and opened the front escape hatch.

At the very point of departure he recalls thinking that, despite wearing a seat-type parachute, he felt strangely comfortable with none of the usual pressure at the back of the legs caused by the equipment. This was an incredibly lucky moment of hesitation. Looking up to the seat he had just vacated, in the little light available, he could see his parachute pack was still there! It was attached to his harness by yards of the thick webbing straps normally folded within the harness, to deploy when the rip-cord was pulled and the canopy opened after some tie-cords were broken. It had detached and was snagged behind the seat-raising handle. If he had exited the aircraft he would have ended up suspended beneath the fuselage on its death fall to the ground. Ken gathered the webbing and toppled through the hatch space.

Once out of the aircraft he let go of his bundle of webbing and pulled the rip-cord. A painful jerk confirmed that the canopy had deployed without mishap. Almost immediately, his Wellington appeared out of the fog heading straight for him but, fortunately, it was banking steeply and passed by very close before disappearing. It struck the ground at Holton-Le-Moor with a horrendous noise, followed by an eerie silence because, with no fuel on board, no explosion occurred.

Despite exiting at fairly low altitude, and hitting the ground quite hard, his injuries were surprisingly light. He suffered concussion and a back injury owing to being unprepared for the landing because the thick fog had obscured everything below on the descent. He thinks he was knocked out for around half an hour and, on regaining consciousness, could see little owing to the poor weather. He fired two shots into the air from his World War I Mauser pistol, which he always carried inside his flying suit, and was soon joined by a member of the Home Guard accompanied by a policeman. (Many years later, he met George Fawcett and Kenneth Hubbard again at an airshow.) They took him to a nearby farmhouse where he was offered a cup of tea. On asking to use the telephone to contact RAF Elsham Wolds, the farmer was very hesitant but on offering to "reverse charges" Ken gained his consent. Ken was relieved to hear that his crew had landed safely along the Caistor-Market Rasen road; the first 103 Squadron crew to bale out over the UK. Around 6 a.m. the housemaid came in so he gave her his bar of chocolate that had been reserved for the flight, hoping that bacon and eggs might materialise in exchange but without any luck.

The next morning Ken's Squadron Commander, Wing Commander Ryan, arrived and they drove back via the crash site where he salvaged the control column from the wreckage plus a piece of fabric from the fin - mementos he still has to this day. They then picked up the crew from nearby cottages and found all to be in good spirits. Ken was taken to the RAF Hospital at Nocton Hall where his spinal injuries were assessed but it seemed that not much could be done so he was given 10-days leave, during which time the swelling reduced. For this escapade he qualified for a gold braid "wound stripe" which he wore on the sleeve of his uniform, but would go on to suffer occasional periods of pain from the injury for years to come. Three other crews from the squadron were lost the same night as his crash.

Soon after this event Ken was made a member of the Caterpillar Club and joined the many aircrew members who have survived a parachute descent from a stricken aeroplane; he wears the small badge with great pride. The reason for choosing the caterpillar emblem may not be obvious: it depicts the origin (the caterpillar) of the silk from which parachutes were made.

Two views of the remains of Wellington L7886. Ken tore off the piece of fabric bearing the national colours and bombing raids from the tail, as seen in the top picture. It now bears his signature along with those of his crew: P/O J E Ward, Sgt E A Fairhurst, Sgt N Rouse, Sgt R Walker and Sgt K Clowes. It is displayed with his parachute rip-cord from that day.

The preceding pages reflect a few of Ken's flying stories, and more follow, but what of the time spent preparing for an operation and moments of reflection before stepping into the aeroplane - perhaps for the last time? Ken penned a few lines for me and his words convey something of the mixed the emotions of crew' members as tension builds before and during a raid:

'It is very difficult to describe what it was like to be aircrew on a Bomber Station. We all knew, well enough, what was likely to happen, though, initially, there was some feeling that this happened to others. However, after seeing what happened after a few operations, that feeling of confidence passed. Anyone who said they were not afraid would surely be a liar, and certainly not a reliable member of the crew. We were intent on not "letting the side down" in the important and difficult task we necessarily had to conduct. Strangely, I do not particularly remember any real feeling of being the "aggressor" while flying a bomber on a raid. Rather, it was such a task to fly a heavily-laden Wellington in dangerous weather conditions it seemed the *"flak"* defences were the "aggressors". It was certainly satisfying on those few occasions when the target could be clearly identified and effectively attacked. Thankfully, we would not know any personal details concerning those unfortunate enough to be in the target area.

On a night when the squadron was on operations there would be many RAF and WAAF Officers in the Ante-Room of the Mess, all quietly engaged in something. Aircrew would often be writing letters; all too often the last they would write. There was a definite awareness that numbers would be reduced by the morning. The "quiet period" would then end and we would have to embark on the aircrew truck, get our kit and, if it had not taken place before, attend a briefing to learn our "Target For Tonight". Some were regarded as "easy meat" but others caused forebodings. It was strange to be in the civilised surroundings of the Ante-Room then, only two or three hours later, to be over the Ruhr in intense *"flak"* and with the sight of others being shot down.

At that stage of the bomber campaign the crews had some choice of the route to the target and the bombing run. I think a very primitive instinct could sometimes take over. When we were preparing for the run-in over the target, we would often not start it until we saw a bomber caught in the *"flak"* and searchlights and on fire. When enemy concentration was on that it seemed to be the time to go in over the targets for "Bombs Gone!" Upon the relief of a safe return there was then the question of who else had returned and who had not. There was often no quick answer, some having "flopped in" elsewhere; others being missing for a long while.

One of the worst jobs in the WAAF must have been that of the girl who drove the truck taking the crews, with all their kit, to their aircraft. A few hours later she had to collect them on their return, to take them to the de-Briefing Room. She would be well aware that she had been the last to see some crews alive. In short, on such a

Station and whether Aircrew or not, there was an awareness that the chance of survival of a "tour" of Bomber Operations was not good. There were so many widows in such a short time.

After a particular operation the returned aircrew would discuss their various experiences. There were some who were convinced that they had survived by adoption of some form of course changing, thinking it fooled the *"flak"* and searchlights. Others might be tempted to adopt some similar tactics, until the originator of the tactic failed to return.'

Pilot Officer Wallis was put back on the operations list on the 10th October and, on the 22nd, he was returning from a raid on Mannheim in Wellington Mk.1C R1459 when it became the subject of intense German *"flak"*. It turned out that this was the least of his problems. The aircraft had been struck by lightning during a bad storm on departing the English coast during the outward flight over the North Sea. This had put the radio out of action, leaving only Morse for communications. As the flight continued, further problems developed which included frozen oil coolers, a broken oil pump - this had come away in the hands of the Second Pilot (Ken Winchester) who was on his first operational flight - severe icing, inoperative Air Speed Indicator, and being forced to fly mostly on one engine.

Limping home on the return leg in very poor weather conditions, one engine suddenly cut out and Ken took over control from the Second Pilot with some difficulty, hoping to bring the iced-up engine back to life by feeding de-icing fluid into the intake. At this point the second engine also iced-up and there was relative silence, with no outside vision possible. The WOp/AG hurriedly sent out an S.O.S. Miraculously, one engine then restarted in fine pitch followed by the second a little later as the aircraft descended below the freezing level, only just above a stormy North Sea, and the screen defrosted. The S.O.S. was cancelled and they headed for home.

The strange noise produced by the aircraft as it neared the coast then attracted anti-aircraft fire from a "friendly" gun battery at Harwich. Not an uncommon happening, and this activity provided something of a beacon for other homecoming bombers. His Navigator told him to fly north, eventually calling for a due west course for Elsham Wolds which was just south of the Humber and Kingston-upon-Hull. On this course, Ken knew they were approaching the Humber balloon barrage, which could be seen from the station, and that it might be illuminated when friendly aircraft only were in the vicinity. Obviously they did not qualify in the eyes, or rather the ears, of the operators.

Ken's thoughts lingered on the danger of the barrage balloons in the area as, with the R/T out of action, there would not be the usual warning sound of the "squeakers" in the headset to indicate their proximity. Suddenly, the Navigator called *"Due west, now, Skipper"* and Ken saw a flashing light in the distance straight ahead (a "Pundit" beacon). He called out its letters to the Navigator and asked if it was their beacon but, before an answer could be given, the aircraft encountered a "Lethal Type" balloon cable near to Immingham Docks north-west of Grimsby, at the mouth of the Humber. If the radio had been working it would have picked up the "squeakers" that were supposed to warn friendly aircraft of their approach to a barrage. Also, searchlights should have illuminated the balloons.

On contact with the wing of an unsuspecting aircraft, friend or foe, this type released 5,000 feet of cable with a drogue on both ends. It then worked on a similar principle to a wire cheese-cutter to sever the wing. As planned, the cable duly engaged the leading edge of the aircraft's port wing, within a foot of the fuselage, and commenced cutting through half of the chord. On contact, the aircraft was almost brought to a stall in a shower of sparks and tearing sounds, and Ken had to apply full power to both engines to maintain control. The engine controls to the port engine were soon severed, together with the fuel pipes and hydraulics, thus cutting out that engine and allowing the bomb doors to open and wheels to hang down. Luckily, the cable broke on cutting through the front main spar tube, top and bottom, before reaching the second but with full power in fine pitch on the starboard engine alone it was not possible to maintain height.

By now the port wing was oscillating up and down, reacting on the control wheel, but miraculously remained attached. With this severe damage, Ken struggled to make headway towards the Elsham Wolds "Pundit" airfield identification beacon to then set course for home. (These beacons were placed at different positions about five miles from airfields to reduce the risk of attacks. The heading from the "Pundit" to the airfield would be known by aircrews for the night concerned).

Despite efforts to attract attention, no airfield lights were switched on but, in the glow of the Very Lights they were firing, Ken spotted some Wellington bombers on the ground. He attempted to pull the aircraft round in a tight circuit to make an approach for a crash landing but height could not be maintained and the aircraft began shuddering before onset of a stall. In the darkness something light-coloured passed just underneath the aircraft and he called to the crew to brace for a crash-landing.

The aircraft struck the ground and Ken was thrown forward with great force as there had not been an opportunity to do up the straps. His face hit the de-icing levers below the windscreen and his left hand was caught up in the throttle levers, causing permanent damage to a finger, but no one else was hurt. The Second Pilot (Pilot Officer Winchester) had been standing beside Ken and now found himself trapped up to his waist in mud that had entered through the damaged nose. Ken hastily opened the escape hatch at the top and ordered everyone out in case of fire but his "number two" almost required a shovel to extricate himself. Luckily, the aircraft had missed recently erected anti-landing poles extending along the top of a deep quarry by passing through a gap in the work - the quarry face being the "something light-coloured" Ken had seen and just managed to clear.

By way of compensation, the Balloon Command personnel at Grimsby made Ken and his crew guests of honour at a party organised for the next day; obviously they were very pleased to have a live RAF crew to entertain. Each member received a piece of the offending balloon cable as a memento of the occasion before leaving, somewhat worse for wear, from the hospitality provided. Ken recalls that Balloon Command had brought down some 42 RAF aircraft against 7 German ones by that time but, importantly, they were preventing the Luftwaffe from bombing at low altitude. At much the same time, another crew from 103 Squadron had survived a balloon cable, crash-landing near Yate (Bristol Barrage). Ken and the Captain of that aircraft were then ordered to report to the Air Ministry to describe their experiences. The weekend stay in London allowed their fiancées to go along too for a rare treat. Unfortunately, the other pilot would soon lose his life.

Ken later found out that the sound of his single engine in fine pitch did not readily identify the aircraft as being a Wellington so the airfield runway lights had not been turned on for him. In the circumstances it was the best thing to do. Ken judges that if he had attempted a crash landing on the runway, rather than the wet, ploughed field, the sparks could well have ignited the fuel that had been released by the fractured pipes.

Ken recalls that most of his Wellingtons came to a sad end. R1459 was repaired following her encounter with the barrage balloon and was operational at RAF North Luffenham in 1944. It was soon to crash after take-off and burn, with the loss of all crew.

The effectiveness of the balloon cable can be seen by the extent of damage inflicted upon the leading edge of the Wellington's port wing.

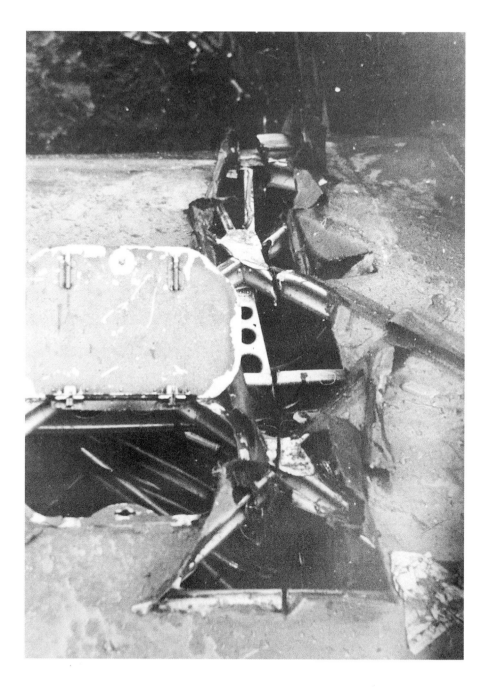

This photograph was taken from the trailing edge and shows that the wing
was very nearly cut through.

Wellington 1C R1459 PM-X at rest following Ken's skilful landing.

Between the 11th and 17th November Ken was on a Blind Approach Training Course at RAF Mildenhall, using the Lorenz Beam but never had to use it in operations. His next operation was on the 26th to Emden with incendiaries. His Log Book records that they *bombed at 16,000 feet, 10/10 cloud, Medium/Heavy "flak", no oil in starboard oil tank on landing due to a fractured pipe.* Early in December there was formation flying and "Fighter Cooperation" in connection with "Wings For Victory", etc. A photograph of his Wellington "PM-X" was used for the 103 Squadron Christmas card.

On the 23rd December 1941, Ken was required to take his Second Pilot P/O Ward and crew to Colerne, Wiltshire, in Wellington Mk.Ic W5664, to collect another Wellington but the weather became so appalling that he was soon flying just above the ground. The aircraft then hit a large bird with the spinner of the port airscrew and it was put badly out of balance, causing serious vibration. When Ken saw a grass airfield at Watchfield he decided to put down immediately but the wheel-brakes had virtually no effect on the wet grass. The aircraft carried on through the boundary fence and finally came to rest. The report that followed said *"Pilot not to blame....the officer who authorised the flight should have obtained the latest Met. information before authorising the flight and should have given the pilot more definite instructions, and should not have left it to the pilot's discretion. Officer responsible notified'.* Ken saw this report only a few years ago.

Through the fence at Watchfield - Wellington W5664.

60

Another of Ken's lucky escapes (or *"major adventures"* in his words!) occurred on the night of 21/22 January 1942 in Wellington Mk.1C L7819 when the target was Bremen Docks. There was to be an early experiment at indicating the route to the target by dropping parachute flares – an important role successfully carried out later in the war by the Pathfinder Force. On this occasion, Ken's aeroplane carried some 41/2 inch reconnaissance flares in the bomb bay in addition to a load of incendiary bombs; this was instead of the usual launch method for a flare or Photo-Flash which would be down the flare chute. The intention was to drop the first flare over Emden en route to Bremen.

The Navigator went to the Bomb Aimer's position and called for Ken to open the bomb doors and he selected them "Open". He then called out that the flare had gone and for the bomb doors to be closed. The Navigator then asked the Rear Gunner to advise when the flare lit up. As a sighting was not made it was presumed to have been a "dud" and the request was repeated for the bomb doors to be opened. *"Flare Gone"* was then reported by the Navigator/Bomb Aimer so the doors were closed again.

Within seconds Ken could smell burning and called out to the crew to investigate. Before they could reply a mighty explosion rocked the aircraft and the blast blew the plywood bulkhead at the front end of the bomb bay into the lower area of the cockpit. At the same moment, an intense white light and smoke filled the cockpit. The smell must have been from the fuze which would have given about 14 seconds delay after the flare safety pin had been withdrawn on launch and before the burning magnesium flare, with its parachute, would be blown from the flare container tube. The Navigator/Bomb Aimer yelled *"Jettison, Skipper"* and Ken immediately pulled the bomb-load jettison knob. The magnesium flare had ignited the incendiary bomb load but, fortunately, the combined weight of the bombs carried the flaming mass away from the aircraft. The aircraft continued to burn brightly, however, and this attracted considerable enemy "flak" from the ground. The cockpit was full of fumes and smoke so Ken opened the side windows in order to see and breathe properly in spite of having on his oxygen mask. The fire burned for some time, consuming fabric on the underside of the fuselage before finally being extinguished, leaving a good view of the North Sea below when walking down the narrow cat-walk to the rear turret.

In reality, the doors had been iced-up and had not opened on being selected "Open". The flare, with its time fuze initiated, had fallen on to the iced-up doors. They only opened when Ken pulled the "Jettison" knob and the full weight of the incendiary bomb load fell on them.

On returning to base the temperature of the burning magnesium was evident from the melted bomb bay beams, and the crew had been fortunate that the flames had not reached nearby fuel pipes. In short, the dangerous situation had been created because the bomb doors had iced up, causing the flare to be retained after it left its rack. In the case of the first flare, it was possible that the safety pin had not been withdrawn by the wire lanyard fixed to the bomb rack. The second flare had operated properly and the pyrotechnic time-fuze had ignited.

Having outlined the event to me, Ken then went on to provide a more detailed assessment on the situation. He explained that the 41/2 inch Reconnaissance Flare had a pyrotechnic delay that would be initiated by a wire lanyard attached to the roof of the aircraft as the flare was pushed down the flare chute or, in this case, a lanyard attached to the bomb rack. The flare would only have to drop a little before the delay, which could be of about 14 seconds according to the dropping altitude, and would start burning. After the pre-selected delay the big magnesium flare would be ignited and be blown out of the 41/2 inch steel tube, together with its parachute. All this happened with quite a bit of force.

In the case of flares carried on the bomb racks, in connection with this early experiment in lighting the way to the target, it was possible that in some positions in the bomb-bay the lanyard would be long enough to prevent initiation, even if the flare were to fall from the rack on to the closed bomb doors. There were other positions, however, where the lanyard would initiate the flare, perhaps as the flare rolled a little on the doors. In the circumstances of Ken's mishap, he had dropped the flares and selected "Bomb Doors Closed" after their release, not realising that the doors were iced-up. It was the pull of the wire lanyard at the flare that started the delay fuze. As with a bomb, had it been decided to drop the flare or a bomb "Safe", the Bomb Aimer could have selected to release the lanyard from its link to the bomb rack.

Ken recalls that a number of Wellington bombers were lost when the 41/2 inch Photo-Flash got stuck in the flare chute after the delay fuze had been initiated by the short wire lanyard. The tail would then be blown off the aircraft. This occurred twice when he was later with No.21 Operational Training Unit so it was decreed that a Staff Air Gunner should fly with pupil crews when photoflashes were to be launched. On one such flight, F/O

"Larry" Mole went to the waist of the Wellington with an axe in case of an emergency. The pupil gunner went to the flare-chute and plugged in his intercom lead, then lifted the photo-flash to the chute before attaching the wire lanyard to the time-fuze. On receiving the Navigator's order to launch, he pushed to photo-flash down the chute and its fuze was ignited but his intercom leads caught on the tail-fin and the flash was retained! The poor pupil was frantically trying to get clear of the leads with his head pulled down to the top of the chute. "Larry" Mole felt he ought to use the axe to chop off his head to free the flash and save the rest of the crew! Fortunately, the flash was freed just in time and it detonated behind the aircraft.

In talking of his flying experiences in the RAF, Ken will make passing reference, usually with a chuckle, to aircraft under his "pilotage" being encouraged to perform feats not found in Pilots Notes for type.   When at Advanced Flying Training School and flying North American Harvards, he experimented with one by holding the aircraft on its back in a gliding descent lasting for over a minute, from 10,000 feet to 6,000 feet, in the full knowledge that the engine would not run inverted.

Whilst at the School of Army Co-operation, Ken had enjoyed looping the Westland Lysanders - very few pilots attempted this. He recalls that some of these aircraft were quite happy to turn on their backs and his Flight Gunner did not complain! He admits though to nearly being caught out with one *"Lizzie"* owing to insufficient friction on the trimming wheel when the control column was pulled back to the nose-up setting. Luckily, he spotted it as he tried to pull it over in a loop and grabbed the trim wheel in time. Ken explained that the trim wheel on a *"Lizzie"* had more authority than the control column. If full power were applied so as to go round again, with the trim set for landing, the aircraft would go vertically nose-up even with the stick hard forward. This was the cause of a number of fatal accidents for young pilots during training.

These exploits are some indication of the approach to life Ken has usually followed. Whilst displaying an obvious respect for all things mechanical, he clearly feels the need to probe and to experiment with generally accepted boundaries and limitations.   Whilst others might well not venture, or necessarily succeed, Ken has always possessed a natural "feel" for the degree to which an aeroplane can be encouraged to perform better than the norm; a skill very much required when flying the autogyro.

Ken was always grateful to his namesake, Barnes Wallis, for the Wellington's tremendous strength in design and construction that had enabled him and his crew to survive this deadly contact. Cable cutters had been fitted to the aircraft in 1941 to prevent such damage but the "friendly" cable obviously did not know that it was supposed to slide along the wing towards the tip where it should have entered and triggered the explosive cutter. Ken recalls that the modification to the aircraft was probably supposed to include the fitting of a harder wing leading edge but his aircraft still had one of the original type made of aluminium alloy.

It is worth recording that the late Sir Barnes Wallis, the brilliant engineer and inventor, was possibly a distant relative to Ken as he had, on one or two occasions, referred to there being "second cousins" in Cambridge who had constructed an early flying machine. Had they met each other I suspect that they would have got on very well together. In 2006 Ken did meet a number of BW's family members at an event and they discussed possible blood links but it would require genealogical research to verify this.

In February 1942 the German battleships *Scharnhorst and Gneisenau* made their famous "Channel dash" and Ken was supposed to have taken part in 103 Squadron's attack on the ships. It so happened that the Wellington being flown by his Flight Commander, Squadron Leader Ian Cross, went *"u/s"* just before take-off and he promptly commandeered Ken's aircraft, telling him to stand in as Squadron Adjutant. The aircraft then had the misfortune to be shot down by one of the ships and *"Crossy"* was captured.

Whilst a prisoner-of-war, Cross wrote a letter home that appeared to recount a game of golf he had once played but it was not difficult to "read between the lines" that it was a disguised account of the way the aircraft was lost. Later, Ian Cross and another officer from the squadron were within the group of fifty selected and shot on Hitler's direct orders after their mass escape and recapture from the notorious Stalag Luft III.

I have wondered what Ken's fate might have been if he had made the flight as planned. Would his aircraft have been hit and would he then have been captured and interned? If so, I can quite imagine that he would have spent much of his time designing and making all manner of ingenious tools and equipment for escape attempts - and possibly something with wings! It is then interesting to contemplate the choice of actor who would have played Ken's role in the classic film *"The Great Escape"*.

Whilst hugely entertaining, the script was a mish-mash of true events and people and fiction, with Steve McQueen portraying a very dramatised version of the real "Cooler King", London-born Squadron Leader Eric Foster. He had been a serial escaper but did not take part in the actual breakout from the camp as he was planning another escape method - feigning mental illness! Using stolen text books, he acted out the role so well that he was diagnosed insane by medics from a visiting Swedish Red Cross delegation and handed over. On reaching England, however, he was very annoyed to be placed in a lunatic asylum and had to convince a War Office medical board of his sanity. He died in Gloucestershire in March 2006 aged 102 - never having ridden a motorcycle! His fascinating autobiography is named *"Life Hangs By A Silken Thread"*.

Ken remembers being frustrated that he sometimes missed out on operations during the first part of 1942, when he really wanted to "get on with the job" and also complete the tour. At this time he was the "Squadron Instructor and Engine Control Officer". Though he had no formal training as an instructor, his interest in technical matters shone through and one of his duties was to check out Second Pilots on night flying, circuits and landings, before they became Captains with a crew of their own.

The duty of the Engine Control Officer was primarily that of instructing on fuel conservation to get the best performance out of the two Bristol Pegasus engines of the Wellington Mk.1C. At the time there were a number of losses of aircraft sustained after the loss of one engine on operations. Pilots found that they could not maintain height even though every pound of excess weight, even parachutes, had been jettisoned as the aircraft lost height to just above the ground or sea. Often the "ground effect" and moist air just above the sea would enable an aircraft to just stay airborne until it reached our coast but then it would not be possible for it to climb over the sea wall and land. A crash landing on the beach could be hazardous because beaches were mined in case of enemy invasion.

The Station Commander at Elsham Wolds, Group Captain Constantine, seldom flew, being absorbed by the ground duties on this operational station. The growing loss of crews attempting to return on one engine must have spurred him to say to Ken, as the Squadron Engine Control Officer, *"Come up with me Wallis and I will show you that a Wellington will stay up on one engine"*. They took off with *"Connie"* at the controls and, at 5,000 feet, he shut down one engine and feathered the propeller. *"There you are Wallis. It is maintaining height on one"*. Ken knew he had yet to face the problem so suggested that they carry on for a while longer and then watched for a gradual increase in the cylinder head temperature of the working engine. *"There you are. What's the problem?"* repeated *"Connie"*. Ken again asked him to carry on a little longer even though his superior was obviously a bit displeased at Ken's doubts. It was not long before the altimeter began to unwind, in spite of *"Connie's"* efforts, and soon he had to restart the second engine to save the aircraft! Whilst he had "got the message", Ken does not think that the test improved his own popularity with his Station Commander.

The Engine Control Officer's task was placed on Ken because of his interest in engines and previous experience with aircraft. For much of the time it entailed giving advice on how to conserve fuel and be kind to the engines on the long bombing flights. An excess of fuel was not carried as this would be to the detriment of the bomb load. It was always a bit worrying for a pilot, therefore, to see that more than half the available fuel had been consumed before reaching the target. This was of course due to the excess weight being carried in the bombs and fuel at that stage. The policy of not being allowed to drop the bombs if the military target could not be positively identified caused many losses before a more realistic solution was adopted.

One embarrassing incident occurred on the 28th January 1942 when Ken was instructing. A Pilot Officer Smith, an Australian, was at the controls, with a Flight Lieutenant Gillespie on board to be checked out after Smith. During the flight, Smith did everything according to the book and ended with a good landing, so Ken called Gillespie for him to take over when the aircraft had rolled to a stop. The next moment there was a mighty bang as *"G" George*, a very tatty old Wellington, dropped onto the runway and promptly broke her back. The very competent Smith had raised the undercarriage instead of the flaps!

Ken flew eight more operations in April 1942, starting on the 2nd with the low-level attack on the Matford Works at Poissy, near Paris. He recalls the bright moonlight and seeing the Eiffel Tower for the first time. Interestingly, it was directly ahead and above rather than below but he had ample time to avoid it. On the 12th the target had been Dortmund but the rear turret doors broke away when the turret turned fully to one side. It could not be moved and there was no way to get the gunner safely into the aircraft and prevent him freezing to death on a long flight so it was aborted. Just before touching down on the slightly downhill runway a lorry drove across the runway in front of them. Ken just managed to lift the fully laden bomber off the ground and touch down again for a longer landing roll. In the circumstances, the WAAF driver had no reason to expect air traffic at that time.

The bombing of Cologne, Hamburg, and Dortmund came next, then Dortmund and Hamburg again, followed by Rostock on the 23rd/24th April and again on the 25th/26th, flying Wellington Mk.1C Z8533 to end his first tour. On this occasion, a German night-fighter passed dangerously close with guns blazing but the target was another Wimpy below and it was hit. Ken then realised it was his 26th birthday.

The year 1942 also saw Ken purchase a 1925 Rolls-Royce from the widow of an architect in Hove, a Mrs. Garrett. News of its availability had come from Peggy's father, who was then Manager of the National Westminster Bank in Brighton. Mrs. Garrett wanted to retain the dashboard clock and sell the vehicle for £20; Ken gave her £25. He intended to remove the coachwork and make it another of his "specials" and still has the drawing he made in 1943 incorporating the proposed changes. After the purchase, however, he realised *"it was a dreary old car"* so used it as a "hack" until about 1949, when it was superseded by the 71/2 litre "Wallis Silver Ghost Special" - he recalls selling it for £230.

In November 2001, Ken was surprised to see the same vehicle featured in *The Daily Telegraph*, having been found in a potato shed on a farm in Buckinghamshire. Expected to make £30,000 at Bonhams' auction the following month, it was withdrawn from the sale at the last minute.

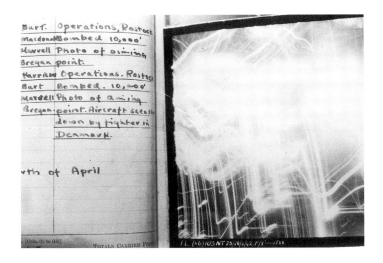

Photograph from Ken's Log Book showing the target area of Rostock on the 25/26th April 1942.

The 20 hp Faux Cabriolet (chassis number GEN82X) had been purchased for £80 by the vendor from the owner of a wallpaper shop in Woolwich in 1956. He then used it as a family car until it was laid up in the shed and remained there for the next thirty-six years. It turned out to be a development model, driven by Sir Henry Royce as his personal car until 1927, and considered to be a very important piece of Rolls-Royce memorabilia. Research found that it was built in 1925 as 10-G-111 and ran without a body for 1,200 miles before a Barker Cabriolet body was fitted.

In 1926, after various adjustments had been made, Royce ran it for a few days in Le Canadel and then it was driven back to Paris and handed over to the testers for a 10,000 miles endurance test. This was carried out by two teams of two drivers and completed in 34 days - an average of 294 miles per day - in spite of a number of breakages to such things as the battery box brackets, spare wheel bracket, water temperature tube connection on the dashboard, exhaust flanges; also, both back springs cracked and a back axle thrust race failed.

In 1927, the body was removed to be repainted and the chassis updated to the latest 20 hp standard, being fitted with vertical shutters, a new bonnet and a 10x47 back axle. It then went back to Le Canadel for more endurance testing under a George Hancock. There had been complaints of poor performance from the car and it was thought this was due to the body so a new Hooper Saloon Cabriolet (aka Faux Cabriolet) was fitted - a considerable improvement was noted. The car spent the next twelve months with Royce at West Wittering, then put into good order and sold to a Mr Thomas Garrett with the new chassis number GEN82X.

It is interesting that Ken, as the next owner, described it as *"a dreary old car"* so the improvements had not achieved too much. When owned by him at Moreton-in-the-Marsh, a squirrel managed to get inside the body and set up home. Later, on a return trip from Farnborough, a fire started under the back seat - the top of the inverted "U" of the tail pipe had rusted through and hot gases set the floor alight. On another trip he spotted a 7 1/2 litre Rolls-Royce "Silver Ghost" chassis dumped on the verge south of Farnborough and this provided some spares such as a coil ignition distributor. Ken believes the vehicle is with the Rolls-Royce Enthusiasts Club, Paulerspury, near Towcester. When changing a wheel on his old David Brown tractor recently, he suddenly realised that the jack he was using, and its handle, had been part of the car's toolkit. Ken has since reunited it with the car.

Behind every great man....

…. there is usually a good woman and Ken was no exception but, sadly, Peggy died in November 2003. We had persuaded her to contribute a section in this book at an early stage, in order to link with the period of the next chapter, as it includes Ken meeting her and marriage. I felt a few words on events in her life leading up to this happy union would be appropriate.

Ken's reputation had reached Peggy Stapley even before they actually met, when she was stationed in the Women's Auxiliary Air Force quarters at Barnetly le Wolds. This was some distance away from his station at Elsham Wolds - no doubt a sensible precaution! *"Crasher"* Wallis (as he was now known) had "pranged" two Wellington bombers in little more than a month and as this was not too common she was probably a little concerned at the sort of man she would meet on their first date. This was a dinner-dance in late October/early November, 1941 at the Berkeley Hotel in Scunthorpe where they went with another couple. Obviously she was impressed for, from then on, she recalls it was all "downhill" but they decided not get married until Ken had finished his tour of "ops" on the 26th April 1942.

Previous to this, on the 12th September 1938, the crisis over Czechoslovakia put in motion the events that led up to Peggy's first meeting with Ken. Before hostilities arose, life had been pleasant and uncomplicated for her but the dramatic events of the time brought home the seriousness of the situation and she felt obliged to do something useful. Nursing seemed to be the obvious career and she enjoyed her time in this noble profession. In 1940, however, she suffered a bad riding accident and received five broken bones in a foot plus a cracked ankle.

Nursing was now out of the question as continual standing on the wards was too painful so she applied to the W.A.A.F. as a potential Motor Transport Driver. On being called up, however, she was told that the intake for driving was full to overflowing; they also had too many plotters, cooks and cipher operators. Applying to become a Cartographer was suggested so Peggy agreed but on telephoning the W.A.A.F. officer found that this trade was also fully subscribed. The officer added that a new trade had just opened although details were not available - a sparking plug tester - and if Peggy applied she would be "No.3". This was enough to attract her and during the course at Melksham she became firm friends with her two companions.

69

They successfully completed their course to become Assistant Instructors with immediate promotion to Corporal. Peggy then re-instated to Administration and became a Sergeant at Melksham before being posted to Elsham Wolds which was then a new bomber station. A dispute followed as Melksham wanted to hold on to her, and she was also happy to stay, but Bomber Command won in the end and she started on her "fateful mission" with Ken the ultimate target.

On arrival at the W.A.A.F. section she was surprised to find that a state of panic existed. A young A.C.W.2, whose home was in Grimsby, had gone "AWOL" (Absent Without Leave) for 48 hours following 24 hours' official leave. Her excuse being that she could not find where to get off the bus for the W.A.A.F. Section between Grimsby and Scunthorpe.

The W.A.A.F. officer, Flight Lieutenant Harthan, gave her 14 days "Confined to Barracks" as punishment. As was required in King's Regulations, the culprit was asked if she would accept the award or opt for a Court Martial. Not knowing anything about Courts Martial, but feeling that the award was unfair, the A.C.W.2 promptly demanded the CM! The fury with which this was viewed by H.Q. can only be imagined and the Flight Officer was told to "sort it out" in no uncertain terms. She duly called in help from all the other W.A.A.F. officers - Codes & Ciphers, Intelligence, Met., etc. - but the miscreant would have none of it and stuck to her guns, no doubt impressed by the reaction to her decision and sensing that it could be the road to fair play.

Before Peggy had even sipped a cup of tea, therefore, she was asked if she would try and talk the girl out of her demand. In Peggy's words *"Things were clear from the start. 1) She was not accustomed to travel. 2) She was telling the truth and had tried to get back. 3) She was feeling unfairly treated. 4) She had 'her rights'"*. She clearly felt that all in "authority" were against her and Peggy appeared to be another one.

Peggy's solution was to sit her down in the tiny office and send the Corporal for mugs of cocoa. She took off her jacket saying *"forget I am a Sergeant and tell me all about it"* and listened patiently to the tale of woe. She then explained to her what a Court Martial would mean, how it worked, and the time it would take when everybody was busy trying to fight a war. Peggy sympathised with the girl over the loss of privileges but pointed out there were plenty of young men who would be going on missions and not returning, never to go home again so those on the ground had a duty not to complicate things further. Peggy knew she had won her over when tears began to flow, and then the girl agreed to abide by the punishment.

Peggy's Commission Course came within two days of arrival at Elsham Wolds and she was sure this was due to her success with the A.C.W.2 in preventing a waste of time and effort in wartime conditions! After this, Peggy was posted back to the station as an officer and judged that if she had been posted to the station when the order was first issued, she would have been resident there too long as an NCO to return with a Commission. This was obviously another important part of the "plot" to ensure her meeting with "Crasher" Wallis.

Peggy was first commissioned as an Assistant Section Officer in the Administration Branch and later promoted to Section Officer.

Peggy and Ken plus *"Jock"* in 1942

Between tours

Ken duly completed his first tour of operational duty a few months after he met Peggy at Elsham Wolds, where she had been since around early November 1941, and they married on the 29th April the next year. The best man was Ken Winchester from 103 Squadron - the Second Pilot who had shared the near-lethal encounter earlier on with the barrage balloon cable.

Following one week's honeymoon leave in London, Ken was posted to No 21 Operational Training Unit at Moreton-in-the-Marsh in the Navigation Training Flight, flying trainee Navigators in Ansons. During early May, however, much of his flying was with six ex-operational Wireless Operators/Air Gunners on board. They would take turns at the Morse key, sending messages with different call signs as they flew over the UK and North Sea on typical Operational Training routes. This was to fool the Germans monitoring such transmissions into thinking that training was proceeding normally, whereas the Wellingtons with these call signs were being bombed-up ready for the first 1000 Bomber Raid on 30/31 May.

One of Ken's crew, F/Sgt Marvell, who lived up to his name, was also posted to 21 O.T.U. and was awarded the Distinguished Flying Medal for his service with 103 Squadron. On the second raid, to Essen on June 1/2, he was required to fly with a 20 O.T.U. crew but the aircraft was lost at sea. His was the only body recovered. Ken felt sad that this should have happened so soon after he had completed his first tour.

Although a very sedate aircraft, Ken enjoyed regularly delivering a sharp lesson by turning the *"Annie"* almost on to her back in taking controlled, evasive action when pupils repeatedly failed to advise the appropriate course as the aircraft steadily advanced upon the Cardington "Pundit" beacon. Cardington was a test and development site for barrage balloons and, whilst pupils could identify the beacon correctly, they often failed to recognise the attendant lethal peril of balloon cables. Ken made sure they did not forget and gave them some bruises as a reminder!

On one of the daytime training flights he spotted a barrage balloon that had broken away from its moorings and it was trailing its cable along the ground. The *"Annie"* had a forward firing machine-gun (fixed) under the pilot's control and Ken felt this would be a great opportunity to get revenge but his radio calls failed to produce the necessary permission to destroy it. He returned, very disappointed, to Moreton-in-the-Marsh.

Some staff pilots said they had found an engine in one of the *"Annies"* sometimes cut out. They had reported this to the Engineer Officer but he did not seem to believe them. Accordingly, Ken invited the E.O. to go up with him in the suspect aircraft (20.11.42 - Anson 985 - per Log Book). All went well for a time so Ken thought he would have some fun. The wings of an Anson are quite flexible in torsion, and engines are in nacelles extending well forward of the wings. By small movement of the control wheel, suitably tuned, the engine nacelles can be induced to rock up and down to an increasing degree. (Ken said he thought that it could be potentially dangerous!). Ken looked out over the suspect engine while inducing this movement and the Engineer Officer followed his gaze, not noticing Ken's small movement of the control wheel; he was clearly frightened. Then, during some steep turns under power, the suspect engine did indeed cut out for a while. On landing, a major investigation was conducted because pilots were obviously not simply "making a fuss". The cause was then discovered.

There had been an air-raid on Moreton-in-the Marsh some time before and various aircraft had been badly damaged. This particular aircraft was one assemble from "cannibalised" parts which included one wing. When this had been removed from a damaged fuselage, the fuel pipe had been sealed off from debris by inserting a plug of rag. This obstruction had not been seen when the wing was fitted to the new fuselage and had acted as a filter for a while, then was completely sealing off flow under high power settings.

Ken would occasionally "drop in" for a chat back at Elsham Wolds with old friends and had done so on the 15th October specifically to see Ken Winchester, then a Captain of a Handley Page Halifax bomber. They made arrangements to meet up the next evening for a celebratory drink to mark the end of Winchester's tour but on his arrival, around lunch-time, Ken was told the sad news that his friend had been shot down by a German night-fighter and killed on his last operation which was to Koln. Ken had spent that very morning flying an unsuccessful North Sea search for a missing crew believed to have ditched in a particular area when returning from the raid on the night of the 15/16th October.

Ken can remember some good parties in the Mess at Elsham Wolds, especially when Polish flyers attended as they produced some very potent alcoholic mixtures and were good company. On an earlier occasion, with 103 Squadron, there were a few moments when he had not felt so relaxed in their

73

company, however, although all was well in the end. On this occasion, he had "been a bit lost" on returning from operations and was pleased to get permission to land at a UK airfield. He landed his Wellington bomber at this darkened airfield and taxied-in, with directions coming by torchlight. Having shut down the engines and opened the cockpit hatch there was a brief moment of concern for Ken when voices called out in a foreign language.

His first thought was the length of time needed to restart the engines and take off again whilst in a possible hostile environment but calm was quickly restored when the voices changed to the English language. Ken had landed at a Polish station where the squadrons also flew Wellingtons. The resident ground crew had presumed the aircraft was one of theirs and had asked what sort of trip it had been for them. In those few seconds, Ken had also wondered how they could have strayed so far from home and what punishment to award the Navigator!

Fun often had to be manufactured during wartime and his time at 21 O.T.U. was no exception. No doubt as a deliberate piece of devilment, Ken chose the 180 feet tall, and naked "Cerne Abbas Giant" on a Dorset hillside as one of the targets for photographing in the bomb-aimers' training exercise. This ancient, chalk figure was therefore captured on film by each pupil and, on landing, the output went to the girls of the W.A.A.F. to assess the bombing training results. After a while Ken received a stern telephone call from the W.A.A.F. officer in charge, complaining that repeated exposure to this well-endowed figure was *"disturbing her girls"* and it was to stop forthwith!

In Ken's absence, his father managed the business whilst undertaking the additional duties of a Divisional Commander in the Special Constabulary so was "doing his bit". He had been a Special Constable during World War I and risen to the rank of Superintendent during World War II with Ely Section, "A" Division, Ely Special Constabulary. Ken laughs at this because of all the summonses his father had received for speeding during the early days of his motorcycling career. In addition to having concern for the safety of loved-ones in the Services, hardships of every kind were endured on the Home Front, plus there was the risk of injury or death from enemy bombing.

One leave period, Ken visited his parents and witnessed the difficulties caused by rationing and the fuel shortage so he used his skills to make a small contribution to the war effort, and life a little easier for his father. He converted a BSA Bantam motorcycle to electric power, which could be put on trickle-charge after each journey; the power source came from a Hotchkiss-Morris dyno-starter motor and worked well. Many a pedal cyclist was surprised when overtaken by Wallis senior on his "silent-bicycle". Ken similarly converted the garden lawnmower. Both were ahead of their time of course but likely to have been thrown away after the war when his father ran down the family business.

For most of 1943, Ken served as Officer Commanding "X" Aerial Gunnery Training Flight at 21 O.T.U., based on the satellite field at Enstone. Here he flew Wellington's and Miles Martinets, the latter for target-towing. After the guns in the rear turret of the attacking Wellington had fired at the drogue target and their ammunition was expended they were supposed to be made "safe". The drogue and cable attached to the Martinet would then be wound back in or jettisoned over a safe part of the airfield. The trainee Gunner in the Wellington would then use a camera-gun as the Martinet carried out simulated fighter attacks. With a chuckle, Ken remarked that *"there were some funny moments!"*

Before take-off on such a flight the gunner, with the guns at "safe", was required to select some suitable object for a sighting shot by the camera-gun. This would be used in the assessment as the aiming point when the film was subsequently projected. One pupil Gunner decided to use the propeller spinner of one of the Flight's parked Lysander aircraft as the aiming point. Unfortunately, he had omitted to ensure that the guns were first rendered "safe" and several rounds were fired into its Bristol Mercury engine.

The BSA Bantam motorcycle Ken converted to electric power.

Ken had a very competent and enthusiastic pilot in the Flight, a Warrant Officer Bosher. He accepted the many jokes arising from his name and was a great asset to the Flight. One day, Ken received an urgent telephone call from air Traffic Control to say W/O Bosher had reported that the green lights were not coming on to indicate the wheels were locked down on his Martinet aircraft after his target towing sortie. Ken rushed to the control tower and W/O Bosher was ordered to make a low pass, close to the tower, so that the position of the wheels could be seen. Bosher obviously thought that this would be a marvellous opportunity for a light-hearted "beat-up" of the tower. Unfortunately, for some unknown reason, after the target drogue had been shot away the towing cable had not been wound in or jettisoned safely. The sound of the aircraft passing very close to the tower was followed by a loud "swishing" noise as the cable slashed past objects on the ground, and through the telephone wires at the edge of the field. Some fierce radio messages followed and Bosher's wheels stayed down after he had landed.

Although *"a naughty incident"* per Ken, he considered W/O Bosher, and many others in the O.T.U., had the right spirit. They were always keen to fly and to do the job, including realistic simulated attacks on the Wellington for camera-gun recordings after completion of gunfire at the towed target. Sometimes Bosher would be so close to the rear turret with the Martinet that detail of the radial engine would completely fill the projection screen.

Ken's Log Book for this period produced an interesting insert: an instruction to pilots from the Chief Instructor of No. 21 O.T.U. dated 26th July 1943. It concerned "corkscrewing" and instructed that this would not be practiced by aircraft of the unit pending further instructions; the only evasive action permitted against fighter attacks was to be *'a gentle turn towards the oncoming enemy'* (!) and directed that, *under no circumstances, could Flight Commanders communicate the reason for this to flying instructors or pupils;* Ken recalls that this order followed some nasty wing failures.

Whilst with the Flight Ken found a problem existed with the towing cable to the drogue target. It was often cut by gunfire and then the drogues fell over the range area of open country quite near to Moreton-on-the-Marsh and Gloucester. When the drogue had been located, Ken would often jump on a Service motorcycle and retrieve it. These live firing activities were not always popular with local inhabitants and he was sometimes accosted by an angry farmer. He could not help but feel some sympathy was due when the cause of concern might be a neat row of bullet holes across a barn door, or other evidence that some bullets were not just falling from the sky! Whilst the gun firing was always supposed to be upwards - above horizontal - this was clearly not the case in reality.

There was a problem with the towing cable being cut through by gunfire. When this happened it required a very tedious wire-splicing of a new loop on the end by an Airframe Rigger who had to be specially summoned to "X" Flight to do the job. This process could waste quite a lot of the training time available so Ken looked for a solution. He devised a new type of fitting from two small steel plates through which three 5/16 inch bolts were suitably placed. The cable was fed around the bolts to form a loop between the two plates, and the bolts were then tightened to bring the two plates together to form a "sandwich". This provided a simple and speedy method to re-attach the cable each time.

Twice, when making dummy attacks with a Miles Martinet on the Wellington for cine gun recordings, an escape hatch detached from the waist of the Wellington just missing Ken's aircraft. The escape hatches had detached as a pupil Gunner was walking down the very narrow "cat-walk" to the rear turret. It was necessary to move to one side to allow another Gunner to pass and this sometimes resulted in stepping on the escape hatch. Such hatches had to be replaced and, needless to say, Ken took a poor view of such "carelessness" but was later to suffer a similar experience for himself.

In 1950, he attended the No.3 Senior Specialist Armament Officer's Course at RAF Lindholme, practising bombing and aerial gunnery in Avro Lincoln aircraft. One day, after gunnery in the rear turret, Ken politely stepped to one side to allow the next Gunner to move down to the turret. He stood on a quite large escape hatch and promptly fell through it up to his waist. The slipstream carried his legs back and parallel to the underside of the aircraft whilst he just managed to support himself on his elbows.

Luckily, the hatch was jammed sideways in the opening and had not dropped away. With memories of the loss of hatches from his Wellingtons in the Gunnery Flight, and the need to indent for replacements, he was more interested in saving the hatch than getting himself back into the aircraft. He finally managed to pull his legs back inside and placed them either side of the opening, in order to release the hatch and heave it back into the aircraft for re-fitting. He was thankful the hatch had been saved and that he had avoided some humiliation, so reflected upon the bad time he had given some of his less fortunate pupils in the past.

Whilst in the Navigation Flight he decided to apply to go back on "Ops", on Mosquito night fighters. He successfully completed the decompression tests, and other requirements but was caught out on the night vision tests on each eye. This time he was not able to fiddle the results and the consequences were more serious. The discovery of his eyesight defect caused considerable concern at the Operational Training Unit and he was whisked off to the Central Medical Board at Bristol.

Expecting the worst, Ken was relieved to hear the "top medic", an Air Commodore, say that he would rather have a pilot with a bit of fire in his belly than some of the perfect specimens who did not want to fly. He prescribed a pair of flying goggles with a corrected lens for Ken's defective eye but told Ken not to put them on and added *"Always have them with you and if you get your good eye shot out, put the goggles on and bring the aircraft home!"*

With three other previously "tour-expired" aircrew members, and a Sergeant Bombardier who had not been operational, they formed a crew to go back on "ops". Previously, Ken had a Wellington crew of six with a Captain and Second Pilot. This later crew consisted of five, with the Bombardier having some flying skill but not to Second Pilot standard. His Navigator was Pilot Officer George Morgan who had been badly burned in a Wellington in his first "tour" so a brave man to go back on ops in a *"Wimpy"*. Pilot Officer "Larry" Mole was his WOp/AG; the Rear Gunner was Warrant Officer John Ball - both gunners coming from his "X" Flight. Sadly, the "Bombardier" was increasingly useless per Ken and, in Italy "gave up" after the first raid.

Top: The Miles Martinet target-tug with Bristol Mercury engine. The first aircraft to enter RAF service having been designed specifically for this purpose, rather than being an obsolescent first-line type or the modification of an aircraft originally designed for a quite different role. This is the Mk 11. (photo: *M.A.P. via P. Amos of the Miles Aircraft Collection*).
Bottom: Ken when O.C. "X" Aerial Gunnery Flight at Enstone, 1943, with Miles Martinet aircraft in the background.

Flying operations over Italy

In January 1944, Ken returned to Operations and flew a new Wellington Mk.X (LN976) from Melton Mowbray to Italy to join 37 Squadron at Tortorella. The aircraft had 14-cylinder, sleeve-valve Bristol *"Hercules"* engines with ample single-engine performance. After some flight-testing, they left Portreath, Cornwall on the night of the 29th January and touched down at Rabat Sale in Morocco. He recalls that this was his first time on foreign soil.

During the flight from Rabat Sale they flew over the Atlas Mountains for a stop-over at Raison Blanche Airport in Algiers, and the Bombadier/Second Pilot was sent aft to change the fuel tanks as the fuel was being consumed. Suddenly, both engines stopped and Ken had to say, very calmly on the intercom., *"Whatever it is that you have done, put things back to where they were"*. Silent engines were hardly suited to the terrain! Fortunately, the engines came back on power and the Navigator then went aft to make the correct fuel tank connections. They stayed overnight at Maison Blanche and Ken has memories of an evening in Algiers, plus a visit to its popular "Sphinx Club" to see *"Exposition Fantastique"*.

The journey was not without some hazards in crossing the Bay of Biscay. The Germans were operating their Focke-Wolfe "Condors" over the area, occasionally picking off Wellingtons. It happened that, when he arrived at Rabat Sale, he was told that a German aircraft had been shot down in the Bay of Biscay that very night. On this subject, there was an occasion when Ken's mother stayed at Moreton-in-theMarsh for a few days. One evening he went to her hotel for dinner and she told him that *"Those boys at that table are going to Africa tonight"*. She had heard them talking. Ken immediately contacted the OTU and they did not leave for Africa that night. Ken believes it quite likely that some such security leak had led to some of the bomber losses to the "Condors".

Prior to Ken's flight they had all been provided with a *"Goolie-Chit"* in case of a crash-landing, to be handed to "All Arab Peoples", promising a reward if the holder was returned "complete and in good order!" They also had photographs taken wearing civilian clothes and "looking foreign", to attach to a false passport should they find themselves in occupied territory.

Operations in Italy were very different to those over the well-defended territory of Germany. Also the Wellington Mk.X would maintain height on one engine, unlike the Mk.IC where the remaining engine would gradually heat up and lose power. The main target at the time was the Anzio Beach Head, which would be "visited" twice a night. The two ops each lasted around 3 hours 20 minutes and, on landing back from the first, the crew would stay in the aircraft and consume a snack meal before taking off again.

There was not much effective enemy anti-aircraft fire in the Anzio area so Ken would indulge in a little low flying, with W/O Ball machine-gunning the roads. There could be some nasty storms and some aircraft were lost in the Appenine Mountains. On the airfield, the Squadron Carpenter seemed to spend much of his time making little white wooden crosses since so many of the crews were buried at their crash-sites.

On the night of 3rd April, Ken's Wellington X (LN976 - collected new by Ken from Melton Mowbray on the 14th January) was flown by Squadron Leader H H Beale DFC, one of two Flight Commanders in 37 Squadron, for a raid on the Manfred Weiss Works, Budapest. The aircraft was shot down and three members of the crew were killed; Beale died later of his wounds in Belgrade. Two others were made prisoners-of-war after baling out.

Compared with life on an operational Bomber Station in the U.K., the living conditions were very different. The Officers had taken over the living quarters of an Italian farmhouse, with the local farmer and his family required to take up residence with the animals on the ground floor. Four Officers shared the one small bedroom; three enjoying camp beds whereas Ken's resting place was a blood-stained stretcher.

After the usual two trips to the Anzio Beach-head, they would try to get some sleep and an Orderly would bring them a "basic" breakfast in bed. The empty plates would then be put on the stone floor, while they tried to get more sleep. Ken's stretcher had the disadvantage of being much closer to the floor than the camp beds of his colleagues, giving him a clear view under all of them. No sooner had the plates been put on the floor and quietness returned, than an army of mice appeared from nowhere and raid the remains.

Ken decided to purchase a number of mice traps and, later that day, set the traps in the bedroom. He then turned off the light so that he could open his camera to wind the film into the developing tank he used for the black and white film. As soon as he started to extract the film from the camera the traps went off all around him but they did not always kill the mice. He struggled to

81

get the film back into the camera in order to finish off any mice still living, and then re-set the traps. Yet again the same thing happened. Only after the third re-setting of the traps could he process the film.

Ken recalled some other amusing moments, such as when two pigs escaped from an adjacent civilian enclosure next to the Tortorella airfield and strayed onto the metal runway. An airman ran up to report their presence as a potential danger to aircraft. Ken agreed and also saw the chance to vary the Mess menu so went to the Parachute Section and asked to borrow a rifle but instead he was given a STEN gun. Not having fired one before he pulled back the bolt and fed a round into the chamber as with a normal weapon but the bolt appeared to be stuck so Ken pulled the trigger. The bolt went forward at speed and promptly discharged a shot into the ground an inch or two from his foot. Having fathomed out how it worked, Ken commandeered a lorry with an opening in the cab roof and, in true African safari style, chased the pigs until they were finally dispatched by his shots.

The carcases were taken to the Mess where one of the airmen, who had been a butcher, strung them up from a tree and expertly dissected them to provide a welcome source of extra rations. The Italian owner of the pigs was not so pleased, however, and made a formal complaint to the "authorities" but it was agreed they had presented 'a danger to the airfield' and had to be destroyed immediately.

On another occasion, two South African members of the squadron decided to boil eggs over a Primus stove in a second-storey room they occupied within a rough old farmhouse. As the "water" began to boil it caught fire. One of the airman grabbed a "Jerrycan" of what he thought was also water and threw it over the flames to extinguish them. Instead, they both shot out of the window a little shaken. It transpired that they were unaware they had been using petrol to boil the eggs, and had then thrown the remaining contents of the same can over the fire to douse it. Ken recalls a sad occasion in nearby Foggia when a building housing many NCO's collapsed with heavy loss of life.

The second Flight Commander on 37 Squadron had served a long spell on operations in the desert before the squadron moved to Tortorella, and slept in the same room as Ken. He will be referred to as Squadron Leader "X" for the sake of the stories that follow. On one particular night he stayed up drinking long after the rest of the occupants had returned to bed. Eventually he staggered into the room waving his .45" "Colt" pistol at Ken and colleagues, calling them *"******* Volunteer Reservists"*, etc. As he held a Permanent Commission, he clearly did not approve of the other officers. It was the first time a pistol had been directly pointed at Ken, and he recalled he could see the nickel-clad nose of the bullet in the barrel. The gun was being aimed at everybody in turn and Ken recalls the expressions on the faces of his companions as they looked up from their camp beds. Eventually, their drunken Flight Commander decided to remove his pullover whilst still holding the pistol, and as he got it over his head he fell down. Ken said that he had never seen people move so quickly; as one, they fell upon the body, disarmed him and dismantled the weapon.

As a Flight Commander, "X" had an open lorry, a *"Gharry"* as they called it, for his use. One evening he suggested that Ken and Flight Lieutenant Jackson, accompany him to the Officers' Mess at Bari, on the Adriatic Coast. They duly arrived, had a meal and a few drinks, before being told that there was a party at the Military Field Hospital at Trani, along the coast on their return route. The trio "gatecrashed" the lively party and were warmly welcomed. There appeared to be a shortage of glasses as Ken recalls being handed a bowl full of Brandy by one of the nurses. The majority of those at the party, and the residents of the hospital, were Army personnel; many of whom had been injured in the crossing of Salerno, etc. Ken and his colleague were enjoying the company and the refreshments and had not noticed that "X" was missing. There was then a sudden disturbance and a blood-stained "X" was dragged in by some of the party-goers. They had caught him trying to cut through the electricity cables feeding power into the hospital with an axe. He was mouthing rude opinions about the *"******* "Pongos"* (RAF slang for Army personnel: small brown monkeys), and showing as much disdain for the Army as he had for Volunteer Reservists! Ken was told they should remove themselves before something serious occurred.

Having got "X" outside there was still the problem of what to do to quieten him down. Jackson had been an amateur boxer and it was decided that a bare-knuckle knockout was called for; the return journey was very peaceful as a result. On reaching camp "X" was carried upstairs and dumped on his bed. Fortunately, he had no recollection of past events the next morning so the striking of a senior officer went without punishment. Ken refers to his time in Italy as *"still quite hectic days"* and recalls that things there sometimes a bit rough. Many of the crews were "Desert Happy" after their time in Africa and their unpredictable moods sometimes caused some tense situations.

For light relief, the Officers' Mess radio was always tuned to a German station for the good music, to which they sometimes sang. On other occasions they turned to flying the kite from a dinghy that would normally be used to carry an aerial aloft for an aircrew after ditching at sea. Ken soon extended this amusement with an open-topped tin can, on a wire, being carried some way beneath the kite. One or two Very Light cartridges would be placed in it, and then the can would be topped up with petrol. With the kite in flight, and trying to lift the now quite heavy can, they would light the petrol and release the can. The flaming petrol ascending skywards was quite spectacular but when the Very Light cartridges heated up and ignited in the can of fluid the results were really special. Ken has photographs of these escapades and one shows Flying Officer "Larry" Mole holding a kite ready for take-off. This little show was generally staged in the evening from the balcony of the Officers' Mess for full benefit and when there was a good breeze. Some of the local inhabitants did not know the true source of these lights in the sky and could be seen fervently making the sign of the cross!

When Ken got a few days leave he would grab a parachute bag, put in a tin of *Spam* and some other goods, and hitch-hike to see other parts of Italy – "and the war on the ground". There were plenty of military vehicles around so it was easy to get a lift but sometimes it could be a bit bad for the nerves! His travels took him to Cassino while the battle was still going on, and he once got a lift in a Jeep driven by a Pole. They were soon going quite madly down a zig-zag road on a steep mountainside and the Jeep was literally leaning over the edge. The Polish driver probably thought it was good fun compared with some of his experiences in the war.

On another occasion Ken was hitch-hiking on the roads along the Adriatic Coast when he had to start walking because the vehicle he had been in was going to a different destination. After walking alone for quite a while he came across a lone soldier holding a rifle. He thought it wise to check that he was on the correct road for Ortona and the soldier confirmed it, adding that he would be on his own from then on because it was the "front line"! Ken would have innocently strolled into enemy occupied territory.

One difficult task recalled by Ken was when he was when placed in charge of a funeral party in Foggia for the crew of another Wellington. It had suffered engine failure on take-off, failed to get down again safely on the airfield at Tortorella, and the 4,000lb "cookie" bomb had then exploded. The remains of the bomber's crew were but small fragments and the burial was somewhat daunting for men following the same trade.

Ken well remembers that storms, lightning strikes and the Appenines were all natural hazards but one incident provided another escape from certain death. On the night of the 17/18 February, the bomb load was the usual eighteen, 250lb N.I.Rs (Nose Initiated Rodded) for the two raids on the Albano, Anzio area. This type of bomb had a rod extending about two feet from the nose, designed to set it off as soon as it touched the ground, for maximum anti-personnel effect. (Although there will be ex-Service personnel around who will have clear memories of this bomb, I have not found any articles written about it to refer to).

Ken was returning to base in the first light of dawn and selected wheels down but found that the green light for the tail wheel did not come on so proceeded to go round again. Aware of the likely danger for the Rear Gunner, he told him to leave the turret; this was in case the tail wheel still refused to drop, and caused the tail of the aircraft to drag along the runway. At the last moment before touchdown, however, the green light came on so he presumed that the wheel was iced up and had then released itself in the warmer air. The aircraft landed and he taxied in to the hard standing.

The usual procedure then would have been to switch off the engines and select bomb doors to 'Open' in order to relieve the hydraulic pressure. At this very point, he spotted an airman running towards the aircraft giving the "Bomb Doors Closed" signal with his arms. Ken wondered what was wrong so switched off the engines, left the bomb doors closed, and climbed down the ladder to investigate. He was shocked to find before him the nose of a 250lb bomb protruding through a gap it had forced between the edges of the bomb doors, with its lethal rod sticking forward and down towards the ground. The safety fork had pulled out of the bomb the moment it fell from the rack so one touch on the rod would have caused its detonation.

For this to have happened Ken deduced that it must have been iced-up on release and later fallen on to the closed bomb doors as the aircraft descended. Ken recalls his double slice of luck in that the tail wheel had finally lowered, plus the chance presence of the observant, and very brave, airman who had managed to warn him. He deserved a medal in Ken's eyes but, typical for the time, the crew simply slapped him on the back with a promise of a drink if they saw him in Foggia!

Following this incident, Ken made the mistake of leaving his goggles on the seat-raising handle in his Wellington after landing. An observant airman must have come across them and, on noticing that there was a correcting lens for the right eye, promptly sent them to the Squadron Medical Officer. The first Ken knew of the discovery was when he was summoned from his bed for an explanation. The M.O. was not satisfied with Ken's explanation and promptly decided to send him to the military hospital at Torre del Greco, by the base of Vesuvius where it was decided he would have to go to the Medical Centre for the Middle East Air Force at Heliopolis, Cairo.

Whilst waiting for transport, Ken was standing by the hospital entrance and looking up at the usual wisp of smoke coming out of the crater. He asked the Italian door-keeper if he was not worried about being so close to the volcano but the local replied that he felt no fear as there was an observatory that kept a careful watch. Later that day Ken flew on to the RAF Hospital at Heliopolis in Egypt for further checks. That night, Vesuvius had its most devastating eruption since the destruction of Pompeii. At least this time there was ample transport available to move people from critical areas but Ken believes that three Allied aircraft were brought down by the volcanic dust. He hoped that the door-keeper did not think he had somehow induced the eruption!

Ken managed to get a break at Sorrento, not long after Vesuvius had erupted. Though some distance from the volcano, there were many very thick deposits of black ash on every roof and flat surface. Officers could stay in the rest camp there, actually in Hotel *"Cocumella"*. The staff always proudly announced that it was where Lord Nelson and Lady Hamilton had stayed.

It was possible to hire a canoe from the harbour, or some places at the bottom of the cliffs where there were caves, and on one occasion Ken was some way out from shore when a storm occurred. He remembers having serious doubts if he would ever make it back to the harbour, or anywhere along the coast, and it was a great relief to reach land. On another occasion he took a trip to Capri where the Americans had a rest camp. For a catholic country, it was a surprise for him to see so many condoms floating out to sea. Ken added with a chuckle that those on issue from the RAF doctor at that time had been liberated from Italian supplies during the North African campaign. The packets intended for Italian troops were very educational, being printed with orders and illustrations on the way to don …. a gas mask! I have resisted the urge to include a cartoon at this point on the grounds of decency but I have to wonder what instructions supported their gas masks.

At a meeting with No 2 Medical Board at Heliopolis, he was told that *"they did not have to answer to No 1 Central Medical Board, and that there were plenty of healthy pilots who had not yet had the chance of flying on*

Operations". He was taken off Operations and, amongst other duties while waiting for the next move, served on a Court Martial in Naples. He then received a posting as a Test Pilot to Setif in North Africa. Ken hitchhiked the 40 kilometres up to Caserta (No 2 Middle East Air Force Headquarters) and, on arrival, cheekily proclaimed that he *"had volunteered to go on Ops in Italy and not to do some dogs-body job in Africa"*.

Ken was taken at his word for soon after this he was boarding *"The Empress of Australia"* in Naples for the voyage back to the UK. By then, he had flown a total of 36 Operational Missions over Germany and Italy.

Top: Ken beside a wrecked German aircraft at Tortorella in 1944.
Bottom: Wellington X aircraft of 205 Group in Italy. Taken during the early part of 1944. *(IWM)*

Back in the UK

On docking in the UK on the 1st June, Ken went from Glasgow to the Middle East Dispersal Station at West Kirby and then to Catfoss in Yorkshire. On the 16th June 1944, as a Flight Lieutenant, he took up the post of Deputy Flight Commander and pilot at the Central Gunnery School, engaged on advanced aerial gunnery training for fighters and bombers.

At Catfoss he greatly enjoyed taking violent evasive action in his Wellington to avoid cine-camera "hits" by fighter pilots on training sorties but was told to damp down his tactics to give them a chance! A number of Ken's near "brushes with death" have been recorded in earlier pages and if he had been a cat there is little doubt that all fabled nine lives would have been exhausted by this point. I suspect that he experienced many other "close encounters" and a glance at his Log Book identifies that the prospect of death, or serious injury, was always present and not necessarily through enemy fire. Entries for the 12th August 1944 are good examples: *'Wellington III "X": Varied (attacks) low level. Starboard engine u/s. Emergency landing - duration 10 minutes"*. There followed another flight: *'Wellington III' "P": Quarter attacks - duration 1 hour*. Next, the same morning: *'Wellington III' "T": Air test. Emergency landing - starboard engine u/s - duration 15 minutes."* Ken quickly points out that these were not minor engine failures but real "blow ups" with cylinders detaching and bits going through the crankcase.

He does recall another lucky escape whilst at Catfoss. On one particular fine and sunny morning he was given a "Green" on the Aldis Lamp for take-off by the Control Caravan positioned just at the entrance to the runway in use so commenced to get airborne. The Wellington III was accelerating down the runway, well into takeoff, when he suddenly became aware that the bright sunlight streaming into the cockpit had strangely commenced to flicker. There was a second or two of puzzlement before he looked upwards - and found himself immediately below, and looking through, the idling propeller of a Spitfire with its wheels and flaps down, close to landing on his cockpit. All he could do at this critical point was to swing off the runway, thereby crashing through some of the ground lighting equipment in the process, to eventually complete take-off from the rough ground to the side as the fighter landed unscathed. Ken does not recall meeting up with that pilot at a later date to exchange views.

Whilst serving in Italy, it had become obvious to Ken that he would have no future in the RAF in the General Duties Branch when the war ended. Thinking ahead to avoid this, he had applied for a permanent commission in the soon to be formed "Technical Branch" of the RAF, specialising in Air Armament. Thus, in September 1944 he left Catfoss for the School of Aeronautical Engineering at Henlow to start his Armament Training, then to the Empire Air Armament School, Manby in the November. He took up his post with the Ministry of Aircraft Production in Thames House, Millbank in London as RDArm(1c): Research & Development - Armament - Fixed Gun Installations. Pyrotechnics were readily to hand for VE Day celebrations!

One attractive benefit of this post was that aircraft could be borrowed from RAF Hendon for travel to sites of weapon testing, so he applied to the Central Medical Board to continue flying in such roles. As a result, he was granted permission to fly *"Non-Operational, Daylight Only, With Passenger"*. Although he suspected the wording of the document he decided not to raise a query and retained it for possible future reference. Ken then flew Percival Proctors and other aircraft, carrying Naval and Army officers from Hendon to see weapon testing at sites such as Pendine, where he would land on the Pendine Sands.

On Ken's posting to 21 Operational Training Unit, Peggy had managed to transfer to nearby Innsworth but after becoming pregnant with Vicky their first child she left the W.A.A.F., in January 1943, and went to live with her parents in Brighton. When Ken took up the post in London, they moved to a maisonette in Brunswick Square, Hove, and he commuted daily to Millbank. Even with these responsibilities, daily travel and family distractions, Ken still found time to install a 7$1/2$ litre Rolls-Royce "Silver Ghost" engine in an old "Chris-Craft" hull. He also acquired and renovated a 4$1/2$ ton cutter, *"Manola II"*, originally built in 1918.

Later that year, he enjoyed a short break and sailed from Shoreham to Dieppe, and then to St Valery-en-Caux. Even here he was not far away from ordnance and danger for, whilst moored in the harbour, he was fascinated to see the number of unexploded mortar bombs around the keel when the tide went out! Hostilities had ended not too long before this trip and clearance had yet to begin. The boat had been gaff-rigged but in 1947 he rigged her along the lines of a Bermudan Cutter with new masts and sails. He was very happy with the results and there followed many Channel crossings.

A fine shot of *"Manola II"*

Post-war armament research and development work

On the 25th September 1945 Ken took up a post in the Armament Design Establishment, Small Arms, Enfield, as Acting Squadron Leader. Here he was set the task to design the British equivalent of the German Mauser MG 213c, a 30mm "revolver" gun. The British development of this was later to be designated the "ADEN" – Armament Design Enfield.

The background to this weapon was that, in 1944, an engineer by the name of Dr Maier who was working for IWKA Mauser at Oberndorf in Germany had devised a new feed system to cope with a very fast cyclic rate of fire for the company's new 30mm gun. The Luftwaffe desperately needed the weapon but its development had been shelved in 1943 because the ammunition feed of the prototype - the 20mm MG213a - had not coped beyond 900 rounds per minute. Early tests with Maier's new system achieved 1,200 rounds per minute but then snags occurred with excessive barrel wear and this held up production so it was never used operationally. On the 3rd May 1945 the Oberndorf complex was captured, intact, by Free French Forces and armament experts quickly realised the importance of the weapon so the machinery and other contents of the centre were promptly transported to France. Details were then made available to the Allied authorities and, in time, several countries developed the weapon independently to great success.

At this stage, however, the German gun had not been acquired for the A.D.E. so Ken was put in charge of the first firing tests of a 47mm aircraft gun that had been designed as a "tank buster", amongst other things. The weapon was novel in that the long (47cm) ammunition was arranged across and above the barrel. The next round to be fired would drop into a *"Geneva"* mechanism, and, as the gun was fired, the recoil would turn this mechanism through 90 degrees. The round would then be fed into the breech as the bolt moved forward. The trials were held at the Royal Ordnance Factory, Llanishen, Cardiff, but only one or two firings were required to prove that the idea was fundamentally unsound. The recoil turned the "Geneva" mechanism so rapidly that the centrifugal force on the shell caused the projectile to separate from the cartridge case with the propellant being flung all around. The cams operating the "Geneva" mechanism were bent under the shock loads on the recoil. Ken had the rather sad task of writing a detailed Report, completely killing off that project but, happily, the war was over and the requirement had eased.

Whilst at A.D.E., Enfield, he had shared an office with a Mr. Turpin, a superb model engineer, who made large-scale steam locomotives and gave children rides on his trains at Sunday School fetes and the like. Early in the war Colonel Shepherd, Commanding the Design Establishment, took Mr. Turpin to a meeting at the War Office and on the table was a German Schmeisser MP40 9mm Maschinenpistole. The objective was to make an equivalent sub-machine gun, taking the same ammunition, but it had to be manufactured at extremely low cost.

The Colonel had made an excellent choice when he selected Turpin for the job and the low-cost prototypes were made in his own model workshop. Although it is likely that few people would have heard of the unassuming Mr. Turpin, the partnership of "Shepherd Turpin & Enfield" when shortened produced the very famous name of "STEN". This British machine carbine was widely used during World War II from mid-1941 and nearly four million had been made by 1945 in several different marks and variants. The per unit production cost was unbelievably low at around £2 10s. (£2.50 today). Although it was not a popular weapon with the Armed Forces, it remained in service until phase-out commenced in 1953 when the 9mm Sterling was introduced. I can well remember the first time I fired the STEN and my nervousness at the prospect of losing fingertips in the exposed spring if the weapon was not held correctly but improved upon with the Sterling.

At the A.D.E., Ken spent a brief time studying enemy ammunition but was soon summoned for a meeting with the Chief Engineer, Armament Design (C.E.A.D.) at Fort Halstead where he was asked if he would be prepared to spend a further eighteen months in Armament, rather than be released at the end of his RAFVR Service. Ken had by then already applied for a permanent Commission in the RAF but it would be quite a while before that came to pass. While at the A.D.E. which was based at Cheshunt, he had foregone the daily commuting to Hove to be with Peggy and his growing family, and had been in "digs" so, rather cheekily, he said that he would be pleased to serve the period provided he could be posted back to London. Accordingly, on the 12th December 1945 he took up the post of R.D.Arm9 at the Ministry of Aircraft Production still as an Acting Squadron Leader.

The post was concerned with ammunition of all types, including enemy munitions, extending to that used in the new ejector seats. In this respect he was very pleased to meet Jimmy Martin of Martin-Baker Limited (whom he described as *"that most practical of engineers"*) and to take a ride on one of his ejection seats. From Ken's description it seemed that volunteers were welcomed to try out the new test equipment in the early days and he witnessed some interesting scenes, including one chap accelerating at such a pace that the heels of his shoes, with nails protruding, were left on the ground! Ken remained in contact over many years and Jimmy helped on the WA-116 autogyro project by colour anodising of some parts.

On the 18th March 1946, Ken was posted, again as Acting Squadron Leader, to the Ammunition Division, The Ordnance Board; a prestigious posting. Again, his duties involved the assessment of enemy munitions. He flew to RAF Seighford for the Royal Ordnance Factory, Radway Green in a Percival Proctor on a number of occasions.

One task he was set concerned an ingenious enemy aircraft shell with a hydrodynamic fuze. This was designed to penetrate the wing skins of an aircraft and only to detonate when it came into contact with the fuel. The question posed was how to prove that it functioned when striking the fuel and in his Ordnance Board post he was called upon to find a way. The shell had a light alloy nose that was intended to be torn away when it hit the structure, thus exposing passages leading to the hydrodynamic fuze; this should then activate by the pressure of the fuel entering the passages.

The best way to prove it really did function hydro-dynamically was by Ken's suggestion that the shell be fired through a balloon filled with fuel after the light alloy nose cone had been removed. Having made the suggestion he has strong memories of having to take the live shell into a deserted workshop at Radway Green and putting it into a large lathe. Then, very carefully, he took the cutting tool into the base of the light alloy nose cone until it could be removed to expose the passages leading to the fuze. It was considered the only practical method and, according to Ken, was *"a bit hard on the nerves"*. A typical understatement! On test, the fuze did detonate the shell when it struck the balloon filled with jet fuel as he had predicted.

Ken was soon to join the Lethality Division of the Ordnance Board, and engaged in work to find the best way to achieve a "K" (Kill the threat of the day) as represented by the twin-engine German jet bomber the Arado Ar 234 *Blitz (Lightning)*. The tests involved attending the "killing" of jet engines, shooting at fuel tanks with jet fuel in them, under decompression as at altitude, etc. Ken says that finding the best warhead fragment size and velocity to "kill" a jet engine was a most interesting and memorable experience. He thinks back with some sadness, however, at the many Spitfires, Lancasters, and other aircraft supplied to them for dismantling,

93

simply to provide small components to be used in the experiments. Almost new Spitfires were used just to fire at their wing leading edges to assess the lethality of warhead fragments. These Lethality Trials were conducted at the Proof & Experimental Establishment, Shoeburyness on Foulness Island.

The jet engine would be set up on a suitable stand beside which was an armour-plate shelter of very thick steel, and the engine could be viewed through a tiny slit. A 20mm cannon was positioned close to the engine and it could fire a typical anti-aircraft missile warhead fragment at the chosen velocity, using a specially-prepared cartridge. A high-speed camera viewing on the line of the cannon would record the effects of the fragment strike. During Ken's four years on this job, he saw 180 engines "killed".

Being exposed to the wind coming off the North Sea, the work was often conducted in bitterly cold temperatures, and visiting "brass hats" could become bored if the engine did not falter, as sometime happened. Ken would sometimes decide to put an engine "out of its misery" and told the assembly that the next fragment would be fired into the air intake area and not at rotating parts. Sounding even more boring to the visitors, they would return to their own protective shelter, having had enough of this pointless exercise. On firing there was no dramatic effect but the structure of the air intake also served as the oil tank, benefiting from the cooling air. The fragment would firstly cause a leak of oil into the intake, being burned in the wrong place and causing a small change in the engine note. Loss of oil would cause the hydraulic governor to fail and the engine to "run away"so the note would soon start to rise, and the paint on the main body to blister. As the note rose higher, the blisters became a red glow which then turned brilliant white as the "Elektron" magnesium-based alloy started to burn, to be carried away downstream with the jet efflux and setting fire to wet grass for about 200 yards. The rest of the engine would be reduced to an intensely, hot glowing mass. The "bods" would then emerge from their shelter to warm up at some distance from the magnesium pyre and leave, commenting on the marvellous job being done by the Division!

Though the German jet engine, in Ken's view, represented the future with their axial-flow design, it was decided that some lethality trials should be held against axial-flow engines as represented by Rolls-Royce "Derwents". Six engines were purchased (rather "through the nose" Ken recalls). On firing a fragment into the turbine area, it momentarily "coughed" and then continued running normally. On shut-down, clunking noises could be heard as it drew to a halt. There was obviously some distortion of a turbine and a blade,

94

causing the contact when not under power. Following discussion with the engineer who had set up the engine, they decided to fire a fragment into some other part of the engine to "kill it off" rather than exchange it.

On pressing the starter button nothing happened and Ken quickly realised the problem to be that of a bent turbine and stator blade in contact. He grabbed a large crowbar intended for use in emergencies, ran to the rear of the engine and jammed it into the turbine blades, resting it on the cruciform section in the jet outlet. With a "thumbs up" sign to the engineer to use the electric starter, and by levering the turbine over the locked blades plus helping the turning by more jamming into the turbine disk, they got the engine to speed up and start. They then "killed it off" by a fragment into the combustion area. Ken doubts his starting method would have had Rolls-Royce approval.

Ken observed it might be thought that warhead fragments striking such an axial-flow jet engine at very high velocity might achieve the most lethality but this was certainly not always the case. The high velocity fragment could well bury itself in the rotating parts and be retained in them, rather than breaking such as a compressor blade. Such a breakage is more likely to occur from a fragment that just enters the compressor and gets between the rotating and stator vanes, causing an increasing scale of destruction. Sometimes, to the accompaniment of dramatic sound, the entire set of broken stator and rotating blades would erupt from the air intake, with the engine note quickly dying down and much scrap to be cleared away before the next engine was installed to be "killed" in some way.

For many of these Lethality tests, Ken had the company of representatives of the Vulnerability Panel of the Royal Aircraft Establishment, Farnborough. He explained *"the matter was of as much interest to those who wished to ensure a resistance to vulnerability of our aircraft as those of us who were designing for Lethality"*. Ken commuted daily from Hove to London for office days at the Ordnance Board but, when Lethality trials were on, he would drive his *"dreary old Rolls-Royce Twenty"*, purchased for £25 in 1942, to Farnborough to pick up the Panel members. Travelling via the North Circular Road to Southend, they stayed at the Palace Hotel before attending trials.

Ken particularly recalls a trial at the Orfordness Research Station in which the R.A.E. had made a "representative pressurised cockpit", as for a jet bomber. The aim was to fire a warhead fragment at it and see if that would lead to a dramatic tearing of the cockpit. The "hit" must have been rather low because the next thing they saw was it taking off and climbing like a released balloon! That possibility had been overlooked and it went about 300 feet in the air. That was the only firing against a pressurised compartment so Ken presumed the Panel members were satisfied.

In 1980, Ken produced some fascinating notes from memory on the Arado Ar 234 and its *Kurzkoppler* automatic navigation and bombing system - part of this equipment is on loan from him and displayed at Flixton and we had asked for some information. He was clearly greatly impressed with the aircraft's systems so I have recorded his personal views for general interest:

'The aircraft was a one-man bomber of extremely advanced design, powered by two Jumo 004 turbo-jet, axial-flow engines of some 2,000 lbs static thrust. The automatic navigation and bombing system, the various "black boxes" (actually grey boxes) were grouped together under the reference BZA-1. A magnetic compass well outboard in one wing, hence well clear of ferrous material in the airframe, was used to monitor an electric gyro-compass. The equipment was provided with multiple accelerometers. Wind-speed and direction, and target height above ground, and barometric pressure, could be fed into the computers.

A complex computer solved the bomb aiming equations, virtually all parameters being computed, and the information was fed to a sighting head in the bomb-aimers position. For the bombing run, the pilot would leave his position and take up the task of bomb-aimer. The entire system was an incredibly complex and a beautiful piece of electro-mechanical engineering, continuously changing three-dimensional triangles of velocities being   set up in the bomb-aiming computer. D.C. selsyns, using watch scale 360 degree potentiometers had fine silver wire pickup brushes. 22 volts A.C. was used to power other selsyns and the various gyros.

Most of the frame castings and beautifully machined parts were in Elektron, a magnesium alloy. Virtually all shafts and sliding parts were carried on miniature ball and roller bearings. The system was normally assembled, the cover screws then being wire-locked and fastened with a lead seal. Maintenance of the system would obviously need extremely skilled workers. By comparison, Ken compared the British Mk.14 Bomb Sight and Computor to *"something like a Junior Meccano Set. However, it may have been more practical"*.

According to research by colleagues at the Flixton museum, the Arado Ar 234 was the first German jet aircraft to operate over the East Anglia region. The reconnaissance aircraft came from the Luftwaffe's Kommando Sperling unit based at Rheine in Germany. Several sorties were claimed to have taken place during September and October 1944, and an aerial photograph exists of Horsham St Faith dated the 11th September.

At the foot of Ken's report there is also a brief outline of another interesting invention he had come across and this time by the British: an experimental air-to-air, anti-aircraft bomb. As I suspect that little has been published about such a weapon I include Ken's report here:

'It is believed that this equipment was for use against enemy aircraft in formation. A bomb (likely 250 lb) would be dropped above the formation and a photo-electric cell with all-round view would be energised. As the bomb passed through the aircraft formation there would be a sudden change in light level and the electronic pulse from the P.E. cell would be amplified to operate a relay to detonate the bomb. The amplifier equipment, complete with battery pack, was fitted in the tail fins of the bomb and cushioned from vibration by (an outer band of) felt'

Ken has the remains of one of these bomb systems, including the P.E. cell, in his hangar museum but gained it only by chance. He was always looking for bits of brass and other metal for his own inventions and regularly acquired discarded assemblies such as this from an adjacent department - the Ministry of Aircraft Production - when he was based in London. In fact, often when I meet Ken he will produce an intricate object from his pocket and ask *"What do you think this is?"* Sometimes he doesn't know the answer himself and had been attracted to it because of its fine machining or intricate design. Being a skilled engineer, Ken is fascinated by all manner of inventions, machines and designs; he particularly admires production techniques and quality finishing of products. He also marvels at the high standards achieved under wartime conditions.

This aerial bomb was of 1940 vintage and did not reach production. In the *"Daily Telegraph"* obituary for the famous RAF flyer and post-war test pilot Group Captain John *"Cats Eyes"* Cunningham, mention was made of him testing such a bomb. Ken thinks that it would have been dropped from an aircraft flying over a barrage balloon. Ken went on to serve four years at the Ordnance Board, twice the normal service posting time, and says that he experienced many interesting incidents, plus a few laughs. Sounds a little understated to me!

Some other hobbies and interests

Peacetime service also gave Ken the opportunity to return to some of his hobbies and other interests, plus experimentation. For example, in 1947 he installed an adapted *"Riedel"* 270 cc two cylinder, two stroke starter engine from a Junkers Jumo jet engine in the rear of a Slingsby *"Petrel"* sailplane owned by his friend John Morris. The whole unit, including the propeller he had designed and made himself, weighed only 11 lbs. He had carried the complete assembly, together with a champagne bottle filled with fuel, on a train from Brighton to London, on the underground to his Kensington office, and then by train to Redhill in the evening.

The gliding fraternity did not approve of Ken putting an engine into a glider and comments such as *"not the sort of thing to expect of a gentleman"* were to be heard which he felt was strange being that he had flown, pre-war, the BAC Drone, a glider powered by a modified Douglas motorcycle engine. He turned to Hugh Kendall the Chief Test Pilot for Handley Page Ltd. at Woodley for support and, eventually, approval from the Air Registration Board to conduct tests was obtained. Ten successful take-offs were achieved at Redhill using the tiny engine. The same year saw Ken construct a tiny hydroplane, powered by the same type of starter motor, for pure speed and not for racing. His model-making interests had also embraced a tiny, double-acting "marine" steam engine with boiler, fitted into a small hull and, in 1942, an electrically powered scale model of HMS *Hood* - the ill-fated Royal Navy capital ship. By turning one of the gun turrets to the side it would move forward; turning the other way would result in reversed motor.

Whilst there he met Lorne Welch who was the Chief Gliding instructor and not initially supportive of Ken's work. Lorne had been incarcerated in Colditz Castle during World War II and was one of the team of British prisoners-of-war who had constructed a two-man glider for a daring rooftop escape. The Castle was liberated by the allies, however, before it could be put to the test. A full size, airworthy reproduction is on display at Flixton.

Ken also enjoyed competition shooting and represented the RAF as a pistol and rifle marksman. He achieved a 2nd in the RAF Small-Bore Championship of 1951, gaining medals for Service Rifle and Light Machine Gun at Bisley. He also won the Bomber Command Small-Bore Championship one year. All this probably followed on from his interest in firearms at an early age. When a schoolboy he had made a quite lethal

3/8 inch smoothbore, muzzle-loader using odds and ends, including wireless set terminals with pieces of toy caps in parts of bicycle valves - these were then screwed into the "breech" of a steel tube "barrel" as the initiator. All this was before he really understood how a proper muzzle-loader with cap nipples, etc., was made. Looking back, he wonders how he did not receive serious injury with these early experiments.

Top: Ken standing (left) talking to the pilot of the *"Petrel"* glider powered by a *"Riedel"* 270 cc starter engine he had modified, plus a 27 inch propeller. Bottom: The *"Petrel"* glider in flight.

An interest in pistol shooting had developed around 1933, and Ken shot a variety of revolvers from .22 inch to .455 inch, plus .22 rifles. In 1935, he was shooting with the Cambridge Small-bore Rifle Club and went on to be quite active in national competitions at venues such as the Alexandra Palace. He was Captain of the City of Ely Rifle Club at its inauguration in March 1939. Around this time his father also took an interest in target shooting and, in fact, learned to shoot very well. Local newspaper reports of the time disclose that their individual competition scores were very similar.

Ken was also shooting full-bore rifle at Barton Range and elsewhere from the mid-thirties and he rather liked the unusual straight-pull, bolt-action of the Canadian .280 Ross rifle. Being poorly-sighted in the right eye meant that he had to shoot left-handed and this was by no means an easy thing to achieve with a heavy, bolt-action rifle such as the P-14, especially when under the pressure of rapid-fire competition. It just so happens that, in 1948 whilst with the Ordnance Board, Ken designed a modification to the zeroing device fitted to the telescopic sniper sight for the Enfield No.4 Rifle. This was to overcome serious operational problems brought about by it loosening in action.

Whilst his passion for solving engineering problems had given rise to an interest in making steam engines pre-war, he also much enjoyed producing the smallest, technically workable objects he could build. In this pursuit he first turned his attention to designing and constructing ultra miniature 16mm cameras, and firearms. On being invited to examine an ebonite case measuring only 1¼ inches x 1 inch the surprise comes on opening it for within will be found an exquisite breech-loading, single-shot pistol measuring 1⅛ inch, complete with pin-fire cartridges of .052 inch (1.32mm) calibre; the grips are ivory and Ken's name and address are finely scribed on the barrel. When fired the bullet will penetrate ¾ inch of hardwood.

Having captivated his audience Ken will then produce two more of .085 inch (2.16mm) calibre. One was tested at the Proof & Experimental Establishment, Orfordness, and had a mean velocity of 970 feet per second recorded over a 20 feet base. The source of the metal naturally being from an anonymous aeroplane! The urge to make miniature pistols came from a simple gesture by Peggy. She had given him a little silver pistol to hang on his watch chain, acting as a key to wind a pocket watch. Ken had decided that it would be a challenge to make a working model to the same scale.

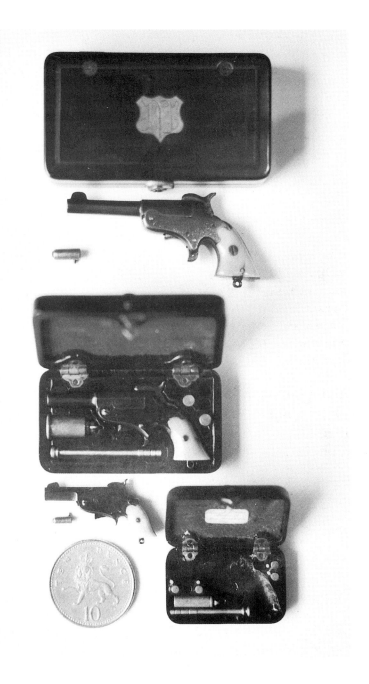

The craftsmanship required to make these superb pistols cannot be fully appreciated from the photograph.

This unusual wartime hobby for creating miniatures also embraced model racing cars and, again in 1942, he designed and constructed the first electric slot-car racing circuit. The model racing cars were 3 inches in length with self-steering front wheels that followed a slot in the track; an idea developed later by others and commercially produced for considerable profit. He had to make the electric motors with $\frac{5}{16}$ inch diameter armatures and the first track was on the black-out board taken from one of the windows in his billet.

Ken related to me the development of his design in great detail and I think it will be of interest if I follow suit. He had long thought that it would be exciting to have model racing cars, electrically driven and with their speed controlled, remotely by individual "drivers" through a potentiometer operated by a "throttle lever", spring loaded to return to "stop". Such models he felt would hardly be appropriate if running on rails, such as model trains; some freedom to skid on turns and snake in acceleration was needed. Also, he had to make some suitably small electric motors; whilst common nowadays, they were not so in 1942! One of the primary tasks was therefore to make a pair of tiny motors because he felt it was hardly appropriate, when living in a small room in a Nissen Hut, to accommodate a large track, or even to find the plywood on which one might be made.

The motors were made, largely using a little clockmaker's lathe that he had acquired as junk and rebuilt, but only using hand tools on a rest. It was driven by a motor from an old electric fan, driving through a belt to a control cable and made up "change gear" pulleys, via belts. The motor's armatures were 5/16 inch diameter and the commutators were made from a piece of brazing rod, bored through and then cut into three segments, before being mounted and spaced on a suitable insulator on the armature shaft. Then followed the winding of the armature and careful soldering to the commutator, etc.

The question of steering, and of electric current pick-up next had to be translated into hardware. His early experiments included pick-up of the current from metal foil strips stuck to the track via copper wire "tyres" made on the *"Perspex"* wheels. Steering was an important feature and his first experiments were by use of a single copper wire laid on the track. First, a number of brass tacks were driven into the plywood track and the wire would then be soldered on to the heads of the tacks, flush with the surface. The front wheels of the cars were free to steer, as with full-scale cars, with a suitable cross-link to ensure 'Ackermann' geometry.

The steering was by a pivoted bar in the centre of the front axle connected into the wheel-steering system. This pivoted bar was just above the wire laid on the track but at each end it had a sort of fork reaching down and over the wire. Thus, as the car moved forward, the forked bar followed the wire and steered the car. This was the system on which the first model cars were tried and it worked, with the "accelerator pedals" being mounted on potentiometer dimmer switches for the instruments from crashed aircraft. The track had been made on one of the air raid "black out" boards for windows of the hut.

Races were taking place late in 1942 to early '43 but a potential problem was soon apparent. If a car swung outward on a violent turn with a bit too much speed it was mechanically restrained, when the forked steering bar engaged with the guiding wire reaching its limit. It could even result in the copper guiding wire on the track becoming bent. The next experiment dispensed with the rear fork on the steering bar and this produced some improvement but then the rear wheels would hit the guidance wire about the track. Ken decided to make a guidance slot in the track and for this he used a dentist's drill mounted on a motor from a wrecked cine-gun.

Firstly, he used a pin extending down from the front of the steering bar in the centre of the front axle but he then simplified things by arranging a steering pin forward of the nearside front wheel steering axis. This worked well; cars could spin around completely, with no restriction from guidance wires laid on the track. Electricity was soon picked up by a pair of spring-loaded contacts touching a pair of copper wires virtually recessed into the plywood track. With the electricity pick-up via the copper wire "tyres" on the early versions there would be quite a few sparks on acceleration. The first pair of tiny racing cars created much enjoyment to Ken's colleagues at Moreton-in-the-Marsh, and at Enstone, and on another "bodged up" track after he returned to the U.K. from "ops" in Italy and was living in his maisonette in Hove. Ken could see that there was obviously potential for model racing cars to be complimentary to, if not a bit more exciting than, model trains.

After the war ended in Europe there was access to much of the German equipment brought over for study, and then "junked". Thanks to the fine engineer at R.A.E. Farnborough, Miss Shilling, Ken was able to acquire pieces of the German *"Kurzkoppler"* electro-mechanical navigation and bomb-aiming computer from a twin-engine Arado Ar 234 bomber. He was only interested in the beautifully engineered motors and their bevel gear drive systems, tiny ball-races, etc. They were ideal for building a pair of larger model racing cars steered by a slot in the track as with the first, much smaller experiments he had carried out.

Before expanding upon the story of these models, no mention of Miss Shilling can really be made without some reference to her most famous invention: fondly known as "Miss Shilling's Orifice". Beatrice (Tilly) Shilling was a notable aero engineer and a respected scientist at the Royal Aircraft Establishment, Farnborough. She had already gained a reputation as a "feisty female" in the 1930s by racing around the Brookland track at over 100 mph on her Norton 500 motorcycle, to be awarded the prestigious Gold Star. She went on to gain further recognition for solving the fuel-delivery problem in the Rolls-Royce Merlin engine installed in our fighter aircraft.

A potentially fatal defect with the carburettor in the Merlin was its inability to function smoothly in a dog-fight with enemy fighters. Early in World War II, pilots found it necessary to invert their aircraft in the dive because the "negative-G" created by the aircraft being nose-down caused fuel starvation. The engine would otherwise splutter or even cut out. The German Daimler-Benz aero engine, however, had fuel-injection so did not suffer the same problem. Miss Shilling produced a simple, stop-gap device: a metal disc with a small hole in the centre. This was brazed into the fuel pipe so that, when the aircraft accelerated in a dive, the disc prevented any fuel starvation. "Miss Shilling's Orifice" made an important contribution to the war effort and saved lives - coincidentally, it cost less than a shilling. Her biography by Matthew Freudenberg is entitled *"Negative Gravity"*.

Now back to the main story. The first models had the "coachwork" moulded from *"Perspex"* coming from wrecked aircraft but, for the larger scale, he wanted to use suitably shaped brass sheet. In a "junk room" next to the office he shared at the Ministry of Aircraft Production, he found three felt-covered, cylindrical drums made of brass, with some form of electronic system, battery compartments and thermionic valves inside. Ken thought that the brass would be ideal and, being that they were classed as junk, he decided to use them. It transpired that they were the amplifier system to fit inside the cylindrical tails of 250 lb G.P. bombs, for experiments in photo-electrically initiated bombs (as I have mentioned earlier).

The two cars made with these superior motors, and with ball-bearing wheels, etc., represented the "E.R.A." (English Racing Automobiles) in British Racing Green, and the German Mercedes in white. The track was made up from a large plywood packing case, from four hinged segments, making an area of around 9 feet by 4 feet. Much of this was made in 1945 when he was commuting between London and Hove, and it was soon in action, being very popular with visitors to his home. He took it with him when posted to RAF stations, such as Scampton and Binbrook and on "long weekends" there was always the case, at about 04.00 a.m. of *"Let's have one last race before we go to bed!"* Ken said that it went on and on and the two cars must have travelled many hundreds of miles around the quite large track.

During the time they were resident in Hove, Ken met Ellerston Trevor (Ken believes this is the correct spelling) and he was very enthusiastic for the model racing car game. It continued when he lived at nearby Southwick, and he occasionally brought friends over to see the models and have a race. Ken had thought of applying for Patents but, as a serving officer, any Patent awarded would have been the property of the Crown. (Ken says that this is the reason why the Patent for the novel focal plane shutter in his tiny camera was applied for by his father. All his autogyro Patents, while in the Service, had to be made over to the Crown).

To complete this story it is necessary to creep into the period of the next chapter. Everything was made to be transportable so the game went with Ken when they moved to Southwick in the 1950s. Races continued to be a popular feature of visits to Peggy and Ken. By 1956 he was due for his two-year exchange posting to Strategic Air Command so, before leaving, he agreed to leave the model car game to be dealt with as a possible business project, on a 50/50 basis by Ellerston Trevor. Patent Agents were brought in but by February 1956 Ken was serving in the U.S.A.

Ken knew that Ellerston was going to make cars and a track of his own along the same lines but was rather disturbed when Peggy sent a newspaper cutting to him in which Ellerston had publicised the system, in Ken's opinion, prematurely. On a brief visit to the U.K., Ken enquired of the Patent Agents the "state of play" and can recall they said that the "Provisional Applications" had not been followed through, or some such words.

It was not until June 1957 that Ken submitted a Provisional Specification to The Patent Office for a means of steering model cars by a soft-iron wire buried in a non-magnetic material track, to be followed by a permanent magnet attached to the car steering - much as where the pin would normally engage in the track. Ken never followed through with his invention, however, as he was busy with so many other things. The commercially-produced "Scalextric" models first appeared at the 1957 Toy Fair and they have now become one of the most popular games of all time. Ken believes that the person (now deceased) who initiated the manufacture of *"Scalextric"* had been first introduced to the idea by Ellerston Trevor.

Ken concluded by saying that, by accident or design, *"Scalextric"* would not have infringed the Patents applying to his design as these cars are forced to follow a slot in the track by way of a pin extending down from the nose. The pin does not actually steer the front wheels; they are fixed straight ahead and forced to slide a bit on turns although they do follow quite well. He feels that they lack the realism of the over-steer and corrections that sometimes occur in real life, and a deliberate feature in his own design. Even so, I am sure that many millions of pounds have been earned by the less realistic models. Ken now has his racetrack set up in the hangar and happily demonstrates the racing cars, which I found surprisingly heavy.

Obviously, small has always appealed to Ken although he almost dismisses the challenges brought about by his choice. He recalls that as he was married he did not spend leisure time in the "hot-spots" of the nearest town, and he also had only a tiny room in a Nissen hut with few tools to work with so nothing much larger could be attempted. It would seem though that he was well advanced in the art of re-cycling waste!

Ken beside the track set up in his hangar, after demonstrating his cars to visitors in 2006.

The two "slot-car" designs were closely modelled on the real thing.

The early 1950s

Ken left the Ordnance Branch in March 1950 for the Senior Specialist Armament Officer's Course at the RAF Technical College, Armament Division at Lindholme. After more than four years as an Acting Squadron Leader he had to revert to the substantive rank of Flight Lieutenant. In November 1950 he was posted to 230 Operational Conversion Unit at Scampton as Station Armament Officer.

Whilst there, Ken observed the many failures with the 25lb Aircraft Practice Bomb being dropped from Lincoln bombers. On inspection he deduced that the fault probably lay with damp air in the bomb bays turning to ice at operational altitude on the bombs and equipment. The spring would then fail to force out the iced-up plunger. His Report of the 26th November 1951 identified a simpler and more reliable firing system but this was not adopted until seven years later with the introduction of the No.2 Mark 1 Practice Bomb. During this time, disastrous orders were given for the plunger to be attached by a wire lanyard to the bomb rack. This caused the bomb to be "snatched" and tumble, end over end, from the aircraft and fall short of the designated Danger Area, or for the iced-up plunger to be retained on the lanyard and become live whilst resting on the bomb bay doors as the aircraft descended to a warmer altitude. Ken came up with a safe firing mechanism not requiring safety plungers.

The matter was particularly frustrating for Ken as his modification could have been carried out at RAF stations on the existing stocks of the bomb and thus saved injuries. Bureaucracy allowed the matter to drag on and create a large file of papers. It was also very annoying for Ken to learn the Air Ministry had replied to HQ No.1 Group that his solution "was fundamentally unsound and could not possibly work". The Royal Navy eventually presented Ken with a version of the Practice Bomb No.2 Mark 2 incorporating his ideas following successful trials. In 1958 he was awarded the princely sum of £150 by the Air Force Council on the recommendation of the Ministry of Supply Committee on Awards to Inventors.

In 1951, as Senior Armament Officer at RAF Binbrook - the first Canberra jet bomber station - he devised improvements both to the aircraft's armament system and other weapons' systems. Notable amongst these was a completely revised weapons' loading system to greatly simplify and, importantly, speed up the process of bombing-up the aircraft. Here he used a modified WWII Type F trolley allied to the Alvis lifting trolley.

The official system saw an Alvis Bomb Transporting/Lifting Trolley allocated for three Canberra aircraft. As it could carry only three 1,000 lb bombs, half the bomb load of a Canberra, or one 5,000 lb bomb, it would usually have to make six journeys between the aircraft and the Bomb Dump to fully re-arm them. This was not an efficient operational procedure. Ken's solution was to use a sturdy WWII "Type F" bomb transporter trolley to carry a full Canberra load of six 1,000lb, or one 5,000lb bomb.

By suitable modification of both the "Type F" and the Alvis Bomb Trolley, it was possible to manually transfer the bombs on site from one to the other, and the Alvis lifting trolley would then be used solely for bombing up the Canberra. The transfer procedure required the "Type F" to engage with the Alvis and this would then take the weight of the former; manual movement of the bombs from one to the other was achieved by employing roller bearings in steel channels. The bombs were transferred three at a time to the lifting trolley for bombing-up, and arranged as they would be positioned in the bomb bay of the Canberra.

The bomb carriers on the Alvis were also adapted to take three 1,000 lb bombs or a single 5,000 lb bomb; in the latter case, rods with squared ends moved rollers to rotate the bomb to get the attachment at the top. Ken also designed a special "Inching Tool" - this manually engaged with two opposing wheel nuts of one wheel on the trolley so that the operator could make precise movements during the "mating" of the two trolleys. The aircraft manufacturer, English Electric, had incorporated a special system whereby the nose-wheel of the aircraft could be raised allowing the nose to drop, thus lifting the rear of the fuselage to allow access by the Alvis trolley.

This separate selection of the "nose-wheel up", while the main wheels remained down, required the action of an Airframe Fitter during the bombing-up procedure. Ken came up with the idea of using hydraulic jacks with pads engaged in the main-wheel oleo legs to lift the aircraft. Elevation by the legs provided easy access by the bombing-up trolley, and the fuselage was not at such an angle as occurred previously when the nose-wheel had been lifted. Also, the new procedure did not warrant the involvement of an Airframe Fitter *"as even an Armourer was considered sufficiently trustworthy to use a jack!"* (Letters from ex-Armourers to Ken, please!)

Convincing "the authorities" was not easy, however, and recalling clashes with bureaucracy over the years is guaranteed to make Ken's attitude change visibly in conversation. Although a reasonably tolerant person, he clearly finds it extremely difficult to accept the slow-to-grasp, and often negative, attitude of "officialdom". He finally overcame the problem of convincing the decision-makers at H.Q. Bomber Command about the merits of the bomb trolleys by using his skills to make a detailed model to illustrate his idea. The go-ahead was given very quickly as a result of him demonstrating the working model. He was then told to take some personal leave and supervise the necessary work to be undertaken by 4 MU (Maintenance Unit) at Ruislip. The requirement for him to use his own leave to supervise the development of a necessary piece of equipment for the RAF still causes Ken slight annoyance to this day!

Ken did not think to apply for recognition to the Royal Commission on Awards to Inventors for the aircraft-jacking solution until five years later. The formal response, 'As commanded by the Air Council', reached him whilst he was seconded to the Strategic Air Command. It stated that *'his good services had been appreciated but were not regarded as having gone beyond what was expected of an Officer of his status in performance of his duty as the Senior Armament Officer when at RAF Binbrook'*. It went on to state that although the circumstances were not considered to justify special recognition in the form of an award, arrangements would be made for suitable notation in his personal record. Ken's observation to me on this response was *"It seemed that RAF Officers were expected to design the Canberra in service, being better fitted to do so in performance of their duty than English Electric's own design staff"*. Nuff said!

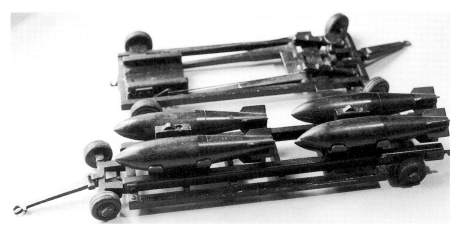

The models Ken made to illustrate his bomb trolley modifications.

Later, he received £400 under the Royal Commission on Awards to Inventors for his bomb transportation and transfer to a lifting trolley solution for the Canberra but was actually more pleased to improve efficiency and gain some recognition than to receive the money itself.

Ken recalls that when at RAF Binbrook he also had to investigate an accident causing injury to an Armourer when he was servicing an ejector seat. One of the explosive charges had functioned. Ken cannot recall all the details but, at that stage, to service a seat it was necessary to remove a safety device that would prevent accidental operation in order to gain access for a spanner. A simple solution was called for so Ken cut away a section of the ring spanner used so that it could be put in position without the need to remove the safety device. The modification was immediately adopted.

"Type F" Bomb Transporter Trolley with 1,000 lb bombs.

Top: 5,000 lb bomb being transferred between trolleys.
Bottom: Alvis bombing-up trolley as modified by Ken.

In the course of his duties, Ken found it necessary to report numerous armament problems with the Canberra and thus felt, at the time, that he was becoming unpopular with the Air Ministry. Eventually, representatives from both the Ministry and English Electric visited him at RAF Binbrook. Although he suspected the visit might have been seen as an opportunity to "put him in his place", he was soon able to convince them that the changes were called for. The English Electric representatives promptly invited him to their Warton factory in order to progress the matters. To his surprise, on arrival there they asked him to resign his commission and join the company as their armament designer. Whilst he felt that this was a tremendous compliment, it was not practical for him to accept the offer at that time.

Ken and Armament Section - RAF Binbrook in 1952. Flying Officer W. K. MacTaggart (third from left front row) later Air Vice-Marshall MacTaggart CBE MBE. Ken gave him his first flight in the Station's Tiger Moth.

Whilst visiting Warton he recalls his excitement at seeing the first drawings of English Electric's P.1 (later *Lightning*) super-sonic jet fighter. In the early 1960s, he was at the Aeroplane & Armament Experimental Establishment, Boscombe Down in Wiltshire and, as Officer Commanding the Tactical Weapons Group, became involved in some of the weapons testing with the English Electric pre-production aircraft.

Ken was particularly interested, when I purchased XG329, one of the three surviving P.1B/Development Batch aircraft, and placed it on display at Flixton with my other aircraft. It was at Boscombe Down for several periods during the 1960s, assigned to supersonic gun-firing trials with the ADEN cannon, and for Firestreak missile tests. Ken had been involved in this work and a document from his files dated November 1960, when serving at Headquarters Fighter Command, records his recommendations and drawings on a modification kit for the re-positioning of the Armament Safety Break for the Lightning's Firestreak Missile Jettison System.

Ken's memories of Binbrook include the very difficult period in the early days of the Canberra when there were several fatal accidents. There was dramatic failure of the tailplane actuator, operated by a switch on the control column, which forced the tailplane to the "down" position and the aircraft into a dive. Ken said that it had been suspected the accidents resulted from the inadvertent firing of the detonator ring that cut the elevator controls if the pilot needed to eject - this prevented the pilot's knees striking the spectacle roll control on the typical bomber-type control column. As this was an armament matter, he had the very unpleasant task of searching the crash site for the detonator ring - he was pleased to find that the ring had not fired. Following the miraculous landing later on by a pilot of 231 OCU after such an incident occurred in flight, the true cause was discovered to be that the single-pole trim switch had a tendency to stick even after the pilot had released it, causing the actuator to run on to full travel.

Whilst at Binbrook Ken had managed to put in an occasional flight on the station's Tiger Moth but something faster was just around the corner. In January 1953 he was posted to A.C.A.S. (Assistant Chief of Air Staff) Operations Training at the Air Ministry in an Armament Technical post as TWI(b) and with the substantive rank of Squadron Leader. His post embraced Training and Weapons, covering gunnery, bombing, targets, and all the allied equipment.

Fortunately, there was a period of around three months before he could take over from his predecessor so he was told that he could undertake a Conversion Course on to jet aircraft if he wished and get his Green Instrument Rating on them. He jumped at the opportunity, undertook a "refresher" on Harvards, and then went on to gain his Green Instrument Rating on Meteors and Vampires with good Reports on his conversion. Ken's job encompassed technical matters with targets towed by aircraft and this aspect of his job was to lead him into a real life "James Bond" situation in his first year.

The assessment of the results of air firing training, with gunfire against towed banner targets, was achieved by colouring the projectiles. The score would be ascertained by counting the number of hits by a given colour on the banner after the training flight. Since a number of attacks might be made by one aircraft on such a flight, however, the attacker would not know which of his attacks had been the most successful despite the number of hits being recorded. The SAAB company then came up with the announcement of their "Near-Miss Recorder".

This was a system in which all projectiles passing within a given distance of a sensor on the target would be recorded on a dial in the target towing aircraft. Thus, the pilot of the attacking aircraft could be advised of the number of successful hits after each attack. There was great interest shown by the Ministry in the system but, understandably, the SAAB company was not willing to lend their system for appraisal in the UK. Testing would have to take place at their base in Linkoping in Sweden. At this time, of course, the "Cold War" was very "cold", and Sweden, of course, is adjacent to Russia. The decision was made for Ken to fly to Sweden in the company of another Squadron Leader (John Peters) in a Meteor target tug. Needless to say, there were intense briefings on the need for secrecy concerning the visit of an RAF jet fighter to neutral territory, in a very sensitive area, and uniform was not to be worn when they were "off base".

On October 10, 1953 they flew to Schleswigland in Germany, and on the 12th took off for Linkoping in the centre of southern Sweden. As they entered Swedish airspace they were immediately surrounded by Swedish J-29 fighters and escorted to the base. The flight-testing of the near-miss recorder soon started but there was a long weekend approaching and as Ken and John Peters were interested in seeing something of the country they asked if they could visit Stockholm. The SAAB company officials immediately said that they had someone who was going there and they could travel with him; they would also arrange accommodation at a hotel. The next day,

115

however, they were told that all the hotels were fully booked, owing to a football match (this may have been true, but it could also have been a security matter) so alternative arrangements had been made for them to stay in a "doublet" - two bedrooms in a private house.

They were duly delivered to the house in Stockholm and shown to the two rooms by the lady of the house who spoke no English. Access to Ken's room was via the room occupied by his companion. His room had a big brass bedstead, with doors either side of the bed-head that, presumably, led into the rest of the house and were not to be used. They were given keys and, naturally, ventured out for drinks and snacks to see what made the city "tick". Both were very still very aware of the need for secrecy, of course, emphasised by the sight of Russian soldiers in uniform.

After a long evening and many drinks they returned to the house and let themselves in. Ken was in bed just after midnight and soon dozing off. He was suddenly alerted by the loud ringing of a telephone from the other side of the door to the left of the bed-head – it was prolonged and insistent. Eventually it was answered and Ken heard a man's voice, with the words *"Flygman"* and *"Flygplan"* being mentioned. He knew enough Swedish to recognise that this meant "Pilot/Airman" and "Aeroplane". In the special circumstances of their presence in Sweden he became apprehensive to say the least. There was then a period of silence.

Ken next sensed someone very quietly attempting to open the door near his head - then a person crept into the room. He felt extremely helpless in the circumstances. He next sensed the door on the right of the bed-head being opened very quietly and recalls asking himself what an RAF officer was supposed to do at this point? Ken felt that some action on his part was called for so he slowly reached up for the pull-cord of the overhead light, pulled it and the room was instantly illuminated. There stood a man with a pistol in his hand. The "assailant" uttered something in a foreign language and dashed for the door to the left of the bed-head and was gone. In the heart-thumping stillness that followed, only gentle snoring came from the next room so Ken felt there was no point in waking his companion to recount the nightmare experience. Next morning, the hostess said a few words of farewell in Swedish as they departed for the return trip and Ken then told John the story.

Ken reported the incident to the SAAB officials but doubted that they believed a word of the episode and probably put it down to the effects of the local ale. A couple of days later, however, their hosts offered the explanation.

It appeared that the room Ken had been given belonged to the son of the house, who was a member of the Swedish Home Guard. That night there had been a surprise exercise and he had been told over the telephone that parachutists had landed, and he was required to report for duty immediately. Unfortunately, his equipment and pistol were in a cupboard in Ken's room and he had tried to retrieve them without disturbing Ken. He was relieved to hear the explanation but it had not been funny at the time.

On another occasion, they were drinking with some SAAB employees in Linkoping and, around eleven in the evening, were told *"And now you go to bed. Tomorrow we hunt the elk and we will call for you at 05.00!"* Next morning they were driven up to a hunting lodge in the hills, to take part in a hunt which is permitted on only a few days in the year. As soon as they reached the lodge, glasses of Schnapps were handed around and after a few drinks the senior SAAB member present said to Ken *"Now we go and hunt the elk"*. He then presented Ken with a loaded rifle, explaining that weapons were always loaded because they were then handled with respect.

After some time in the forest, during which any sensible elk would have been long gone, his companion announced *"Now Squadron Leader, we shoot a pistol competition"*. There was a small bush nearby and he proceeded to tear off every leaf save one, leaving it standing up straight at the top of the bush. He then handed Ken a long-barrelled 9mm Luger pistol, the "Artillery" model, with which Ken was already familiar having carried one during part of World War II (Ken's explanation for this being that 9mm ammunition was more readily available than the normal issue .38). He said to Ken *"Now you shoot"*. Ken duly took aim and still wonders how he managed to put a shot straight through the centre of the leaf at quite a range. On seeing this, his challenger did not even bother to fire! They both went back to the lodge only to find most of the group asleep or in an alcoholic daze. So much for "shooting the elk" but Ken had been pleased to represent the RAF in that particular match whilst overseas!

Ken had been in the Ministry post for some months when he was called to see an Air Commodore who was completing his Annual Confidential Report (Form 1369) - he had spotted Ken's entry regarding flying undertaken. On being asked if he had flown solo, on jets, etc., and confirming it, the AC pointed out to Ken that he was authorised to fly *'Non-Operational, Daylight Only, with a Safety Officer'*. Ken was able to state with complete honesty that he had not received a copy of this letter and would produce the original the next day, wherein it was clearly stipulated that he should fly *'With*

Passenger'. Ken's suspicions of the original wording were thus confirmed but the error had saved him from serious consequences.

The matter was passed to be resolved with the Central Medical Board but, in the knowledge that he had received good Reports from the refresher, the jet conversion and instrument rating courses, he faced the Board with a feeling of bravado. On the basis that attack can often be better than defence in a tight corner, he complained that he had almost faced a Court Marshal through no fault of his own. The facts were considered and within a few minutes he was told that there was no way the Board could give him a full Medical Category in accordance with the RAF Medical bible. A category with no restrictions was possible, however, and Ken gratefully accepted the "offer". The Board then requested that he undertook a distance judgment test for information purposes only and assured him that it would not affect the decision. He complied and when allowed to move his head slightly he was assessed as 'better than normal'!

Many years later, the Aero-Medical Examiner Doctor in Norwich who medically assessed Ken told him that during the training he had undertaken with the Civil Aviation Authority it was said that there might be 'exceptions to the rule'- such as pilots with only one 'good eye' - and his case was actually quoted.

Ken feels that full vindication came on the 14th April 1955 when a serious flying incident occurred. He was serving in Air Ministry Operational Training at the time and was departing RAF Hendon piloting a de Havilland Chipmunk trainer to view a new bombing target at Chesil Beach. Very shortly after take-off the engine mysteriously cut out at 300 feet. Somehow, he managed to land the aeroplane in a tiny tree-studded park beside the A1 road, having to sideslip electric cables and avoid trees. The aircraft came to a silent halt beside a park bench occupied by women with children in prams but they did not appear at all disturbed.

As a result of this skilful avoidance of obstacles, he received a "Green Endorsement" in his Log Book for "great skill and presence of mind in landing without damage and injury to himself or others". It was later found that one of the fuel pump filter cups had come undone and fallen off. He recalls that he travelled home to Peggy later that day and eagerly related, with natural pride, the achievement of making a safe landing under difficult conditions. *"Oh"* she said, followed by a long pause *"I have been wondering what sort of wallpaper to choose for David's bedroom."* Her view being that, as it was peacetime and he had not been shot at, what was all the fuss? Down to earth with a bump this time!

Two views of Chipmunk WG469 after Ken had put it down on the edge of Sunnyfields Park, Hendon, following engine failure.

With Strategic Air Command USAF

In February 1956 Ken went on a two-year exchange posting to the Armament/Electronics Division at Headquarters, Strategic Air Command, USAF; this was at Offutt Air Force Base in Omaha, Nebraska. Here he held a flying/technical appointment and piloted the giant, ten-engine Convair RB-36H bomber.

Ken had a first class cabin in a Cunard liner for the trip to New York and he arrived in style. Such an overseas trip provided the opportunity for some serious leisure motoring so he had taken his rather special Rolls-Royce motorcar (*"The Long Dog"*) with him in the hold of the liner. This model was not to be found in the R-R catalogue and in view of Ken's "modifications" the company might well have shown some concern. For example: the four headlamps were Aldis Lamps (two dipped and two main beam) with their fairings converted from starter-motor cowls normally housed in the jet air-intakes of a Junkers Jumo jet engine; there were around 450 re-profiled Lancaster bomber wing skin bolts in the bonnet hinges; and pieces of flying wires from "Virginia" bombers for door handles. In fact, most of the body was made up from aircraft parts of one sort or another.

If this conjures up in the mind a picture of a "Heath Robinson" contraption then nothing could be further from the truth. The finished product was an extremely sleek, wire wheeled vehicle of classic lines with a, seemingly, everlasting bonnet. The vehicle was a magnificent creation and a credit to its marque. It was christened *"The Long Dog"* by Ken's good friend Squadron Leader John Crampton DFC AFC when they were both at RAF Binbrook. He commanded 101 Squadron and was also a car enthusiast with a racing Maserati.

After a weekend in New York, Ken had to drive to the British Embassy in Washington D.C. for a briefing. He then undertook the long drive to Offutt Air Force Base at Omaha, Nebraska and, being February, the roads were covered in salt. He arrived on a Friday evening and spent the night in the Officers' Club. He had heard of the "Automotive Hobby Shops" on these SAC bases where enthusiasts could work on their cars so, on the Saturday morning, he took the Rolls-Royce down to the Hobby Shop with the intention of washing off the salt encrusted on it.

The car was immediately surrounded by enthusiasts, all wearing working overalls of some sort. Someone said *"Gee, I understand these Royals-Royces will start on the ignition switch without a starter motor"*. Ken happily demonstrated this by switching on the coil and magneto, retarding the ignition advance lever in the centre of the steering wheel, and the engine fired up. The audience was duly impressed so Ken said that he could do better than that, and start it in high gear - he recalls that he was already using American English! - on the ignition switch alone without slipping the clutch. Whilst it works Ken says he still finds it a little difficult to believe but it is a most impressive trick and one he used quite a lot in the States.

As Ken was about to demonstrate, he spotted *"a grey-haired old fool"* in overalls right in front of the vehicle, examining the "Kneeling Lady" mascot. *"Stand aside"* shouted Ken and was promptly obeyed. On moving the ignition lever, the engine first fired with a little "pinking" sound, then the car moved off as though driven by steam. Everyone was now even more impressed, including the grey-haired man. Ken then found that this was General Curtis E LeMay, the famous no-nonsense but effective Commander of Strategic Air Command from October 1948! It was hardly the way for an RAF Squadron Leader to greet his new Commander but the General was forgiving and immediately had an SAC logo stuck on the "windshield". In his leisure time he was a very keen automobile enthusiast and Ken recalls being "ordered" all over the mid-West to automobile rallies to display his "Wallis Silver Ghost Rolls-Royce Special".

For flights in the RB-36H, Ken would travel down to Carswell Air Force Base, Fort Worth, Texas, to be kitted out with clothing intended to ensure survival at the North Pole if necessary. An early morning start would be made on the pre-flight inspection of the huge aircraft and this would involve some climbing in the wings, etc. By the time the inspection was finished it was as though a full day's work had already been done but the long flight was still to come.

When taxiing, the aircraft was steered by a large hand-wheel on the port side of the cockpit. Take-off would be at a very heavy weight and necessitate the employment of all ten engines but at an altitude of 10,000-15,000 feet the jet engines would be shut down. The umbrella-like seals in the jet air intakes would be adjusted to allow just enough air in to keep the engines "windmilling" to prevent icing-up, leaving the six piston engines to sustain a cruising altitude of around 18,000 feet over the USA and Canada on a heading for the North Pole.

The jet engines would then be restarted for a climb to about 45,000 feet for the run over the simulated target. This would be followed by a turn to starboard on a heading for north of Sweden and then another turn for England. Pairs of pilots would work a four-hour shift in flights lasting 33 hours without refuelling.

The cockpit area and forward part of the aircraft was pressurised as was an area aft, accessed via a small, pressurised tunnel 85 feet long. A trolley allowed a crew member to lie flat on his back to propel himself along but such was the aircraft's distinctly nose-up pitch angle, to maintain height at such a weight for the first 10 hours of the flight, a small handbrake down the right side of the trolley was needed to prevent an overshoot at the other end! Small windows in the tunnel allowed the crew to view the atomic bomb on board. Amenities included heating equipment for ready-prepared meals, and hammocks for rest periods when personnel were not at the controls, although sleep was not easy to come by owing to the note of the piston engines, the general noise and cabin pressure changes.

Much of the flying time would be on automatic pilot but occasionally this was disconnected in order to trim hands off, level, before re-engaging autopilot. This was required as huge quantities of fuel were consumed during flight; the maximum fuel capacity of the RB-36H was over 35,500 gallons. Trouble with one or two of the piston engines was not uncommon. These Flights from Carswell Air Force Base to the North Pole, terminated with eventual landings at Yokota in Japan or at Burtonwood. The latter was popular with Ken as it provided an opportunity to nip home for a day or two.

In view of Ken's later and long-term fascination with the diminutive autogyro it is interesting to note that the RB-36H had a wingspan of 230 feet and length of 162 feet. There was a crew of 22 including four pilots, and the aircraft had a maximum speed of over 400 mph. Consequently, he can claim to have flown some of the smallest and largest aircraft around.

Being that this was the time of the Cold War, there was always an A-Bomb on board the aircraft during exercises with an assigned target should "the order" be given whilst they flew over the North Pole towards Russia. This was a tense time for the Allies, especially when in that year Russian tanks entered Hungary and troops landed at its airfields to quell an uprising by those opposed to Prime Minister Nagy's declaration that the country was to leave the Warsaw Pact, and calling for NATO to recognise its neutrality.

On one occasion Ken was one of the four pilots flying an RB-36H on a very long exercise flight from Greenham Common, England, back to Carswell Air Force Base. They had been airborne about 27 hours and were about to land at around 02.00 am. All Ken was thinking about was a hot shower and going to bed but when they landed there was a message waiting: *"Your car is in the Automotive Shop being polished. A T-33 (jet aircraft) is on its way to bring you to Omaha and you are to be in St Louis "Autorama" in the morning"*. When General Curtis E LeMay gave such an order it was to be obeyed! Consequently, Ken had the quite long flight from Fort Worth to Omaha and then a drive of some 400 miles to be present at the "Autorama" that morning - he just made it. Whilst in America, Ken gained nine trophies at car shows with *"The Long Dog"*.

Time in America also afforded him the opportunity to purchase an outboard engine and an old hull, tune them up and enjoy trips on Carter Lake in Omaha, Nebraska. He also was able to race again and recalls that it was much easier in the US. During 1956 and 1957, he gained eight gold-plated die-cast trophies: he achieved 1st place on six occasions, a 2nd and a 3rd. He confesses to have "flipped" *"Per Ardua XI"* once during a race, with one of his shoes still likely to be at the bottom of the Missouri as a result. The headline in the local paper the next day quaintly reported *'Air Force Colonel Flips In Last Race'*.

His very last race was the 56-mile *Missouri Marathon* where he gained 1st place. This was held on the 25th August 1957 with around 60 boats of different classes competing and the local headlines next day reported *'British Pilot Bags Trophy'*. Ken recalls that he *"suffered some small loss of blood that day"* - he had to kneel on a cushion for some protection from the harsh bumps as the craft hit the waves and his knees took a beating in the process.

Following his success, Ken was asked to give a talk to the Inland Outboard Racing Association on the sport in the U.K. There was a large gathering of enthusiasts and their wives, and he started his talk by saying that in the U.K. *"we really enjoyed ourselves on the Norfolk Broads"*. There was a sudden, deathly hush and Ken could see looks of horror on the faces of many in the audience, particularly the ladies. He then realised his error (I wonder!) and quickly explained that the "Norfolk Broads" was the name given to the area of man-made lakes in Norfolk county in the U.K.

Ken still has three boats at home: one is the tiny 1947 experiment with the Jumo starter motor; another is an American three-point racing hydroplane hull that he had flown back to the UK. The last one he built - a stepless hydroplane much along the lines of the craft in which he won the Missouri Marathon - was some time around 1960, when living at Southwick on the south coast.

Ken suspects that he saw more of America during his posting than most "locals" managed to achieve in a life-time, especially because SAC pilots were able to "keep their hand in" during weekends, so long as they shared the flying time with another pilot. His wife Peggy had not ventured to the USA because it would have interrupted schooling for their children so he was always available to share the leisure time flying facilities, piloting a B-25 Mitchell or whatever was available to a different part of the country. During his time with the SAC Ken flew the Beech C-45H, C-47 "Dakota", B-25N, RB-36H and the T-33A jet. He recalls that it was a busy and interesting two-year assignment - something of an understatement!

On returning from the US, Ken took up a post as Command Weapons Officer in Fighter Command, and it was not long before his inventiveness and gift for problem-solving earned him further recognition.

The mighty ten-engined Convair B-36, similar to the one Ken flew in SAC. *(General Dynamics Corporation)*

Top: The Rolls-Royce vehicle as purchased in 1948.
Bottom: Ken with *"The Long Dog"* in the Rocky Mountains 1957.

Top: *"Per Ardua XI"* at speed.
Bottom: Winning the 56 mile *"Missouri Marathon"* in 1957.

Why the autogyro?

'I had no need of sails to drive me, nor oars or wheels to push me, nor rails to give me a faster road. Air is all I wanted, that was all. Air surrounds me as water surrounds the submarine boat, and in it my propellers act like the screws of a steamer. That is how I solved the problem of aviation..............'

- Jules Verne in Robur le conquerant (1886)

As most of Ken's life, from this point on in his story, has centred upon the autogyro I wanted to explore the origins of his interest in designing very small, rotary-winged aircraft. He identified two main sources for me. One was his post-war examination of the un-powered German autogyro kites. These were designed during World War II by Focke-Achgelis, to be flown from the deck of a German U-Boats to lift an observer up to 1,000 feet as an observation platform in the hunt for Allied shipping targets. The tethered aerial observer would thus be towed behind the submarine and needed to exercise care in the way he phrased his radio message to the submarine commander because if an emergency were indicated the order to crash-dive would be given without hesitation. The aerial observer would then hurriedly jettison the rotors and parachute, with the machine, into the sea where (according to one wartime reporter) *"he would drown in the normal way!"*

The second source of inspiration for Ken was the Hafner Rotachute: a towed autogyro glider intended to carry an agent or infantryman to a designated point with greater accuracy than could normally be achieved at that time by a drifting parachute. Raoul Hafner, an Austrian émigré, later became the Chief Designer for the Bristol range of helicopters - in 1935 designed the ARIII gyroplane (or autogyro). This differed from contemporary Cierva designs in that the pilot had full control of the collective pitch of the rotor blades. He formed his own company but commercial development stopped with the outbreak of World War II.

In 1940 Hafner put his talents at the disposal of the Ministry of Aircraft Production and started work on the Rotachute. Around twenty were built but none was used operationally; examples later went to the United States and, post-war, tiny rotor gliders of this type became available in kit form for hobbyists. His most spectacular design to fly was the Rotabuggy: essentially a flying jeep, air-towed into action as an alternative to being transported in a Horsa glider. A number of successful test flights were carried out at the Aeroplane Forces Experimental Establishment, Sherbourn-in-Elmet during the latter part of the war. With the coming of peace, however, development of the two Hafner designs ceased.

The very first practical, rotary-winged aircraft was built by The Cierva "Autogiro" Company, and Juan de la Cierva made the first successful autogyro flight at Gatafe, near Madrid, on 9th January 1923. The Spanish inventor then brought his C.6A machine to England in 1925 at the invitation of the Air Ministry. The design was basically an Avro 504K aeroplane without main-planes, fitted instead with a four bladed rotor mounted on a steel tube pylon. A V Roe & Co. Ltd was given an order to build two similar machines for development purposes, with the second being the first two-seat example.

The first evaluations to be conducted by the Aircraft & Armament Experimental Establishment, then at Martlesham Heath in Suffolk, were early in 1932 on the Avro-built Cierva C.19 Mk.IV Autogiro G-AAYP. A somewhat tentative report was produced. Then the de Havilland-built C.24 G-ABLM followed in the April and gained its C of A the same month. Late the following year, the improved C.30P G-ACKA, built by Airwork with a 140hp Genet Major engine, quickly passed the tests for the Type C of A and many C.30s were built thereafter.

A batch was ordered for Service evaluation as the "Rota" and several aircraft were tested at Martlesham Heath. Problems developed with the rotor blades, however, as they twisted under extreme loads so a maximum speed was imposed but doubts continued to exist about the strength of the blades into the late 1930s. Most of the surviving C.30As were impressed into RAF service during 1939-1940. A civilian 'Autogiro Unit' attached to No 24 Squadron became a service unit on 20th May 1940 and moved to join the Special Duty Flight at Martlesham Heath. This was to form part of a calibration unit within 60 Group and included Rota and Cierva aircraft. It existed for a short period only and closed in November 1940.

Cierva C30 aircraft also saw service with No.1448 Calibration Flight at Crazies Hill, Henley-on-Thames - it formed No.529 Squadron at Halton on 15.6.1943 - and was stationed on Ipswich airfield from November 1944. From here the squadron carried out calibration flights for radar stations and gunners defending the East Coast against V-1 attacks. A particularly slow-flying aircraft was needed for these missions - one that could remain almost stationary over one spot on the ground. The prevalent method had been the use of captive balloons but they proved too unwieldy and inefficient. Twelve of the autogyros survived the war and HM580 is on display at the Imperial War Museum, Duxford.

Autogyros have been produced in all sizes, from G & J Weir's diminutive Weir W.1 to W.4 series built in Scotland between 1932 and 1936, to the multi-engine, all-weather, helicopter Fairey *"Rotodyne"* XE521 which operated in autogyro mode in its 200 mph forward flight. The rotor diameter measured 104 feet, with power provided by two Rolls-Royce Tyne turbo-prop engines and rotor-tip jets to produce a cruising speed of at least 185 mph. All up weight was around 53,500 lbs and it was designed to carry up to 70 passengers. A cornerstone of the country's defence policy at that time was for powerfully-equipped mobile army units to be established at strategic points where they could be quickly transported to areas of conflict.

A major disadvantage, however, was the high noise-level of the tip-jets. The first flight of this giant was in November 1957 and funding for the venture was not forthcoming to begin but, when Fairey and Westland merged in 1960, government support then looked promising. Commercial orders did not materialise, however, and the project lost momentum.

Ken once flew in formation with the *"Rotodyne"* but, unfortunately, does not have a photograph of the occasion. This came about because the *"Rotodyne"* was also at A&AEE Boscombe Down when Ken was there as O.C. Tactical Weapons Group. On the 14th September 1961, he flew his WA-116 (first flight having been 2nd August) to the Royal Military College of Science at Shrivenham in company with the *"Rotodyne"*. It must have been a wonderful sight and very much a "little and large" situation.

In view of Ken's great interest in road vehicles, he might have considered designing a combination vehicle, with Eugene L Vidal's experimental Roadable Autogiro being an example; this appeared in the mid-1930s in America. On landing, the rotor blades were stowed aft and its pilot-driver transferred power from his propeller and rotor to the single-drive wheel by throwing a clutch. It was then ready to merge with road traffic. The combination seriously compromised performance levels in both modes, however, and it never went into production.

In 1934, Westland design staff, in co-operation with Senor Cierva, produced a five-seat cabin autogyro powered by a 600 hp Armstrong Siddeley Panther engine. Westland designed and built the airframe whilst The Cierva Company was responsible for the rotors and mechanism. Named the C.29

Autogyro, tests disclosed vibration problems with the rotor system and the project was shelved on the untimely death of Cierva. He was killed in the take-off crash of a KLM Douglas DC-2 at Croydon in December 1936.

In conjunction with The Cierva Company, Westland also produced the neat, two-seat CL.20 (G-ACYI) and it was successfully flown by Cierva test pilot, R. A. C. Brie. It would likely have been a popular purchase by private owners but growing hostilities in Europe prevented its production. This aircraft is featured in *The Book of Westland Aircraft with these introductory words: 'It is true that man has conquered the air and annihilated distance, but his victory will not be truly complete until he is able to perform with the same degree of skill as Nature's aviators, the birds, with their control of wide speed ranges and ability and take off and land safely in very confined spaces. Many experiments have been made to achieve this desirable end, but only with light rotating-wing – or autogiro – aircraft has any measure of success been attained.'*

The Fairey *"Rotodyne"* XE521 (Westland Helicopters Limited)

The late 1950s

Ken now turned his mind to the design of the first ultra lightweight and powered autogyros: a problem worthy of his engineering genius. Having purchased a pair of McCulloch engines in America his thoughts centred upon the Bensen B.7 gyroglider; a design similar to the wartime Rotachute. Various improvements and modifications to Ken's own standards were introduced and the completed machine was broadly a motorised B.7, with a conventional control column layout replacing the suspended "hanging stick" moving in the "wrong sense". It included a reinforced plastic seat originally from a de Havilland Mosquito of World War II.

After introducing constrained movement to a fixed angle in all directions for the rotor spindle articulation by way of a circular collar, Hafner had used a "Metalastik" rubber bush in his Rotachute for deflection of the rotor spindle axis for control. Presumably, these wartime UK products were not available to Bensen when he designed his B.7 "spindle head". His design allowed movement of the rotor spindle for control purposes and used the features of a self-aligning roller bearing for control by movement of the rotor axis via the hanging control column attached. A pin moving in a slot was arranged so that the control column did not turn around the control bearings.

The available movement in the self-aligning bearing at the B.7 rotor head was plus and minus 10 degrees, and pitch and roll stops were provided. Ken deduced that this could allow the 10 degrees of movement to be exceeded - a very serious matter - when roll and pitch movements were combined. Hence his modification, to include a cylindrical roll stop to limit control movement of the self-aligning roller bearing to 10 degrees misalignment at any position to prevent possible serious damage to the self-aligning bearing by exceeding limitations. (Ken had advised the Bensen Corporation of the changes he had instigated so was interested to discover that, from drawings of the Bensen 7 purchased late in 1960 by another RAF officer, some of Ken's original objections to the design had been eliminated by modifications.)

Ken can still recall the thrill of the first flight in the experimental Wallis-Bensen machine G-APUD in 1959. He was then stationed at Fighter Command Headquarters, Bentley Priory, Stanmore, as the Weapons Officer, and went home at weekends to Church Lane, Southwick in Sussex. For his first "hop" on the 23rd May at Shoreham Airport there was a 25-knot wind and G-APUD was tethered by a short rope to a stake in the ground. He had a long wool tuft and a "horizon indicator" to give an idea of the attitude of the fuselage to the pilot - the Air Speed Indicator was a car speedometer driven by a "windmill".

His main objective was to see if the rotors would start to auto-rotate properly. He had previously tried them in calmer conditions but *"they had not seemed interested"*. Ken further said that he had *"done a bit of a bodge"* to present the blades at a slightly more negative angle and this time they spun up. They were soon giving lift, with 'PUD hovering about three feet off the ground with a stationary engine.

This was watched by Ken's friend, the late Lt Cdr John Sproule R.N., He remarked to Ken that in view of the wind level he did not think it would take much to fly it free and under power. Ken thought that was a good idea so the rope was removed and he fired up the engine. When the rotor blades got up speed 'PUD leapt off the ground to about 50 feet when he eased back the throttle. She then "plonked" back on to the ground and he did a further high leap before shutting down, having decided that there had been enough excitement for the day. Ken then went to the Control Tower and it was quite evident that there was much relief by those who had watched the experiment when the target-plane engine was shut down.

Incidentally, Lt Cdr Sproule was the inventor of the Sproule Net, used by the Royal Navy - firstly by Dragonfly helicopters to rescue disabled casualties at sea. He also designed a deck securing system for the Dragonfly at sea but, as there was no immediate requirement in 1955 for small ship operations, the design was shelved. He went on to design a raised boom (and later a hoist) for the Whirlwind helicopter so that a person could be hoisted and easily swung into the cabin of a helicopter without detaching the boom.

The next flights by Ken were in less windy conditions, starting with straight flights across Shoreham Airfield on the 6th June and "S" turns on the 7th; then the first circuits and landings on the 20th. On the 28th, he demonstrated it for the *"News Chronicle"* in a 20-knot wind. Many more requests followed as the word spread about this strange new flying machine. Consequently, Ken has a mass of archive material from these days, along with the many, very detailed reports he wrote following every flight undertaken, and a record of each modification he made to the machine.

Ken had to learn to fly the autogyro but did not find it difficult, though some potentially deadly features showed up as he "explored the flight envelope".

He found that there were many shortcomings in the design, such as the straight tube on which the main wheels were mounted – this was unsprung and had no compression struts towards the ends. It bent after only gentle use but Ken said he would simply turn it over and bend it back into shape again. He used aircraft quality alloy tube but it still bent.

These early flights caused a great deal of interest and Ken has a thick file of press reports following the many demonstrations he made that year. He was even featured on *Pathe Pictorial* which showed 'PUD arriving for a flight on a trailer pulled by Ken's "mount of the day" a Rolls-Royce Phantom III. He received a particularly good reception from the 40,000 spectators at the RAF Tangmere Battle of Britain Display in the September, and several newspaper headlines reported *"Home-Made Aircraft Stole The Show"*. One likened it to a *"20th Century Witch's Broom"*, and another said that motorists would see it as the answer to overcoming the growing traffic jams!

Ken did have to force-land 'PUD on the 29th October, after taking off from Elstree. He came down beside the Elstree Reservoir but on the wrong side of the fence and a crowd of spectators soon gathered. It took quite a while to find someone with a key to let him out of the compound, despite the fact that the aerodrome should have had provisions for speedy access in case an aircraft ditched there and rescue was needed.

One problem he quickly identified with the prototype was the lack of means of effectively spinning up the rotor blades. With a good wind to start the rotors spinning, things were fine but it was difficult to gain adequate rotor speed for take-off on still days. A fast taxi did not achieve the result - the blades would "sail" and sometimes flex down, striking the rudder or propeller. Only a very slow taxi, with gradual build-up of speed as the rotors gained speed would work but he found this tedious. He often demonstrated his Wallis-Bensen B-7 at Shoreham Airport and, in doing so, discovered that if he waited for an aircraft to taxi and then follow, positioning behind it when the pilot ran up his engine for checks, he would then have the rotors at some speed by the time the aircraft had taken off and it was his turn but this was not always possible. He was well aware of the necessity of a mechanical drive from the engine in a practical autogyro.

Ken said that he did make a preliminary experiment with 'PUD but it could not transmit the torque required at the rotating spindle of the "awful rotor head". With the experience of "borrowed" wind in mind he had experimented with a mechanical drive to the rotor via a friction wheel, and a small shaft

133

connecting with the rotor spindle through universal and splined joints but the torque loads required at the rotor spindle were far too great, sometimes breaking the universal joints. Whilst the required torque to spin up the rotor blades in nil, or low wind conditions, could never be applied through the small spindle which turned the rotors, it did show the potential of a good spin-up system.

With increased confidence on fast runs and pull-ups with the modified Bensen he then experienced, with some concern, unstable pitch at high speed, with the stick force lightening or even reversing when g was pulled. A fast, level pass followed by what was intended to be a gentle climb would result in the aircraft rising more steeply than was intended. As it ran out of speed in the climb there would be "a period of uncertainty" as the nose dropped, regardless of the control input. The reason for the instability was the increased drag on the rotor system as a climb was initiated, acting upon the top of the rotor spindle where the rotor blades were attached by the teeter bolt, and being pulled back so causing a backward load on the control column - or a forward movement on a "hanging control column".

Ken had been flying long enough to recognise the potential danger of an aircraft that was unstable in pitch. In his reports to the various authorities he documented this potentially dangerous feature, and it certainly was the cause of some fatal accidents. The pitch instability of the spindle head, and the problem of providing sufficient torque at the rotor head for spin-up, resulted in Ken having to start with "a blank sheet of paper". A completely new design of rotor head would be needed.

His invention was a rotor head in which a substantial rotor axis bolt was fastened in a thick plate. The plate could be moved for pitch on an axis bolt arranged forward of the rotor axis, with roll being provided for by the fore and aft axis. Thus, in the pitching plane, any increase in drag and lift, resulting from entering a climb, would be countered by the lever arm of the rotor, axis-to-pitch control axis. The new rotor head also provided the opportunity to install a substantial reduction gear for rotor spin-up where the maximum torque was required.

As Ken appears never to throw anything away, materials were easily to hand in his workshop, especially items salted away from his work in armament testing at the Proof & Experimental Establishment, Shoeburyness. By using an epicycle reduction gearbox with a pinion engaging in an internally toothed ring fitted to the rotor hub assembly, a small flexible shaft running at high speed could convey the required power to the rotor blades. The drive was provided with a free-wheel and positive disengagement of the pinion from the internal toothed ring at a pre-set throttle position. The "off-set gymbal" rotor head, together with the spin-up drive, was the subject of a number of UK patents now long expired and the principle is employed in most small autogyros, albeit in different forms.

From this it could be deduced that the geometry of the Bensen "spindle head" (based on the Rotachute head) resulted in a lightening of the stick load required to start a pull-up at speed, leading to virtually "taking over" and forcing the stick further back until all speed was lost. The problem was essentially in the pitching plane. Ken did not undertake further experiments with the Bensen machine and happily sold 'APUD to a person very keen to acquire it. Ken heard later that it had been donated and now resides in the Air & Space Hall of the Museum of Science and Industry in Manchester.

Bensen himself went on to build powered versions, and adopted Ken's Patented "offset gymbal rotor head". In an advert c1964, Bensen announced that hands-off flight was now possible in a rotorcraft thanks to the *"Bensen off-set gymbal rotor-head"*. Ken was philosophical about this and said he had only taken out UK Patents in view of its possible military and other working roles - they had been published with drawings and could be examined by all and sundry. As a serving officer at the time, he had to bequeath his rights to the Patents to the Crown in any case. Ken's off-set gymbal rotor-head has become almost universal but he says that there are still a few tricks of design that can make a difference.

The rotor-head of the prototype, of what became designated the WA-116, was the first part of a very successful design to be completed in 1960. Ken believes he made some "lucky intelligent guesses". Only when the rotor dynamics (plus also, by the wool-tuft method, aerodynamics) were recorded, by a high-speed camera fixed to go around with the rotor head, taking ten photographs per turn, did he realise how lucky his guesses had been. New rotor blades were made by Ken during ten days leave late in 1960 in the then disused Link Trainer Room at H.Q. Fighter Command. This room was more suited to such work than his wooden garage at his home, with varying climatic conditions. Ken undertook research largely with G-ARRT. For later testing he used G-ASDY, and G-AXAS - flown solo and two-up for rotor dynamics recording; other tests were conducted with the 100hp Rolls-Royce WA-117 Mark 2, first flown in 1967.

In March 1961 he was posted to the Armament Division, Aeroplane & Armament Experimental Establishment, Boscombe Down, as the Officer Commanding the Tactical Weapons Group. The WA-116 airframe was completed in a building in the Stop Butts area.

Ken's first tethered flight at Shoreham Airport - 23rd May 1959.

The 1960s

Ken's development activities were rudely interrupted early in 1960 when he was placed in charge of the RAF's participation in the annual Royal Tournament Show at Earls Court in London, from 22nd June to 9th July. The assignment was quite an honour really but no doubt he would have preferred working on his autogyro design. The main task called for a "missile-age display" to show what might have happened if a nuclear attack on the UK had occurred, and the response by the RAF. Ken had never mentioned this episode to me but I happened to notice a model of a very unusual, swept-wing aircraft in his study on one of my visits.

Ken was happy to explain that the "advanced enemy bomber" had been his design for the show but recalled he had to be careful at the time not to make it look similar to any Russian design. Filming of the model, as though part of an attacking enemy force with a swift and successful response from the RAF's new Lightning jet aircraft and missile defence system, had been undertaken at Rank's Film Studios at Denham. Ken's design is very interesting, in that the aircraft is powered by four engines mounted on the rear fuselage with a T-tail on the fin, but he did not recall having seen the revolutionary VC10 being built at that time which employed this very similar design. The first standard VC10 flew in June 1962. With the enemy vanquished and the UK safe, Ken settled back to more mundane challenges.

Ken's model of the enemy bomber for the 1960 Royal Tournament

Ken's quest for serious recognition and official acceptance of a flying machine on the same principle, but designed and built to accepted standards, soon arose. A useful way of gaining attention was participation in airshows and his first outing at RAF Tangmere had been very successful.

Another early public demonstration of his autogyro invention was soon presented but in a light-hearted way on this occasion, according to the programme for the annual Battle of Britain Airshow held at RAF Gaydon on the 17th September 1960. On that day he was also giving demonstrations at Biggin Hill and Tangmere so was picked up at Boscombe Down and transported from show to show by a Blackburn Beverley of RAF Transport Command. His appearance was billed under "Light Entertainment", and promised the assembled masses a demonstration by Ken of *'an unconventional method of becoming airborne in his diminutive "Hoppi-copter"'*. Equal billing went to a Fleet Air Arm officer who would attempt to do the same by way of a pair of hydrogen balloons! "Jack" was not heard of again but Ken would go on to travel a long and dedicated journey to promote the autogyro as (in modern parlance) *"a very serious bit of kit!"*

In 1960, the Miles brothers of Miles Aircraft at Shoreham showed interest in Ken's design and this led to collaboration with them on a military test contract to meet Joint Services Operational Requirement 353 for Light Autogyros for trial by the Army Air Corps. JSOR 353 had resulted from some earlier demonstrations Ken had given Army personnel with the Wallis-Bensen B-7. At the time, the AAC had been trying an "inflatable wing aircraft"; useless in any wind conditions.

F. G. Miles was soon absorbed into Beagle Aircraft Limited and the aircraft thus became the "Beagle Wallis WA.116". The "WA-116" was the original designation given to his design by Miles Aircraft: the first "1" denoted a single engine, and the "16" stood for it being the 16th single-engine aircraft in which the company had been involved.

In 1961, formal flight-testing of the Wallis WA-116 prototype G-ARRT commenced and it made its maiden flight at Boscombe Down on the 2nd August that year; it immediately "felt right". Climb tests started with a flight of 7,000 feet carrying a load of 100 lbs of lead ballast and to Ken, at the time, it seemed quite high in the open-framed aircraft over the town of Worthing. Then, with a cockpit nacelle fitted, he climbed from A&AEE Boscombe Down to 10,000 feet accompanied by a Harvard from the Test Flight. The Flight had suggested to Ken that it would be advisable for him to wear a parachute in case of any problems with the rotor blades over-speeding at altitude but, since there was not room for a seat-type parachute, he elected to wear a chest type.

Top: G-APUD at Middle Wallop in July 1960.
Bottom: Wallis prototype G-ARRT.

During the flight he was very aware of the chromium-plated release handle and the consequences of knocking it and the parachute then deploying into the rotor blades - he has never flown an autogyro whilst wearing a parachute since! His next flight was from Swanton Morley in Norfolk, carrying a Recording Barograph and he soon reached 13,500 feet. At this time, however, he was impressed by the "Service Ceiling" of 16,500 feet quoted in the Brochure for the Bensen B-8. He recalls being very surprised to see in 1967 an announcement of World Records achieved by Dr. Bensen in his B-8 including one for Altitude of only 7,280 feet, with a 90hp McCulloch engine! An official 3km Speed Record of 73 mph was also claimed, and a non-stop straight-line Distance of 133.3km had been achieved.

On the 16th September 1961 Ken flew G-ARRT at the "Battle of Britain" Air Displays at RAF stations Finningley, Cottesmore and Gaydon. On that day there was a wind so strong that the Service helicopters and Chipmunks were grounded but he recalls G-ARRT was quite well-behaved "hands-off". Aircraft could exceed 115 mph in level flight, carry a 200lb pilot to over 13,000 feet and, from a standing start, reach 5,000 feet in five minutes at part throttle. The WA-116 was fully Certificated at some expense to Beagle in the expectation of securing orders but when the Army Air Corps trials were conducted the aircraft was encumbered with a heavy valve radio taken from a tank plus "wet" batteries; the trials also took place during the very cold and prolonged winter of 1962/3. The open frame of the military version, coupled with carburettor icing, did not warm the pilots to the aircraft so the A.A.C. tried out two makes of two-seater cabin helicopters but they did not accept either one. Finally, they chose the relative comfort of the Agusta-Bell Sioux. More of this later on.

Beagle's main interest had been in a military application but they did issue publicity material extolling the virtues of the aircraft for *'some civil roles for which it is eminently suitable, including traffic control, photography, all forms of search, pipe line, cable or fence inspection, survey, sport and short range communications'*. Possibly, they were not convinced that any likely civil application would solely justify production and, whilst the WA-116 was Certificated, it was a "Special Category" because of the, then, use of the un-Certificated, converted target-plane engine. The lack of a suitable engine at that time probably most affected their views. Whatever, their support lapsed.

Ken says that Miles (soon to be Beagle) did a wonderful job in producing their versions by May 1962, with nearly everything perfectly copied, and with jigs and tools for initial production. Only two serious mistakes were

Ken has adopted a very relaxed pose whilst "flying" G-ARRT in 1961 and approaching the photographer at speed - taken without a telephoto lens! This pose has become Ken's "trademark" ever since.

made in the copying and they were in respect of the nose-wheel stirrup, carrying nose-wheel loads to a, then, rubber-in-compression system to reduce shock loads (compression loads are now taken by springs), and the weight of the rotor blade mass balances. Combined, they caused what could have been a serious accident on the second flight of the Beagle-Wallis WA-116 in May 1962 at Shoreham Airport.

J W C ("Pee Wee") Judge was the pilot. He telephoned Ken at Boscombe Down to say that he had done a short flight on the first Beagle-built version G-ARZA (XR942) and that there was a dreadful vibration and over-speeding of the rotor blades; it was nothing like G-ARRT which he had flown a number of times. Ken replied that he would like to look at it at the weekend but that it should not be flown again before then - although he did not offer to do the test himself so as to avoid an upset.

On the day, "Pee Wee" performed an incredibly long and high-speed takeoff, just "greasing it around the circuit" and making a very fast landing; those watching were relieved to see it land safely. There was some amazement then when "Pee Wee" taxied back to the take-off point to commence another flight - with an aircraft badly in need of investigation - and his speed on the ground was again excessively high.   Within seconds there was a loud "crack" and G-ARZA somersaulted many times before coming to a stop as a heap of debris.   Dick Stratton of Beagle and Ken ran to the scene and were very relieved to see "Pee Wee" twitching in the wreckage. He was not seriously hurt but spent a weekend under observation in a local hospital. Ken says, that this proved the "crashworthiness" of the design, which has been put to the test a few times since.

When the wreckage was examined it was apparent that the cause of the somersaulting had been the failure of the nose-wheel stirrup. This had resulted in the nose-wheel mounting, and the front of the keel, digging into the ground. Ken had been sent the original Beagle drawings in January 1962 and had scribbled a couple of pages of comment in reply, including mention of more strength being induced on the nose-wheel stirrup on his own G-ARRT. Not only had the Beagle design not changed to that which he had suggested but the unit had not been made according to the Beagle drawing. It employed edge-to-edge brazing, which was then cadmium plated and masked the obvious weakness. Worthing Technical College subsequently carried out tests to discover the Failing Loads of the stirrup as made, as it should have been made according to the Beagle drawing, and as Ken had used on G-ARRT. Ken's design proved the best by far.

By October 1962, G-ARRT was flying with a cockpit nacelle, which was an experiment to see whether it had any adverse effect on handling. All was fine so the temporary nacelle was quickly replaced by one of fibreglass (moulded from a Sea Vixen rocket pack frangible nose-cone) and aircraft plywood. Ken reckons that the streamlining is probably a bit better than some of the shapes that followed, produced from a mould made from a 600 gallon Hunter drop-tank.

After the disturbing start to flight-testing the Beagle versions, Ken insisted upon undertaking the first flights of the rebuilt G-ARZA in July 1962. He recalls a very cautious take-off and flying only a foot or so above the ground. A horrifying vibration set in and continued some time after a straight-ahead landing. It was obvious there was something very wrong.

It came onto rain at this point so the machine was placed in a clear plastic shelter - the Miles brothers always being keen on innovation and the use of plastics, etc. Here, Ken noticed, when looking up through the drilling in the interior rotor blade mass balance (through which the pin to attach the rotor blade to its support passed) that it was more like looking through a tube than a hollow box. Ken questioned this and was told by a company technician that they *"had a bit of a job running that much lead into the mass balance casings"*. Ken pointed out that, 'bit of a job or not', it was the required total weight of the mass balance housing and its lead (or solder) content! The mass balance casings were removed and the lead melted out of them until they were at the required weight. When refitted, G-ARZA flew just as well as G-ARRT.

In February 1963 Ken presented a paper to the Royal Aeronautical Society titled *"The Low Cost Autogyro"* and an enthusiastic audience unanimously congratulated him on his paper, the design of his autogyro and on his flying both at the Farnborough S.B.A.C. Show and as shown in the film covering much of the flight testing which accompanied his lecture. The report of the lecture in the Society Journal states that the Cierva C.30 Autogiro could only be made to descend vertically by *'extreme trickery'*, because the centre of gravity was a little too far forward. It suggests this was a useful safeguard for inexperienced pilots, since it was not easy for everyone to remember to maintain a reasonable minimum speed for landing.

On Ken's design, the stick-back force required to cause vertical descent was considerably greater than the forces required in normal flight. It was considered likely to be applied only deliberately and when vertical descent, rather than landing, was intended. It was further suggested that the small Weir gyroplane, comparable in power, must have been near to achieving a similar performance, but had necessarily been considerably heavier. An outstanding feature of Ken's autogyro was said to be its lightweight and simplicity of design.

Top: Beagle-Wallis WA-116 autogyros on Army evaluation - Ken christened this photograph "The Three Wise Monkeys" The "antique" and heavy radio is mounted low on the starboard side - a better location would have been on the port side to help counter propeller torque.
Bottom: Beagle-Wallis WA-116 XR942 Army autogyro with trial installation cockpit nacelle - the radio is mounted above the engine.

Having flown WA-116/XR942 during the seven days of the 1962 SBAC Show at Farnborough, plus Battle of Britain Displays with G-ARRT at RAF Stations Wyton, Waddington, Cottesmore and Benson all in the September, Ken's thoughts had turned to acquiring a small airstrip of his own. Whilst looking for a house with a piece of land he could use as an airfield for the autogyros, a suitable property inland from Shoreham was found but the purchase fell through at the last minute. Peggy then spotted some adverts in *"Country Life"* magazine for properties in Norfolk and as Ken was to be flying at the RAF Swanton Morley Open Day they decided to stay over and look around. Reymerston Hall, some four miles south of Dereham, was the first property inspected but they went no further and moved in during September 1963. Built in 1780, the interior of the building was not particularly inviting he recalls as it was painted "institution brown" with ugly 1930-style fireplaces in place of the marble originals. The "improvements" having been undertaken by a previous owner post-war.

This work had followed wartime occupation by the Army with a searchlight battery or something similar, and such unsympathetic use explained the absence of the original staircase. Owing to its damaged condition, it had been replaced by the immediate, post-war owner - a Mr. Youle. Peggy later found a large quantity of marble fragments forming a crude pathway leading to a pigsty, along with the remains of marble pillars and carved griffons; all of these came from the original fireplaces, replaced by Mr. Youle. Ken had to remove one of these 1930s style fireplaces, and disguise another, before Peggy would agree to move in! A Mr. Gibb had followed; he felled all the trees in "The Park" and had it ploughed for farmland, using the plot to the rear for growing fruit.

Recently, Ken learned from a neighbour that all manner of military vehicles were seen at the Hall during wartime, and Lysander aircraft had often flown into "The Park" as it was then called; these might even have come from Ken's old 268 Squadron although Ken has no memory of having to land there himself. He thinks that aircraft may have been used to fly in senior Army officers who were checking up on Searchlight units. He added that most of the Army personnel he gave rides to arrived *"almost collapsed, having been very sick after I had enjoyed a bit of low flying practice and a few antics"*! There was no easy way a passenger, or even the Gunner, could communicate with the pilot in any case.

His "runways" are presently about 350 yards long with trees at both ends, although they may not have been there during wartime. Shipdham Airfield is less than one a mile away and was assigned to US Forces in 1942 as Station 115. It was the first US heavy bomber base in Norfolk and thus became the ancestral home of the 8th Air Force Liberator.

Whilst remnants of metalwork and concrete have been found in the garden over the years, possibly from an aerial installation, the most intriguing discovery, made almost by accident, was a small radio aerial indoors. This was on white porcelain insulators and hidden behind what looked like wooden panelling high above an alcove housing a stove in the kitchen, once a cupboard. Ken had spotted hinges to the left of the panelling but no form of handle was evident on the opposite side so it was necessary to prise it open with a screwdriver; inside there was a door catch. The mystery "door" measures around 30 inches by 43 inches. At each corner it has a large nail about 31/2 inches long, around which an insulated wire is wound four times, each turn slightly spaced. These were insulated but not well covered. Ken cannot now recall the exact layout but the wire on the insulators formed a diamond shape a little way in from the door edges. Its purpose has remained a complete mystery to Ken but he found the insulators useful for something else and they were promptly re-cycled!

The section for the county of Suffolk in my copy of *"The Complete English Traveller - A NEW SURVEY AND DESCRIPTION OF ENGLAND AND WALES"* - a fairly rare publication of 1771, mentions the area was visited, and particularly the village of Hingham which is about two miles from Reymerston Hall. It is interesting to read the description as *'a small place but one of the most agreeable in the county owing we suppose to a fire which happened here in the beginning of the present century, when all the houses which were built of wood were consumed, and most elegant ones erected on the spot. Some of the best families have made choice of this town as a place of retirement, so that there are always good company to be found, and many of them and their servants, coming from the capital having brought the politest fashions along with them, it was some years ago called by the people of neighbouring towns, Little London'.*

Reymerston Hall was built shortly after this report was published so there is little doubt that the site had been carefully chosen and, when completed, the building would have contributed to this salubrious image of rural life. The present Hall is on the site of the original Hall, and this was essentially a stone and brick structure rather than one of wood. It is believed that this earlier building was destroyed by fire.

146

A discarded newspaper clipping found during the move also divulged an interesting modern story for Peggy and Ken. It reported that the third, and last post-war owner had been Sir Charles Musgrave; he had lived there for around one year. In 1963, as a 49-year old fourteenth baronet, he had advertised for a wife: *'an attractive lady, under 35'*. The clipping, taken from the Daily Mirror for the 17th July 1963, reported that *'a £700 per week, New York strip-girl named Dior Angel'* considered herself the best candidate for the post and had announced her intention to pursue Sir Charles *"and become his wife before the end of the year even if I have to use father's shotgun!"*

When approached by the newspaper for his response it was reported that Sir Charles briefly contemplated her talents and replied along the lines that he doubted her ability to be an outdoor girl, or to be on the same mental wavelength! When told of this, the delectable Ms. Angel retorted in plain English that she was very much a person who enjoyed wide-open spaces and could learn to play croquet with a little practice as good as any English lady. In her mind, little else was required of the lady of the manor!

Ken did not find later editions so we do not know what happened although marriage would seem to have been unlikely. Ken made the point of adding that he was sure he would have noticed if the young lady had turned up at the house since their occupation. If she had ventured there, looking for the owner, I have a mental picture of Ken being confronted by this nubile maiden in his workshop, and quickly enthralling her with his off-set gymbal, or some other new and fascinating invention, in the hope that Peggy would soon come to the rescue.

Early in 1964, Ken had a meeting with the Air Secretary's Branch at Air Ministry to discuss his future. After nearly seven years as a Wing Commander, promotion to Group Captain might soon have been expected. The Air Secretary, however, observed *"You have had too much time in Research & Development; you need some time at the sharp end."* Ken admitted that he had indeed occupied various R&D posts but that was because of a special interest and capability. He asked what "time at the sharp end" might mean and the response was: *"Wing Commander, Engineering, on an Operational Station"*. Ken's view was that the sort of "sharp end" decision to be made in that role could well be what to do about a WAAF who had become pregnant! It was obvious that the future was not bright for him.

Ken returned to the Armament Division at the A&AEE, Boscombe Down, and related the conversation to the Group Captain in charge, who promptly asked *"What were you doing before you replaced me as Weapons Officer, H.Q., Fighter Command in 1958?"* Ken had been on an Exchange Post at Headquarters, Strategic Air Command, USAF, as an Armament/Electronics Officer, of course. His superior then pointed out that *"Were you not also flying as a Pilot in Convair B-36s, always with an 'A' Bomb aboard, and with an allocated target as you flew over the North Pole on "Exercises" should you get the message - wasn't that the Sharp End?"* Ken was annoyed that he had overlooked the perfect put-down but it was now too late. With the cancellation of advanced projects, such as the Fairey Rotodyne and TSR2, he decided it was time to retire early from the RAF, at his own request, and to carry on with his autogyro project.

By the time he left the RAF, aged 47, he had flown many different types of aircraft including Magister, Martinet, Master, Tiger Moth, Moth Minor, Harvard II, Miles Whitney Straight, Anson, Proctor, Chipmunk, Lysander I/II/III, Wellington 1/1A/1C/III/X/18, Meteor III/VII, and Vampire, plus the American types mentioned earlier.

Looking back over Ken's service, I am not alone in finding it very strange that he did not receive at least a gallantry award. The need to demonstrate outstanding flying skills on several occasions suggests that the Distinguished Flying Cross would have been the minimum award appropriate on completing his first tour of ops. Many deserving people did lose out on awards during wartime for various reasons, of course, including sudden changes in the senior squadron personnel responsible for making such recommendations "upstairs" in respect of subordinates. Some squadron requests were sent to Group but returned with a direction for them to be presented again at the end of the officer's tour, only then to be overlooked. This may be the explanation.

Back to "civvy" life and the quest for a perfect engine

With his cousin Geoffrey, the son of the other brother and builder of the Wallis Monoplane, *Wallis Autogyros Limited* was formed at Cambridge in 1964. This was with the object of building small numbers of autogyros and also to test the waters as to potential markets and roles. Ken acquired three ex-military versions of the WA-116 (XR942/943/944) and they started work on other versions with a carpenter, a car engineer and three apprentices. One WA-116 was sold under special terms to the Norfolk & Norwich Aero Club then based at RAF Swanton Morley nearby. More than 100 pilots flew the aircraft after only a verbal briefing so this tends to speak volumes. This particular autogyro is now owned by Nigel de Ferranti in Portugal.

In 1965, Ken replaced the McCulloch engine in G-ASDY with a Hillman "Imp" car engine he had modified. The object was to find an off-the-shelf engine for aero-club use. The WA-116 at the Norfolk and Norwich Aero Club, with the noisy McCulloch engine, had become unpopular with RAF Swanton Morley where the club was based. Performance with the new engine was good but the noise of the un-geared propeller was unacceptable. As reduction gearing would have increased weight and added complication, G-ASDY was left to gather dust for some years. In 1971, it was converted to the American 44.7kW (60hp) Franklin two-cylinder aero engine and this was a good marriage. Cruise performance was excellent and the low exhaust note and noise intensity was acceptable. Ken found the 60 hp Franklin to be the best engine but, sadly, the company went bankrupt and he lost a reliable source. More of all this later in the chapter.

Another autogyro was sold to an ex-RAF Squadron Leader who was keen on aerial archaeology but he became tired of the noisy two-stroke, target-plane engine. The third aircraft (G-ATHM) went to the Chairman of Air Ceylon as he had some interest in possible production there and this was registered 4R-ACK. When Ceylon became Sri Lanka, however, such private flying became illegal and the autogyro was returned in 1970.

In all his years developing the autogyro, a constant problem for Ken has been to find a good engine so I shall go into more detail now on his quest, including the early expendable and un-certificated McCulloch target drone engine from America, and the similar Italian 4-cylinder, supercharged 2-stroke Meteor - both quite noisy in operation so unsuitable for general use to Rolls-Royce examples. Some small duplication might occur as engine issues are touched upon, necessarily, elsewhere in the book.

Trials by the Army Air Corps in 1962/3 of his prototype G-ARRT and the Beagle-built derivatives relied upon the McCulloch Type 4318 of 1,634 cc - a converted target-drone horizontally-opposed engine. A 4-cylinder, 2 stroke with rotary inlet valve disks as part of the crankshaft, single ignition by magneto, with impulse coupling and fixed advance, plus fuel injection at constant full power of 72 hp at 4,100 rpm. This was converted to a throttled automotive carburettor.

During the AAC trials, mostly conducted in a prolonged and very cold winter, carburettor ice was a common cause of trouble. Less so with his prototype however, using a different make of converted carburettor and with heat transfer to it from the crankcase by replacement of asbestos cylinder base and carburettor manifold gaskets with light alloy gaskets of similar thickness. One of the problems soon encountered was engine failure following the overheating and burning of the pistons in a pair of opposite cylinders in this "flat-four" engine. This was discovered to be due to the fuel/oil mixture burning rich on one side of the throttle butterfly at part throttle settings, the other side being weak; hence causing piston burning.

Ken later cured the problem by mounting the carburettor above the intake port of the crankcase rotary valves so that the carburettor butterfly axis was parallel to the crankshaft, and the mixture strength would be equal between the front and rear crank-chambers, regardless of the throttle butterfly position. This was achieved by cutting off the normal flange mounting and brazing on a new one at the appropriate angle, using a carburettor with a brass body rather than the usual zinc alloy casting.

Ken has written up his summary of events in great detail and, whilst naturally disappointed that his aircraft was not adopted, he was fully aware that a number of engine problems at the time did not create a favourable impression. The converted two-stroke either made too much noise or went suddenly silent (which, to a pilot, seems even louder!) The "prangs" did at least demonstrate the "crashworthiness" of the design and Ken went on to overcome all the difficulties. He judged, however, the pilots would have to be sympathetic to two-strokes in order to operate the McCulloch-powered Type WA-116. In his opinion, the A.A.C. Trial was undoubtedly premature owing to the need for engine refinements, and that the open frame machines were flown during the very cold winter of 1962/3. No protection was offered the pilot and it was hardly practical to read a map in the wind.

Just prior to this, however, the A.A.C. had been testing the "inflatable wing" (christened *"The Durex Delta"* by the RAF!) that could only be flown in virtually "no wind" conditions. The very new Wallis WA-116 therefore had obvious advantages as its original Certification specified a maximum surface wind for operations of 43 knots. The helmets then being used gave no ear protection, however, and there were problems hearing the "antique" A-41 radio. Instead of coming up with more practical helmets, an extra amplifier stage was fitted to the radio - speech in the earphones could then even be heard by bystanders above the noise of the engine! It is interesting to note that 20 years after the original trial, XR944 - "updated" with a cockpit nacelle, and fitted with a Certificated Franklin aero-engine - participated very successfully in further military roles as covered elsewhere.

A quite humorous but instructive article was written by one of the pilots, Major T. M. Deans, RA, and, despite all the problems, he concluded that *"for the sheer fun of flying there is nothing to beat the Wallis Autogyro"*. A colleague of his was a Major Warburton and Ken recalls reading that an airline pilot was disturbed to find he was flying in company with "Warby" at 10,000 feet. In his furry clothing, the airline pilot described the sight as that of "a teddy bear on a motorbike!"

Ken still likes the McCulloch for special roles and his examples have been subject to much modification. They certainly were not acceptable for general use in the roles in which the Wallis autogyro has special attributes so a more suitable engine had to be found.

A 90 hp version was to follow of similar capacity but with improved porting and pistons less liable to burning due to the top piston ring being nearer to the piston crown. Ken says that the McCulloch is a two-stroke engine that quickly induces a "love-hate relationship" with its operators. To some it could be frightening to hand-start it by swinging the small propeller. It was very noisy in use but with the occasional sudden stops it would sound even louder to the pilot.

By 1965, Rolls-Royce Motors at Crewe had started to produce a 100 hp engine under Licence to Continental-Teledyne, of the USA. It was a proven design of light aero-engine of 100 hp at 2,750 rpm with recommended cruise at 2,000 rpm. That was a lot lower rpm than the 4,100 of the McCulloch. To absorb the extra power at the lower rpm it would seem that a provision would have to be made for a larger propeller. This could be achieved only by replacing the straight keel tube of the Type WA-116/Mc by a suitably cranked keel for what was to become the Type WA-117/R-R Mark 1. Further, because the rudder would have to be much taller, it would need to be attached to a hinge at its top and bottom, entailing an extra structure from the top of the rotor mast tube. This resulted in a structure that was much taller than the WA-116, with the rotor blades out of reach above the pilot, thus rendering him unable to steady them manually, fore and aft, as when taxiing in confined spaces.

Ken sketched an impression of what a fully-enclosed WA-117/R-R "Series 1" would have looked like but decided to first try it in open frame form to assess its potential. Registered G-ATCV, Ken first flew her for 10 minutes on the 24th March 1965. Apart from increased height, it had a spindly undercarriage that would have folded up when faced with a mole-hill and degraded the proven design typified by the WA-116. He only flew it about three times before deciding to scrap it - this was before the cockpit nacelle was fitted. Ken observed that, in the U.S.A. the "tall tail" has been taken to far greater extremes than the experiment he so quickly abandoned. He presumes that they only operate from long runways - at least, that is what he has seen on trips to America for "giroplane" events

This particular story continues in January 1967 when Ken started to build a successor to his "tall tail". He used many of the components to make the satisfactory Mark 2 version, including the rotor head, rotor blades, wheels, etc. G-AVJV employed a straight keel on the lines of the WA-116. The rotor mast had to be angled aft to keep the fore and aft Centre-of-Gravity with the heavier engine - the (then) new Rolls-Royce Continental 0-200-B of 100 hp - in much the same position relative to the rotor head. The cockpit layout was more on the lines of a glider, with a rather reclining position. A fractionally larger propeller could be accommodated to that on the WA-116.

The first flight of 20 minutes was made on the 27th May 1967 and it was generally satisfactory. Much further testing and some developments, including use of a 4-bladed propeller, followed. On the 18th July she was demonstrated to Mr Durbec of Rolls-Royce Motors, with whom the fine cooperation continued. It was soon apparent that the Mark 2 was a practical working autogyro although, with extra power and weight, she needed to be handled with more respect than the lively Type WA-116. G-AVJV remains as she was in 1967 and has undertaken much serious work.

Returning to Ken's search for a Certificated aero-engine "in scale" with the Type WA-116 airframe, he next tried an 850 cc Hillman "Imp" car engine.

Whilst it would never achieve certification, he wondered if it might prove more acceptable than the noisy and temperamental McCulloch engine for everyday use. This was fitted with a suitably fine pitch propeller on WA-116, G-ASDY and first flown from Reymerston on 6th November 1965, then at Shipdham. The next tests were at RAF Swanton Morley on 23rd June 1966. It was apparent from the start that the high revolutions per minute would render the propeller liable to damage from rain, and that the noise was unacceptable. Tests then had to wait owing to film commitments in Brazil.

On his return, Ken exchanged the engine with an "up-rated" 1,000 cc version and, on the 27th February 1967, he made three flights with G-ASDY at Bourne, totalling 1 hour 5 minutes. He next flew her on the 3rd May in three flights also at Bourne totalling 1 hour 10 minutes. Ken recorded in his Log Book that oil was getting on the friction wheel and affecting rotor spin-up. On the 25th November she was demonstrated in a 20 minutes flight, and again for 25 minutes for ground-to-air photographs. On the 23rd July 1968, in a 20 minutes flight, the "Imp" engine boiled and the propeller was damaged. That was the last flight with the engine that had flown at excessive rpm for the role. About three years later, when the "Imp" was replaced by the first Franklin WA-120, 2-cylinder 60 hp 2A-120, it was noticed that the fuel tank used had been made for pressurisation and that there was no inward venting valve provided!

G-ASDY went on to be used extensively for several different roles as later chapters will reveal and the successful conversion led to the modification of G-ATHM (previously 4R-ACK) for record-breaking. Ken saw the potential of ASDY with the Franklin engine but left it as a "working hack" rather than modify it by fitting a more streamlined undercarriage and other improvements. Instead, he acquired another Franklin and updated G-ATHM for the long distance record attempts in which he gained the closed-circuit records and went on to fly the length of Britain. Later, it was used for long-range photographic work because of its ability to journey some distance especially when road transportation of aircraft and equipment to the site was not convenient. An example being the filming of the 7.10 a.m. train, journeying from Yarmouth to London, for a television documentary. Another documentary necessitated filming "ducks eye" views of landings and take-offs from a tree-encircled duck decoy in Suffolk.

Top: G-ATCV with the "tall tail" - soon abandoned.
Bottom: G-ASDY with a modified Hillman Imp car engine.

With simultaneous research taking place on several engines we now have to go back again to 1965 and Ken's experiments this time with Type WA-118/M G-ATPW. Early that year he had become aware of the range of two-strokes being made for reconnaissance drone aircraft (and targets) by Meteor Costruzioni Aeronautiche, Triest, Italy. One version, the "Alfa 1", was a 2.3 litre, 4 cylinder radial, giving 120 hp for a weight of around 132 lbs - an unusual two-stroke. Being a four cylinder radial there is no crankcase compression. Instead, it has a Rootes-type blower feeding the fuel-air mixture direct into the inlet ports in the cylinders. The engine is normally fuel-injected, with a conventional lubrication system - sump and pump.

Ken went to Triest and found there was a German engineer with Meteor: Rudolf Zinkl who had been a Focke-Wulfe 190 pilot in World War II. They immediately became good friends and during a visit to the UK, in April 1973, he enjoyed a flight with Ken on G-AXAS. Rudolph was in Trieste at that time because there was a possibility his company (BMW) might produce a fully-certificated version of the Meteor for manned flight. In view of Ken's interest in "Alfa 1", a more suitable version was made up with a conventional "Zenith" automotive carburettor, and following modification it was cleared for 50 hours of flight at 104 hp at 3,600 rpm. Some problems developed, overheating of the conventional lubrication system in particular, but Ken felt it was an engine with possibly high speed and altitude capabilities. The magneto, which did not have any impulse coupling, had to be in a very fit condition to give a spark on the hand-swinging speed of the propeller but this was much hampered by one cylinder always being under compression. On drones the engine was started by a powered drive system engaging in a drive dog on the tractor airscrew.

By 1968, Ken's interest was waning and he described the Meteor Alfa 1 as *"an Italian Prima Donna that sings in a very high voice, then sulks and refuses to sing at all!"* He believes that if its problems could be sorted out it might still have some potential but never as a "workhorse".

Ken also looked at the "Fuji 440", which is an air-cooled in-line, two-stroke. It drives a propeller on a separate shaft through a toothed-belt reduction gear. It was briefly tried but found to suffer surges of power when the throttle was opened beyond a certain point, together with some unexpected loss of power when the throttle was returned to what would have been intended as the cruising speed.

Next to come in Ken's detailed record of engine trials undertaken is the

Two views of WA/118M "Meteorite" as G-ATPW.

60 hp Franklin 2-cylinder 2A-120-B. The first flights of the 130 hp Rolls-Royce 0-240 engined WA-120 were made in 1971. At much the same time the Campbell "Cougar", a two-seat cabin autogyro was being built by the Campbell Aircraft Company and it was to be powered by the R-R 0-240 engine. Rolls-Royce Motors recommended to Mr Curzon-Herrick, who was sponsoring the "Cougar", that he visit to see the WA-120/R-R, since this was flying successfully with no cooling problems, etc.; the engine being in the pusher role. The visitor duly flew in to Shipdham airfield in his own fixed-wing aircraft and was then ferried by Ken in G-AXAS to Reymerston. Ken gave a spirited display in G-AYVO and his visitor was suitably impressed with the 0-240 engine.

Ken was then surprised to be asked what sort of propeller he would use on a Franklin 2 cylinder aero-engine. It transpired that they were trying such an engine on a single-seater Campbell "Cricket" but it would not fly! They were having the propeller re-profiled by Hordern-Richmond in the hope of success. Ken offered to buy the engine if it became redundant as he would not have bothered to order one from the U.S. for his own trials. A subsequent telephone call advised Ken that the "Cricket" with the re-profiled propeller would gather speed until lift off but then, at full throttle, it lost speed and sank back to the ground again.

Ken duly purchased the engine and manufactured a suitable mounting for installing on his "test hack" G-ASDY. He needed to trim about 3 inches from the propeller tips in order to clear the keel of his smaller airframe before the engine was installed. Following flight it was clear that the 60 hp Franklin 2A-120 was "in scale" with the WA-116 airframe and two more engines were promptly purchased. One engine went into his cousin Geoffrey's WA-116/Mc G-ATHL, after Ken had made the conversion to take it, and following ground-running it was ready for an air-test on 11 September 1972.

Ken took off to the South-West but, after getting airborne, the engine gradually lost power, though not misfiring. Thinking that if he could gain a little height he might be able to turn back for an emergency landing, the option suddenly expired as the engine stopped with a shudder. With barely a foot to spare and numerous obstacles in his path, including overhanging trees and telephone poles, Ken managed to land on the Mile Road next to his home. A check found the propeller and crankshaft were virtually locked in the crankcase. To avoid duplication I can say that the conclusion of this story is included in the chapter headed *Three Forced Landings But Several World Records*. Needless to say, Ken solved the problem himself with the U.S.

manufacturer's approval and gratitude. The Franklin was adopted by Ken and powered some of his World Record setting aircraft.

Close collaboration in the mid-1970s with Weslake, a company based at Rye in East Sussex, was intended to produce an engine for the WA-116 airframe and other light aircraft. It would have been the first new British light aero-engine for decades but a production design did not materialise. An experiment Ken did try for himself was to take a Rolls-Royce 4-cylinder engine and cut it in half. He then welded the crankcase together to produce possibly the only 2-cylinder Rolls-Royce engine around. This story is worth elaborating upon so here goes.

The Rolls-Royce 0-240 was operating satisfactorily in WA-120/R-R and WA-122. Rolls-Royce had made the horizontally-opposed 6-cylinder 10-360, under licence to Continental and had design authority for their 4-cylinder 0-240. Franklin built a similar 6-cylinder of 360 cubic inch capacity, then a 4-cylinder of 240 cubic inches, so it seemed logical that a 2-cylinder of 120 cubic inches, identical capacity to the 2-cylinder Franklin, should follow. Rolls-Royce, however, did not seem to want to take that step so Ken suggested that they release to him a 4-cylinder 0-240 and he would section the crankcase to make a 2-cylinder. This was agreed to as, if successful, the company might consider putting it into production.

The two-cylinder Rolls-Royce engine with fuel injection. Ken says that a need to install his experiment has never arisen

Ken made up a representative fuselage frame on which to mount the engine for realistic assessment of vibration levels and suchlike. Providing suitable weights for the shortened crankshaft was a problem but it was solved. The engine was soon providing more thrust, using the same propeller, than the Franklin - probably half the 130 hp of the R-R 0-240 compared with the 60 hp of the Franklin 2A-120 - and the cylinder head design of the R-R engine was superior to the Franklin. Unfortunately, Rolls-Royce never reached the stage of producing the 2-cylinder R-R 0-120; in fact, they ceased making all light aircraft engines.

Elsewhere in this book, mention is made of Ken's involvement with the Post-Attack Airfield Damage Reconnaissance Contract. Portsmouth Aviation had connections with this work and recommended the Wallis Autogyro should be assessed for this role. There were further MOD contracts to conduct a survey of available engines and assess them, also additional evaluation of a twin-engined Wallis autogyro to be undertaken. Flight tests were required of the autogyro with Infra-Red Linescan, having real-time imagery transmission, together with other sensors.

Other engines tried were the Bombardier-Rotax 532 UL of 65 hp, the Norton P-67 twin-rotor, "Wankel" type made for the trials of nominal 100 hp, the Limbach L200-0 EA1X of nominal 85 hp with direct drive, and the Subaru EA-81. For the Norton, a 2.2 reduction gear drives this water-cooled engine in its experimental P-67 version and it showed considerable potential in performance but there were problems to be addressed. It was further modified but it has not been tested in its latest form and is "on the shelf".

He regards the 2,000 cc Subaru as a pleasant engine to fly and it is based upon the Volkswagon engine, though made for such as powered gliders. It is air-cooled and Ken never went to the trouble of making cowlings in the hope of improving the cooling of any rather "masked off" cylinder. This meant that, in the very slow flight at high power settings for some working roles, a cylinder head temperature could be too high. Ken had even thought of providing some water-cooling by such as welding aluminium on the cylinder heads. The EA1X versions were made after a visit to the factory in Germany to discuss the need of a version for the Wallis (and then also Vinten) autogyros. WA-116 G-VIEW and G-AVDG are powered by these engines

The Subaru EA-81, a similar horizontally-opposed, 4-cylinder car engine of similar capacity and water-cooled was in existence, however, with all light alloy. Ken subsequently acquired some and soon made up an engine with suitable modifications and a propeller flange. He built Type WA116/S G-BGGU and first flew it in 1994. the version showed considerable promise, though like many other engines it would never be Certificated for working roles. Things were delayed by the need to provide selectable carburettor heat to prevent carburettor ice, resulting in a rather elaborate structure. At the time, Ken says he was having problems with the then "ageist and perfectionist" Policy on Pilot's Medicals and the Subaru development ceased but further trials would be worthwhile after going getting a renewed Permit-To-Test, etc. Ken concludes that he feels by far the best solution for the Subaru EA-81, or some of its derivatives, was a simple fuel injection system.

The Rotax 532-UL was assessed as the most suitable, readily available engine for the role then to hand, and an airframe for a twin-engine autogyro taking these engines was designed, constructed and flight-tested. This was the 100 hp Rolls-Royce powered WA-117/R-R G-AVJV, first flown in 1967. It particularly demonstrated its efficiency in the day and night, all-weather Exercise "*Keswick*", equipped with Miniature Infra-Red Linescan, with real-time imagery transmission to a ground viewing and recording base. Type WA-116, however, carrying video-recording equipment, showed the particular value of imagery in colour recording more easily recognition of Aerial Denial weapons. The official report clearly confirmed the superiority of the Wallis Autogyro in this special military role.

In the late 1980s, under another MOD Contract, to develop an autogyro for military duties such as aerial reconnaissance and photographic, Ken experimented on paper with a number of designs having two engines, which he had first given thought to back in the mid-1960s, and rejected them. The "commercial in confidence" report issued goes into great detail on the advantages and disadvantages of different engine-mounted configurations, including side-by-side pusher, combined puller and pusher, in-line pusher.

Flight testing in 1987 of the Wallis Type 201 G-BNDG, twin-Rotax engine experimental machine is also covered, being built as a means of determining the optimum basic design for possible Post-Attack Airfield Damage Reconnaissance roles. It certainly proved the validity of the design. With its easy take-off on one engine and complete independence of the engine/airscrew units, it is potentially safer than a twin-engined helicopter, having no reliance on a rotor-drive gearbox or a tail rotor. Ken favoured the "push/pull", in-line engines and that proved to be practical in the flight tests, if such power were to be required.

160

Two views of WA-201 G-BNDG twin-engine machine in flight.

Top: G-BNDG climbing at speed.
Bottom: Tucked away at the back of Ken's hangar - minus rotor blades.

Ken also has a "back-of-the envelope sketch from around 1964/5 of a possibly very potent twin-engine version with two 90 hp McCullochs. He feels that it would still be an interesting project for pure performance but, with their hand-swing propellers for starting, it would not be appropriate to build it on the lines of the twin Rotax engined WA-120/2R he flew. The latter are started by pull-cord. It is worth mentioning here too that back in January 1969 Ken went as far as producing a drawing of a 4-seat autogyro, based on the seating geometry in a Mini car, with a streamlined cabin. For power, he had pondered upon a 300-500 shp gas turbine engine, driving a four-bladed pusher propeller.

Ken's latest summary of events is that the Continental/Teledyne 0-200 of 100 hp has proved itself in WA-117 G-AVJV for working roles, day and night and in all weathers, with very sophisticated remote-sensing equipment on board. It seems that it is still being produced to FAA Certificated Standards and Rolls-Royce made versions of which he has flown successfully since 1967 in this autogyro. The rather reclining seating position might be better if a bit more upright in working roles and Ken could easily build a version to include the lessons learned. Apart from being rather heavy and of "antiquated " design, the 0-200 is air-cooled and he fully appreciates the value of a liquid-cooled engine, with the radiator in the nose of the cockpit nacelle. Not only does this ensure there is no localised overheating of an engine during periods of slow flight at high power settings, it also provides the luxury of heating for the pilot in cold weather.

Ken remarked that there had recently been mention of a new Belgian aero-engine, which is very light, water-cooled and of 85 hp. He very much likes the sound of this but there have been many a new engine announced but never to go through the major process of production to Certificated Standards. The Wilsch diesel aero-engine could also be a good bet but that is a long while getting Certificated.

In addition to the "tall tails" mentioned earlier, another modern design feature Ken does not support is the use of horizontal stabilisers. He sees no need for a stabiliser but did experiments in the 1970s following the fatal crash at Farnborough. He found that stabilisers were potentially dangerous. In gusty conditions, that the aircraft would not normally even notice, the lightly loaded "stabiliser" would cause nasty pitch oscillations. Ken believes that he would not have survived the flight through the "Ventana" in Brazil if G-ARRT had been fitted with a so-called "stabiliser". He still has a stabiliser provided with electric trim adjustment, which Ken tried out on

163

G-AYVO, but it was "tried and rejected". His only concession is to have one on the propeller axis and entirely within the outflow from the propeller, and into which a gust cannot easily intrude.

As for the main rotors, Ken expertly makes them himself in wood and steel, with the pusher propeller in carved wood. Ken has tested extruded aluminium blades but superior performance and stability are achieved by steel-cored blades, the steel being surrounded by Hidulignum (a high-density plywood) with an outer skin of aviation plywood. Miles Aircraft studies considered these blades to have "an unlimited fatigue life".

This section concludes with pictures of two unusual engines. Top is the 2-cylinder, horizontally opposed, 2-stroke starter engine as used in all World War II German jet engines. It reaches 20,000 rpm under load.
Bottom is a very rare 6-cylinder, Rotol sleeve-valve made by Rolls-Royce and Bristol following amalgamation, employing Bristol's "Burt" sleeve-valve system.

The name is Wallis …… Ken Wallis!

In 1966, the company was "damped down" and Ken took to working with the aircraft rather than the pursuit of production for amateur use. Whilst several important commissions and tests had been useful promotions for the autogyro it was his flying exploits that year doubling as Secret Agent "007" in *" You Only Live Twice"*, the fifth James Bond film to star Sean Connery, that caught the public's eye most of all. James Bond thrilled cinema audiences worldwide "flying" a heavily armed *"Little Nellie"* and dispatched numerous villains but Ken undertook all the flying sequences.

The background to this assignment was that, before working in Brazil and Italy for Film-Studio Roma on a "spaghetti" spy film called *"Dick Smart 2.007"* flying G-ARRT (more of this later), a radio interview of Ken by Tony Scase on the planned filming for a BBC *Today* programme was heard by Ken Adam, Eon Films' Production Designer and an ex-RAF fighter pilot himself. Around the same time, co-Producer Harry Saltzman had also seen an article on Ken's aircraft in a magazine. Adam got the Aviation Consultant, Group Captain Hamish Mahaddie, to call Ken to request that he demonstrate the autogyro to the producers of the film, Broccoli and Saltzman, at Pinewood Studios.

The only aircraft Ken could take was his Beagle-Wallis WA-116, ex-XR943, which was then demobbed as G-ARZB. It had been rebuilt with a cockpit nacelle and still required some engine adjustments. The aircraft had been returned to Wallis Autogyros after being pranged by cousin Geoffrey on landing it in a rabbit hole. On arrival, Hamish showed Ken a patch of concrete measuring about twenty square feet, telling him that he could take off from it for the demonstration. Having explained that it was not a helicopter so needed a take-off run, Ken spotted a pathway about 100 yards long but with all kinds of junk either side; at the upwind end sat a massive pile of railway sleepers. Following a convivial lunch, Ken duly "performed" and the potential for such a novel new Bond weapon with its likely high audience appeal were quickly spotted. Ken was promptly "booked".

Afterwards, Hamish said that it was one of the most dramatic things he had seen. The noise of the engine echoing around the buildings was deafening, with Ken heading towards the railways sleepers at gathering speed, only to vanish in a massive cloud of dust. Everyone waited for the crash but as soon as he emerged, going straight up, his participation in the film was secured.

On the 19th June, Ken was invited to attend the important Royal Aeronautical Society Centenary Garden Party at Cranfield. In the absence of G-ARRT, he flew G-ARZB, shortly to be transformed into *"Little Nellie"*, together with cousin Geoffrey flying G-ATHL from his field at Madingley.

By mid July he was on his way to Rio de Janiero in Brazil and this episode is picked up in detail later on in the chapter. With cousin Geoffrey booked to fly G-ASDY at the 1966 Farnborough SBAC Show in his place, Ken went to Japan from Brazil to commence filming for Eon Productions. On arrival he found that his WA-116 had arrived at Kagoshima with some changes. Her rotor blades and some parts had been removed for easy air transport in a passenger-carrying airliner but now she had a new paint scheme, and weapons' systems had been attached. (N.B. According to book customer Geraldine McNeish, the paint scheme was applied by Harold Joe Dye at Oxford Airport, Kidlington, whilst with CSE Aviation).

"Little Nellie" is first seen dismantled in the film, within a number of expensive travel boxes to be opened up by "Q", the Ministry Quartermaster responsible for kitting-out and arming the Double-O agents; Ken still has these within his collection of film artefacts. Not all of the components were genuine; some turn out to be replicas made of wood and painted silver.

Ken was puzzled at first to hear the film crew refer to *"Little Nellie"* but then he recalled that those with the surname Wallis or Wallace in the RAF during World War II were nicknamed *"Nellie"* after the famous music hall star Nellie Wallace. Group Captain Mahaddie had christened her thus. Whilst G-ARZB had been selected for the aerial film work, G-AVDH was "made up" in the same way and used at Pinewood Studios for shots of Sean Connery sitting in the cockpit, with a large fan nearby to ruffle his shirt!

Ken saw Connery at the nearby fishing village of Akine, but only really met him once during filming. This was on the road at Yojiro Ga Hama, by Kagoshima. The star sat in the cockpit and "Q" briefed him on the controls for a sequence. He then got out and took off his shirt and helmet for Ken to don for the first flight of the film which entailed taking off down the road and turning back for a "beat up" before going on an armed reconnaissance flight. Soon after this, Connery returned to the UK and the "air unit" got on with filming over the volcanoes. During filming, Connery had announced to the crew that he was resigning from the role of Bond, because he was tired of it and he *"wanted to act"*! Some film critics said his lack of enthusiasm showed in his manner on screen but none denied that the Ken Adam' sets

A studio shot of Sean Connery in G-AVDH - ruffled but not stirred.

were spectacular, with the *"Little Nellie"* flying sequences among some of the most dramatic and best remembered from any of the Bond films.

In the film, Bond sported a short-sleeved summer shirt so Ken was required to do likewise, despite the fact that after starting in the humid heat of the summer, with filming being delayed through the typhoon season of southern Japan, work commenced at 0600 hours and took place in the low temperature at 6,000 feet over the volcanic terrain of Kirishima and the East China Sea. For the film Ken made some eighty-five flights and logged forty-six hours to produce something less than eight minutes screen time.

Some of the flying was pretty "hairy" and at the 6,000 feet, extra care was called for when making passes at other aircraft owing to the thinness of the air. Ken recalls that, a number of times, a difficult flying scene would have to be repeated owing to something faulty with a camera. His narrowest escape occurred whilst filming over an active volcano where Bond is alerted to the presence of hostile aircraft by the sight of shadows racing across the mountainous terrain below. The flight out to the island involved a five-mile journey over the sea and Ken said that they were flying around the volcano's crater, making pass after pass, with John Jordan (the 2nd Unit camera operator) saying *"Do it again Ken, do it again"*. Then, after a while he called *"You must be getting short of fuel"*.

When the aircraft had been prepared for the film, the fuel tank was painted with yellow and black markings but this had also covered the gauge so that it could not be read. Ken therefore decided to use the stopwatch within his pilot's wristwatch to keep track of things. The filming called for considerable concentration on Ken's part and on checking his watch he felt confident that there was plenty of fuel left - probably 25 minutes' worth. Unfortunately, he had not realised that the minutes displayed were appearing for the second time - he had already flown for an hour above the total. The next moment the engine cut!

Ken explained that, being quite high up, he had plenty of thinking time but being over an island afforded no flat patches on the ground to land other than a very narrow road. All he could do was to ask John to tell him if any traffic was coming up behind him and he would "put her down". Given the "all clear" Ken landed and then pulled into a side path to allow a car to pass. John flew back to base to collect a fuel can, which was lowered to Ken on a rope, so that he could refill and take off again. Luckily, it had not happened whilst flying over the sea.

Typical of all *"Q's"* gadgets, the autogyro gained numerous items of "lethal firepower", thanks to Jack Stears the Special Effects Supervisor (an ex-RAF armourer) following discussions with Ken. These included smoke ejectors, parachute grenades, two rear flame-throwers, rocket launchers, heat-seeking air-to-air missiles and two front-mounted machine guns.

Jack had shown Ken a large rocket, propelled by the rocket motor used to carry a line across a sinking ship and offered to demonstrate it on some rough ground in the studio. It whizzed off very impressively but then circled round, heading back towards them before wrapping itself around a post nearby. The weight of the rocket motor was behind the centre of pressure of the dramatic fins and light "warhead" of the studio rocket - it was rather like a dart with the weight behind the feathers. Ken observed that he hoped the problem would be rectified before he had to fire one from the aircraft! Ken did in fact have to purchase some roofing lead whilst they were filming in Spain. He rolled pieces up and stuck them into the hollow "warheads" to give them some much-needed stability.

The original flame-throwers burned away and were jettisoned during filming but this was cut from the film. The non-firing equipment made up for the tail was quite heavy and Ken felt that it was cruel to the aircraft to have to go through all the combat sequences with this fitted. Consequently, he arranged with the film people that the smoke and flame generators would be the first weapons to be employed in the combat and, after use, they would be jettisoned. Ken recovered the remains later on from a ravine and subsequently made replacements.

In the film Ken had the pleasure of blasting the SPECTRE "baddies" flying four Bell 47 helicopters. Ironically, when the production company was filming the flying sequences, the helicopter pilots requested that he slow down so that they could keep up! No doubt he allowed himself a wry smile at this and thought back to the earlier Army Air Corps trials.

Ken may have been slightly bemused to learn that the Japanese pilot of the "camera-ship" (*"Slim"* Nagashima) had trained as *kamikaze* in World War II but had not reached top of the list before the war ended. No doubt he judged that his speed and agility in the air would guarantee his safety should the chap have a pang of conscience and attempt to prove that the time spent learning his earlier trade had not been entirely wasted! Ken speaks highly of the pilot, however, and recalls how he was devastated, although in no way to blame, when one of the SPECTRE helicopters hit his camera helicopter and a rotor blade cut through the leg of John Jordan who was resting his feet on the skid. Ken says that he did a fine job in getting the aircraft down safely with its port side skid cut away. He had called for a pile of concrete slabs to be set up and he put the helicopter down on it without overturning and causing further serious injury to John Jordan.

Film flying ceased in Japan after this accident but the scenic background had been established. They were not permitted to fire weapons over the volcanic National Park area - where Ken happened to notice that naked girls were enjoying sulphur baths below - so filming was completed later in Sierra Nevada, Spain.

It was at Duxford in 1968, during the filming of the classic *"The Battle Of Britain"*, when Ken next met John Jordan and he had been fitted with an artificial leg. He later heard that, whilst filming the anti-war film "Catch 22" over the Pacific Ocean, Jordan had been killed. Ever the perfectionist, he had undone his "monkey strap" in order to lean further out of the camera aircraft for a particular shot and had fallen into the sea.

Group Captain "Hamish" Mahaddie DSO, DFC, AFC, was also connected with this film and, following retirement from the RAF in 1958, he took on a number of aviation consultancies. One was to be retained to find suitable aircraft for film epics and his fantastic success in this task for the *"Battle of Britain"* film needs no explanation here. During World War II, Mahaddie had been appointed Group Training Inspector by the legendary Australian, Donald Bennett - creator of the Pathfinder Force (PFF) for target location and marking. Mahaddie's skills as a bomber pilot came to Bennett's attention and he was given a free hand to visit bomber squadrons in other Groups to poach their best crews. He was not called *"Bennett's Horse-Thief"* for nothing! Later, he was responsible for inaugurating the English Electric Canberra at RAF Binbrook and, in 1953, planned the UK-New Zealand Air Race, which was won by Canberra WE139 (a PR.3 variant) in 23 hours 51 minutes.

Ken was sorry that he only briefly met Desmond Llewelyn, who played "Q" in the Bond films, on the set. Following filming, however, they did enjoy many meetings back in the UK and were of similar age. His death in a head-on car accident, whilst driving near Firle in East Sussex during the winter snow of December 1999, was a sad loss. He might well have been modelled on Ken in view of his love for new inventions.

The film poster for *"You Only Live Twice" (Eon Productions Ltd)*.
See also front cover for a post-film shot of Ken and *"Little Nellie"*

Since his heavy parachute landing from a stricken Wellington, Ken had suffered recurring back problems so he smiles at the image he must have sometimes created as *"007"* when simply rising from a chair after a meeting he would be bent over almost double, or when swinging the propeller! The local interpreter, Michiko San, who made all the arrangements for accommodation, etc., introduced Ken to the local health-giving sulphur baths and also specialist massage treatments but all to no avail. She then arranged for him to enter the hospital at Kagoshima where he was X-rayed and underwent treatment, being placed upon a rig on which his spinal chord was stretched. After a number of sessions the pain was gone and never to return.

Ken left Japan for Italy (via Ceylon where he briefly flew 4-RACK) and completed work on Film Studio Roma's film *"Dick Smart 2.007"*. Flying was at Urbe Airport near Rome and in the Latina area, which happened to be very near to his bombing targets in 1944! He then returned to the UK and met up again with *"Little Nellie"* following her return by airliner from Japan. Ken used the available time before going to Spain to make some modifications to the armament system. For the record, all the missiles were successfully launched in the air and only lacked live warheads.

"Little Nellie" went on to undertake hundreds of demonstrations and exhibitions in many countries following the film's release in June 1967, and it is still a major attraction today. She now resides at Reymerston Hall but is often seen with Ken at the Flixton museum, and many other events around the country in support of various fundraising activities. Her sister, G-AXAS, not to be outdone, undertook several experimental landings and take-offs on/from moving road vehicles. The most exacting descent perhaps was alighting on the small cabin roof of the pleasure boat *"Solent Scene"* off the Isle of Wight. These were not stunts of course but serious experiments as part of the development of the autogyro for military, police and similar serious roles.

The Bond sets are some of the biggest in the film business, and the skills of Ken Adam for visualising and creating the many memorable film scenes are legendary. He may have been influenced to pursue this later career whilst a young RAF fighter pilot in North Africa during World War II, and on seeing the work of Jasper Maskelyn. Maskelyn was one of Britain's most famous magicians in the 1930s and offered his skills to the military to fool enemy aircraft into attacking decoys. He was duly "signed up" as a Major in the Royal Engineers and employed to deceive the enemy during a critical stage in the battles with General Rommel, and tanks of the German Afrika Corps.

Top: About to touch down on a moving lorry with G-AXAS.
Bottom: Safely down on the cabin roof of *"Solent Scene"*.

Maskelyn formed a unit of fourteen men who, between them, embraced many skills and they became known as *"The Magic Gang"*. Their activities included making decoy vehicles, disguising thousands of our tanks as trucks, "moving" the harbour at Alexandria three miles away by re-creating the harbour's lighting and landmark pattern to deceive the German bombers at night. They also "hid" the Suez Canal by building a series of spinning lights to make the German pilots lose their sense of direction.

Closer to home, of course, Colonel Sir John Turner was in charge of the British Decoy and Deception schemes as an Air Ministry department with its headquarters in the Sound City Film Studios at Shepperton in Middlesex. His film set expertise was directed towards creating ingenious methods to deceive Luftwaffe aircraft and lure them to bomb decoys rather than the genuine targets, thus saving materials, fabric and lives. Turner's intriguing story was researched over many years by my Flixton museum colleague Huby Fairhead, and his book (*"Colonel Turner's Department"*) is available from the museum shop. Nearby, there is a small exhibition to illustrate the work of this secret department and includes artefacts recovered from decoy sites and donated by ex-members. Some of the elderly personnel still manage to meet up at the museum and share their memories.

Ken also had a small role in the Bond film *"Live And Let Die"*, starring Roger Moore. There is a scene where Bond is being chased by the usual villains and jumps into a Piper Cub aeroplane in which an elderly lady is waiting for her instructor. He taxies madly around before going through hangar doors as they are closing and consequently loses both wings. The sound effects of the aircraft engine are actually those of Ken's WA-117 with 100 hp Rolls-Royce engine when taxied around his strip at Reymerston. Not many people know that!

Now back to the 1967 film *"Dick Smart 2.007"* and Ken's major role. This was very much a spoof spy film with James Bond in mind but starring Richard Wyler in the lead. The success of the Bond films had not been lost on Film Studio Roma when Ken was invited to visit them with film of his invention to discuss their leading player's extraordinary mode of transport. It was soon decided that G-ARRT was suitable and the shape of the *Vespa 2000*, and the paint schemes, could be matched with the flying version. The film was to be shot in Brazil in the July and Ken returned to the UK but he was then required to fly a WA-116 at the Cannes Air Festival.

Ken was flown to Cannes in a Beagle aeroplane by Lt. Commander Vyrell

Mitchell who was also participating in the event. Sadly, Vyrell was to be killed on the 28th August 1972 with His Royal Highness Prince William of Gloucester in the crash of Piper Cherokee Arrow 200 G-AYPW at the start of the Goodyear Trophy Air Race from Halfpenny Green. In the meantime, G-ARRT was being partly dismantled and boxed up on her road trailer prior to the voyage to Brazil. She was to be carried on a Greek vessel loaded with nitrate fertiliser from Liverpool and Ken delivered her to the dockside. A Dock strike then suddenly arose and the voyage was in jeopardy. Peggy got to hear of this and telephoned the Dock Authority and eventually managed to contact a strike leader. Her skilful and diplomatic explanation of the reason for the urgent shipment somehow persuaded the strikers to load the crate on to the vessel and it sailed.

The film's storyline is confusing and difficult to relate here and perhaps is best left to the reader's imagination. Having seen Ken's video copy of it (in Italian) I shall not be borrowing it again! The most interesting aspect of the film is how it casually features one of the most outlandish designs of any vehicle ever seen, and way beyond even Ken's inventive mind. The front half is a Vespa motor scooter, mated with a Wallis autogyro at the rear. As a road vehicle it looks simply an elongated scooter, with the "flying bit" hidden beneath long body panels. At the touch of a button, however, the autogyro emerges (never fully on camera!) with rotors turning and achieves a swift takeoff for escape, even in the middle of traffic. Other scenes show the machine as a submersible or a powerboat. Clearly, Ken has overlooked developing the full potential of his design!

After some delays clearing Customs, G-ARRT was taken on her road trailer to storage at the base of Hotel Gloria by Gloria Beach. There she was painted to match the *"Vespa 2000"*. Fortunately, she had a UK Certificate of Airworthiness and this eased any problems in dealing with Santos Dumont Airport at Rio. It was soon agreed, however, that flying from the airport for the filming would be inappropriate and that take-off and landings should be from a small pathway by Flamenco Beach, near the hotel. The most dangerous part of this was wheeling the aircraft across the very busy road between the hotel and the beach. The local road traffic was not used to slowing down for anything and crashes seemed to be quite normal.

The original title of the film was to be *"Nick Carter, Agent 2.007"* but it hit copyright problems and was changed. Ken was soon flying around the very impressive mountain scenery by Rio De Janiero, landing and taking off on a minimal space on the Donna Marta mountain, adjoining the Corcovado, topped by the gigantic Statue of Christ. The large birds soaring on the upwind side of these near vertical mountains could be a menace and Ken had sometimes to take hasty avoiding action. Ken described filming as *"a hoot"* and it entailed 21 hours 35 minutes in the air, during 48 flights in Brazil and Italy. The making of the film was quite chaotic with actors being sent to one location, and camera-crews and the Director going to another. Many high-pitched arguments followed. As was to prove the case in making the proper James Bond film, the most exciting parts of the flying were not on screen and involved mountaintop and cliff-edge take-offs and landings, sometimes in strong crosswinds.

One of Ken's most memorable episodes as "Dick Smart" included a scene where the heroine ("Jeanine") gets into a temper and takes off, flying around the statue with "her" arms in the air and out of control, before appearing to crash in a wooded area. Ken was informed that he would have to fly as "Jeanine" only a few minutes before filming commenced. As they were travelling up the zig-zag road to the Donna Marta mountain, an open Cadillac approached with the actress on board. The car was stopped and to the annoyance (no doubt short-lived) of following local drivers, because the road was blocked, she was ordered to remove her clothes for Ken to don! She commenced to strip but Ken insisted upon retaining his trousers in this very public "cross-dressing"!

Wearing all her upper garments, Ken was then given a silk scarf, which was tied over his head to partially conceal his face. As he took off from the top of the Donna Marta he became very aware of the menace the scarf presented. It kept floating high above his head and at risk of becoming entangled in the rotor blades but he managed to pull the scarf down as tightly as possible and hold it under his chin. This crazy flying around the giant statue was not easy since there was nothing else close with which to judge his distance from it and speed of approach. He completed the final "crash" scene with relief. He was also required to fly down the "Cascades" in a very narrow gorge above a waterfall - the gorge twisted and required some very sharp turns as he flew between the near-vertical cliffs on either side. Ken thinks that this was the first time he had used such sharp roll control inputs that the teeter stops of the rotor system contacted, feeding back sharp jerks to the control column.

On the morning of the 23rd July, he took off as normal to fly to Barra da Tijuca but became aware of an increasing wind with strong gusts as he flew along the coastal mountains. The palm trees were starting to bend and pieces were breaking free and flying through the air. The force also kept lifting Ken out of his seat, restrained only by his lap-straps, and he could not prevent his feet rising from the rudder pedals in violent moments of negative "g". Thankfully, G-ARRT rode out these gusts level, and the negative "g" was transient, followed by the reverse! Ken decided that he would have to go over the coast and the sea to avoid the gusts created by an increasing wind from the land and over the mountains.

Whilst the flight had commenced in the usual sunshine, it quickly became dark owing to black storm clouds obscuring the sun. Over the coast at about 500 feet his eyes were filled with sand, and salt water whipped into the air. Ken said that at this point he started to wonder about erosion of the rotor blades. Further out to sea he soon reached the stage at which it was advisable to head towards land whilst "crabbing" along the coast towards the destination. To go further out, in the hope of reducing the violence of the gusts, would have entailed leaving sight of land, being carried out by a wind far stronger than the maximum safe speed that could be used in storm conditions. Briefly, he thought he might avoid some of the awful gusts if he flew closer to the sea but this contemplation lasted only a second or two.

He looked below at the sea on the port side and noted a large depression with big waves on its edge. Then a black, twisting "thing" joined sea and sky in a waterspout about 100 yards away. All he could do was to try and ride it out, "crabbing" along the beach but off-shore. In addition to any sand and salt water in the air, some quite large pieces of the mountain trees were flying past. Gradually the sun started to break through as the storm eased off. Ken eventually reached Barra da Tijuca and, luckily, remembered where there was a piece of road for the landing even though it was obscured by a layer of sand. Having ridden out the enormous vertical gusts of wind, the experience re-affirmed the findings of Ken's experiments with horizontal stabilisers on his aircraft. They had been tried and then discarded!

The aerial sequences have Ken flying a standard autogyro so the audience is not supposed to notice the dramatic transformation - the loss of handlebars and road wheels, and a reduced overall length. Nor should the viewer dwell too closely upon the "chrysalis-to-butterfly", metamorphic transformation, employing some unseen but ingenious methods to "uncurl" the rotors and engine propellers to achieve instant flight! Armament consisted of forward firing rockets but one scene has Ken dispatching thugs firing semi-automatic weapons at him by flying "hands-off" and dropping bombs on them – not always perfectly synchronised he recalls!.

177

After the filming, Ken flew back to Flamengo Beach where he gathered that there had been some damaged caused at Rio De Janeiro by the storm. Realising that the experience would be worth recounting in his Annual Report he provided the Ministry of Aviation, and other authorities, he took a taxi to Santos Dumont Airport to enquire the gust velocities involved in the morning's storm. The reply was *"Senor, we do not know"*. They said that the *"Ventana"* had been expected so there had been no airline flights to and from the airport as *"no aircraft can fly through the Ventana!"* They refused to believe Ken when he outlined what had happened and simply repeated the negative phrase. Ken was pleased to note that G-ARRT had suffered no damage whatsoever to the rotor blades from the sand and saltwater.

Another "memorable occasion" was when the Directors suddenly informed Ken that they wanted a helicopter to carry a cameraman for filming the *"Vespa 2000"* as Ken flew along the beaches and road to the "Sugar Loaf" Mountain. Ken suggested that it would be a good idea if he met with the helicopter crew and got some idea how the scenes would be captured before the flight commenced. The meeting took place but, because of language difficulties, it did not achieve much.

As usual, when Ken was flying as *"2.007"*, he wore dark glasses and was told that he must avoid looking at the camera in flight as that would reveal someone was standing in for "2.007" The flying around the "Sugar Loaf" mountain with its cable car system went without any problem, and that was to be followed by a flight along the beaches - the *"Vespa 2000"* being seen from the sea. Flying parallel to the beach he became sensitive to the sound and feel of the helicopter very close on his port side but was well aware that he must not look at the it. Eventually, in the interests of safety, he broke the rules and glanced towards the helicopter … and almost into the shutter of the camera filming him! The helicopter pilot was not looking at Ken at all; he was just looking straight ahead. All Ken could do was edge a bit closer to the beach to avoid risk of collision but he was now along the famous Copacobana beach and getting very low, with a high sea wall and buildings cutting off any further escape to starboard.

Ken could still sense the camera helicopter very close by. Then, as he flew very low along the beach, some budding young footballer kicked a ball high into the air directly ahead of Ken's autogyro. It was a great relief that the ball fell below his aircraft with a split second to spare. It was a greater relief to Ken when the air-to-air filming session was over. Further "interesting" flying per Ken involved flight along the front at Rio, dodging the giant light

178

standards and going under bridges in company with road traffic. Flights under arches of the viaduct supporting the funicular railway to the Corcovado Mountain were also required.

Whilst in Brazil, Ken soon started to receive messages from Eon Productions saying the *"Little Nellie"* was in Japan and that his presence was required. Ken's last flight in Brazil was in the air-to-air filming, and then for ground-to-air photographs for *"Time Life"* Magazine on the 4th August. Ken went straight to Japan and assembled *"Little Nellie"* at Kagoshima Airport, on the Isle of Kyushu in Southern Japan. He did a test flight there on the 7th August and started filming as *"007"* on the 8th.

When filming was over Ken went back again to Italy to finish off the Dick Smart film. Here he discovered that G-ARRT had been loaded on to a lorry for transportation from the port of arrival to Film Studios Roma. The driver of the lorry had driven the vehicle under a bridge that was too low to clear the top of the mast on the autogyro. It was badly "bashed back" and quite a lot of damage had been done. Fortunately, the rotor blades were not fitted and were in a box. Ken's cousin Geoffrey had been told of this and had driven to Italy with a mast tube and other parts for the necessary repairs. (After Ken had returned to the UK there was an ongoing battle with the company about the damage caused to G-ARRT. Peggy even took a short holiday to Rome with youngest daughter *"Dizzie"* and met the boss of the studio to discuss compensation but none was ever forthcoming). Ken arrived just in time to see to this and to continue the quite hair-raising experience of flying as *"Agent 2.007"*.

From Rome they travelled to Latina, quite close to the Anzio area that he had bombed back in 1944. The first shot was to be a simulated rocket attack by the *"Vespa 2000"* on a bridge. The bridge was set up with special effects explosives intended to throw much debris into the air after Ken had appeared to fire the rockets and flown over the bridge. He was to take off and wait for a visual signal to commence the attack, while a pair of rockets would be launched towards the bridge from nearby scaffolding, thus giving the impression they had been fired by Ken. He took off and was circling around looking for the sign to attack. Suddenly, when his back was towards the area of attack, the air shook and he turned to see masses of debris in the air after a mighty explosion of special effects. Ken landed and there was a heated argument going on as to who had pressed the button prematurely. Ken was relieved that this had not happened during any low flight towards the bridge in a simulated attack; it would have wrecked G-ARRT - and no doubt bent

Ken a little too. Everything was set up again and he took off but the same thing happened. Ken landed to even more high frequency Italian altercation. The bridge was then set up for the third time, with what little explosive and debris was left. This time Ken made his low pass over the bridge after getting the signal to attack and heard the explosion behind the aircraft with some relief. Further flying over the beach area at Latina was followed by scenes shot at Urbe Airport, Rome. The flights included firing a signal pistol towards the camera, and the dropping of "grenades".

Then, out of the blue, he was asked to lower a nylon net beneath the *"Vespa 2000"* to "scoop up a girl!" Ken pointed out that girls were far too valuable for any such stunt and that there was a risk of cables being caught in the propeller or rotor blades, with probable dire consequences. The only way he could include such a scene would be if a suitable "tailor's dummy" could be obtained. Ken could then take off with it draped over the nose of the cockpit, with the rope carefully taped to the structure so that it would feed out without being drawn into any moving parts.

The attractive dummy, suitably dressed, was provided and Ken took off without any trouble. When he tried to lift "her" over the to the port side, however, and drop "her" it felt just as though he was doing it with a real girl. Then her legs wrapped around his neck and her knickers got caught up in the throttle controls. He eventually managed to lower "her" over the side and the cable paid out as planned. At first the dummy spun round at the end of the cable until he found the speed at which it sailed along steadily, looking ahead. Ken was quite pleased when he received the "thumbs up" from the Director and was able to cut the dummy free to make a normal landing.

The *"Vespa Alpha"*, courtesy of the Piaggio Foundation. This studio "prop" is displayed in their museum in Pontedera, Italy. The autogyro is a mock-up.

Hiccups, problems and prangs!

Ken observes that film sequences may appear to be great fun but he was always well aware that it was akin to walking a tight-rope; it has to be visually exciting but the risks must always be observed.

Flying in the Bond film was necessarily a little hazardous because much of it was exceeding 6,000 feet, and over the most rugged volcanic country. The effect of that altitude on control responses had to be experienced - then borne in mind. The collision between one of the SPECTRE helicopters and the camera-ship may well have resulted from reduced response at altitude.

Once the Bond film was made, needless to say, it was *"Little Nellie"* rather than WA-116 prototype G-ARRT that was required to fly in air shows worldwide. Just flying her was not enough though, and some sort of combat sequence was naturally expected of her. Travels commenced with *"Little Nellie"* being transported to America in the hold of a Boeing 707 as accompanied luggage" to New York, with her rotor blades removed and stowed, undercarriage legs folded, and the fuselage carefully angled through the access narrow door. On arrival, Ken quickly re-assembled her and she was placed on a truck to be taken over Brooklyn Bridge. He flew from Morristown Airport, New Jersey, for Hugh Moran's *"Today"* Show, and again for Johnny Carson's *"Tonite"* Show, being interviewed in both. These were to publicise the Premiere of *"You Only Live Twice"*, which Ken went on to attend in New York. The test flight was on the 6th June 1967 and the two demonstrations on the 7th June.

On his return to the UK, Ken said that *"something of "a dream came true"*. He and Peggy had lived in a maisonette in Brunswick Square, Hove, for around seven years and he had often looked out on the magnificent lawns along the Hove Front, thinking it would be wonderful to land an aeroplane on them. (I am not convinced that the Council Gardner would agree with him!). UK publicity was next and a big party was planned in the Dudley Hotel, Hove, for this purpose. Ken was required to fly *"Little Nellie"* and land on the Brunswick Lawns for an interview, take off for a demonstration, and then return to Shoreham Airfield.

After this, Ken was called upon to give demonstrations all over Germany. He transported the aircraft behind his Mini van to Harwich, and then went by sea to Hamburg. On arrival at Hamburg Airport on the 17th August 1967, it was agreed that the first flight would take place over an area of grass, clear of the normal air traffic. Here he met the lady in charge of the publicity and she was also the interpreter. On being interviewed, Ken was first asked if, when in the RAF, he had flown Spitfires. He had to say "no" and when asked what he did fly Ken replied *"Wellingtons"*. He was then asked if he had ever bombed Hamburg and responded *"Yes, more than once"* and was pleased to find that his response did not attract any unpleasantness.

Ken then asked the lady organising the event to ensure that all the Press photographers kept together with the television cameramen. He explained that he would fly slowly round the group for still photos for the Press. He would then "fling" *"Little Nellie"* around for the television cameras. Finally, he would dive towards the group and press the gunfire button. The interpreter gave out all this detail and everyone behaved exactly as they were told. After the slow, then lively performance, Ken commenced the dive towards the group and pressed the gunfire button, which produced the usual pyrotechnic flashes from the guns.

Ken with a fully-armed *"Little Nellie"* fulfilling a dream at Hove with barely a mark on the grass, and thus following in the "footsteps" of the aviation pioneer Gustav Hamel. Hamel, incidentally, was the winner of the first aerial race in a Bleriot from Brooklands to Brighton on 6th May 1911.

He was horrified to see a dramatic reaction below as large television cameras were knocked over and the Press and television personnel threw themselves to the ground, obviously to escape the "gunfire". As Ken flew away from the site he realised he had no choice but to turn and face the scene of devastation. He did so and was surprised to see all the equipment still on the ground but the personnel were jumping to their feet and clapping!

On landing, the interpreter explained she had omitted to say that the "gunfire" would employ *"platzpatronen"* ("play cartridges" or blanks). Everyone had been very impressed and the demonstration was very successful, as was evident from the Press and television coverage given. After this, he was required to fly for air-to-air Hamburg Television shots.

The 19th saw the Baltic Air Rally in Lubeck, in celebration of its 50 years as an airfield. Ken was delighted to meet Generalleutnant Adolph Galland, the famed Luftwaffe air-ace of World War II, and enjoy a tipple with him. He was renowned for his very humane treatment of captured RAF personnel and many became personal friends after the war. Ken was pleased to be pictured with Galland who sat in *"Little Nellie"* to "try her for size". The 21st saw Ken at Kussel, followed by Frankfurt, Mannheim, Mulheim, Koln, Munich, Nuremburg and then finally Stuttgart on the 30th.

Adolph Galland getting acquainted with *"Little Nellie"*- possibly weighing up the advantages he would have had with such armament in an Me109!

Back in the UK, his first appearance was on the 2nd September, requiring a landing on the beach near the pier at Great Yarmouth for the press. On the 16th there were Battle of Britain Displays at Biggin Hill and Coltishall, with an RAF "Argosy" aircraft for transportation. On the 26th, there was to be a demonstration in Cardiff for local television. On arrival at Pontcanna, the groundsman there was not at all helpful and complained that the aircraft would spoil his beautiful turf. Ken explained that the marks left would be no greater than those of a person walking on the grass and, after much pressure from all and sundry, he relented so Ken was allowed to take-off. Unfortunately... there was to be a mishap.

Just after landing, the aircraft encountered a sharp, upward slope in the grass between two bowling greens, which had not been not evident to Ken because of the smoothness of the greens. *"Little Nellie"* was flung sharply back up into the air and then pitched nose-down to contact the ground again at a very steep angle, with the nosewheel and tips of the missiles digging in to scar the ground. Whilst the aircraft was undamaged, the same could not be said for the grass. Then a Police car arrived .....and promptly drove straight over the manicured turf of the bowling greens! It transpired that a lady in Cardiff had reported seeing an aircraft diving on the Pontcanna area "firing its guns". Ken did not mention the reaction of the groundsman!

Three flights for local television in Birmingham followed, and then on to Manchester Airport on the 28th for a press call. Having completed the flying demonstration in quite windy conditions Ken landed. After photographs had been taken he decided to fly the few hundred yards to where his car and trailer were parked. He started the spin-up of the rotor blades, which was achieved quite quickly in the wind, and the nosewheel lifted off, tilting the aircraft back as is usual just prior to take-off. The port wheel followed, however, and *"Nellie"* was almost flying with the starboard wheel staying on the ground through the torque reaction. In such a situation, the pilot's natural reaction is to put the control column over to port in an attempt to level the aircraft.

With the starboard wheel still in contact with the ground, the fuselage cannot swing out to starboard, achieving the desired control response. Instead, the rotor system continues to turn in much the same plane and the fuselage rolls yet further over to starboard until disaster strikes. The press pictured the tip-over with headlines such as *"Oh! Oh! 7"* and *"00PS 007!* After this embarrassing mistake, Ken explained that he puts the control more over to port once spin-up has started. This counters the torque reaction from rotor spin-up and the propeller torque reaction on the usual aircraft so the roll-over to starboard risk is virtually eliminated. After a quick drive back to Reymerston with the wreckage, rebuilding with another pair of rotors and propeller, an air-test on the 30th September, Ken performed a scheduled demonstration at Zurich on the 3rd October at the start of his Swiss tour. The old propeller hub was presented to the museum at Flixton.

In Switzerland, "BLIK" newspaper said that it would sponsor a series of demonstrations, publicise the event locations beforehand and report upon them afterwards. These were set for the weekend of the 7th and 8th October. After demonstrations at Grenchen and Olten, they arrived behind the BLIK newspaper van with loudspeakers on top, followed by *"Nellie"* on a trailer pulled by Ken's Mini van, at a new piece of Autobahn by Horgen, south of Zurich. The road was not completed and it ended some 3km further on from where they stopped. A large crowd had gathered on one side of the carriageway, the site of the display having been announced in the BLIK newspaper. A Police car, blue light on top, was keeping the audience in order behind the central barrier. Where they stopped there were adjacent bridges over the road and many masts with cables across it.

Ken approached the usual lady who was acting as interpreter/organiser and remarked that it was not a good site for a demonstration. In response to her next two questions Ken said that he could fly from the location although it was hardly suitable, and "Yes" he could race the Police car but it would not be permitted! She promptly approached the Police officers, had a long natter, and then they made some radio calls. She soon returned and told Ken that permission had been given for the race to his surprise. Game for anything, Ken said that he would take off and give *"Nellie"* a fling, fire his guns, and then give a "thumbs up" signal to the Police. They would race to the end of the autobahn, wherever that was, and then race back. Eventually Ken reached the "thumbs up" point and the car roared away under the bridges and cables with Ken flying over the top. They were too far apart vertically for it to look like a race so, on the return journey Ken flew UNDER the bridges, closely behind the Police car.

Ken finished the "BLIK" flying assignment on the 8th October and called in at the film promotion office early the Monday morning, before returning to Germany for more demonstrations. He found chaos in the office *because* the "BLIK" newspaper had printed a full-page picture of *"Little Nellie"* chasing the Police car under the bridges. Apparently, the Swiss Air Board was not at all amused! Someone said *"Show the Wing Commander to the Frontier Post at* (a location he does not recall), *as they don't even have a 'phone there!"*

It had become apparent that, at major air displays, more was required of *"Little Nellie"* than simply flying around. Accordingly, Ken made up a pair of shoulder-launched "anti-aircraft weapons" which would make a large flash when discharged, plus a "sub-machine gun" using 30-round electrically-initiated blanks, as in *"Little Nellie's"* machine guns. He also made up an electrical firing box with four press-buttons to detonate large maroons and special effects. This would be used on a car driven by local volunteers posing as "SPECTRE" agents. The car would be an "old banger" which could be written-off.

The maroons and simulated machinegun-fire strikes would be set up on the rear bumper and the back of the car for Buttons 1 and 2. Buttons 3 and 4 would initiate maroons and smoke generators; number 4 being under the bonnet where it could well start a fire - that would all be part of the act. The plan was for the commentator of the air show to be well briefed, together, of course, with the two local volunteer "SPECTRE agents".

A fine shot of Ken "chasing" the Police car approaching thousands of spectators lining the closed autobahn and standing on its bridges.

After Ken's normal take-off to start the show, the "agents" would drive on to the airfield, stop, and then jump out with their "ground-to-air" weapons. The commentator would react by announcing that the "SPECTRE agents" were about to attack "007" in *"Little Nellie"*. The moment Ken saw the flashes from their "weapons" he would initiate a small explosion on her, followed by a smoke generator and she would appear to fall, out of control streaming smoke. The villains then would jump into their car to make their getaway. At the last moment, however, "007" would regain control and return to attack the villains from behind. The passenger then watched for gunfire flashes from *"Little Nellie"* and pressed Buttons 1 and 2 and simulated "hits" would occur on the back of the car.

The final two attacks were head-on, normally ending with the smoke pouring from under the bonnet and the car catching fire. The villains then jumped out of the car but are "gunned down" by "007" in a final attack. A slow pass along the crowd line, giving a wave, etc., would followed. Then, flying slowly behind the "dead agents", "007" pointed to them, indicating they should get up and receive applause for their part in the act.

Ken remarked that he was well aware that the required special effect maroons and other explosive were potentially dangerous, and that the volunteers would mostly have little prior knowledge of such devices. Consequently, there was always some apprehension in case a firing button was pressed while another person was close to one of the pyrotechnics.

At one such display in Germany all went well, with the car ablaze and the two "villains" apparently "dead" on the ground. When he flew behind them and gave the sign for them to stand up and take applause, only one did so. The other lay "very dead". Ken was worried and more so when he saw the flashing blue light of an ambulance approaching. The "dead villain" was then lifted on to a stretcher and carried off. On landing he was told that the organisers had thought the ambulance personnel should get some publicity. He only wished that they had told him beforehand!

On the 14th June 1968, Ken was in Hoganas, Sweden, for an airshow and another of the participants was a large Russian military helicopter, a Kamov, with contra-rotating rotor blades. These were very much the days of the "Cold War" so Ken was surprised to see it. He was further taken aback to be asked by the airshow organisers if he would like a flight in it. He responded that it would not likely be approved but they promptly spoke to the Russian pilot and he agreed. Ken was introduced to the pilot who spoke as much

English as Ken spoke Russian, and once on board he was ushered to a seat at the dual controls. The pilot started the engine and the drive to the rotors; the very large contra-rotating blades began to turn, followed by some rocking of the fuselage as the sound and vibration increased.

The helicopter lifted off the ground to a height of about ten feet in the hover and the pilot then indicated to Ken "you have control", while letting go of his controls to concentrate on looking out of the port window on his side. Ken had no means of communicating his lack of familiarity with flying any helicopter, let alone the giant Kamov, so all he could do was to concentrate intensely and try to maintain the hover whilst "not letting his country down". After a long period of vibratory hover, the pilot turned back to Ken and indicated that he was taking control. No doubt very unimpressed with Ken's efforts, there followed quite a low "beat up" of nearby gardens and some lively flying. After this unnerving but interesting experience, Ken realised that his Swedish hosts must have described him as an experienced helicopter pilot. Obviously, some sort of misunderstanding had occurred but Ken felt very privileged to have flown in a Russian military helicopter at the time of the Cold War.

On the 31st August 1980, Ken experienced another "hiccup" in Germany. He had reached Damme, having flown fifty miles across country from Munster-Telgte and much had been over forested areas; not good for a possible forced-landing. He arrived after a 50-minute flight and immediately set about fixing up the "SPECTRE" agents' car with special effects. When ready, he took off and made a sharp, full throttle climb … the engine suddenly stopped. He made an easy but rather embarrassing landing on the runway where a check showed that a fuel tap, on the carburettor, was partly turned off. He turned it on, started the engine and undertook the display with its rather worrying climax. He completed his flying by applying a final burst of power and a steep climb at the end of the runway. At this point another sudden silence occurred, followed by a rather solid landing. The fuel tap was again turned off.

After all the years it had been in use it suddenly became subject to the engine vibration frequency. Ken found that it turned itself off in a subsequent full throttle ground test so he had been lucky during the cross-country flight that he had applied only "cruise power". The fuel tap on the carburettor on the McCulloch engine, as modified with a throttle carburettor for use on the Wallis autogyro, was placed there because if the engine got over-rich mixture, and it would not start, it was best to turn off the fuel at the carburettor. The brass tap with its brass lever for fuel "ON" and "OFF" had been in use on the carburettor for years without giving any problems. Ken said it became obvious, however, that the friction retaining the tap in the "ON" position must have reduced, possibly by some weakening of the spring retaining the tapered tap body in its housing. Certain engine vibration frequencies then influenced the tap lever, shaking it to the position at which the fuel was cut off. The lesson was learned and action taken. After that, fuel taps were always on the fuselage.

In 1988 there was an International Motor Show at a huge exhibition hall in the centre of Essen in Germany. The *"James Bond"* cars were there, together with *"Little Nellie"* on static view, plus one of the travel cases from which she appears in the film prior to assembly. Before the show started, Ken was asked if he could fly over the cars with "guns blazing" for television publicity for the show. It was suggested that he could fly from the car park in the centre of Essen but it was totally unsuitable. Ken suggested to the organiser that he should go to an airfield nearby, at Mulheim, where he had previously displayed.

The next morning Ken was told that Mulheim would not allow it but he could fly from the Sports Stadium about 300 metres away. *"Permission had been given and it was all OK"*. Ken inspected the stadium with some doubts - there were high terraces all round and lamps on very tall standards - but decided that he would fly from there although it was hardly suitable. The cars were lined up and he took off. He was quickly flying towards them, "firing the guns", then climbing away - all for the benefit of the cameras.

As soon as he climbed, the whole of the crowded centre of Essen, with its high office blocks and the traffic in the streets, came into view. It was like doing a demonstration in Trafalgar Square in London, only more so. In no time, the blue flashing lights of Police cars could be seen converging upon the sports stadium are. By the time he had landed *"Little Nellie"* was surrounded by armed Police with their guns rather shakily pointed at Ken.

Ken was asked by a German, who spoke little English, to produce his papers and permission, etc. It was obviously a very difficult situation and, clearly, the organiser had not advised "the appropriate authority". Ken was tempted to say that he had not gained permission from Essen when he flew over and bombed the city in 1941 but thought better of it. Eventually, things quietened down and he was released.

On the 8th February 1991, *"Little Nellie"* was at a similar International Motor Show in France for static display. He was again asked if he would fly her for prior television publicity - over the cars, with "guns blazing", etc. The flight could be made from the quite adequate car park by the show hall at Le Bourget Airfield. The television people discussed the matter on the morning of the 8th and it was expected things would be set up so that the flying could soon be undertaken. It was almost 1700 hours before the television crew arrived and then there was a delay extracting *"Nellie"* and the cars out of the hall because a large lorry had been left unattended and blocking the doorway. Eventually everything was in place and Ken took off, almost in darkness. The "gunfire" showed up very brightly. With filming complete, Ken landed and wheeled *"Little Nellie"* back inside, accompanied by the truck driver who had transported the cars to the show. On cue, there then came the familiar sound of Police cars arriving from all around, and the sight of blue flashing lights. De-ja vu!

The young truck driver was immediately pounced upon by armed gendarmes and roughly handled. Ken sensed that there must have been some mistake and that they had thought he was too old to have been the pilot. In his best schoolboy French Ken enquired *"Desiree vous le pilot?"* It was then Ken's turn and he was put into a police car and taken off to the local station. Many animated telephone calls followed and the cause of the panic soon became apparent. The Gulf War was on at that time - Charles de Gaulle Airport was only just across the road and there was a helicopter on stand-by in case of terrorist activity. Naturally, when *"Little Nellie"* was seen, apparently making machine gun attacks nearby, it caused quite a stir.

Ken admits that *"Little Nellie"* had been somewhat embarrassed when she tipped over while still on the ground, spinning up the rotor blades prior to flight at Manchester back in 1967. Much worse was to come, however, at the Ulster Airshow in Newtownards, on 7th June 1986; a venue she had flown at previously. In the programme, Ken was flying immediately before the RAF Red Arrows and at the briefing it was made absolutely clear she had to be landed at a very precise time because the Red Arrows would start their display with a low-level pass over the field at a precise time and not on radio orders from Air Traffic Control.

With the SPECTRE agents' car set up with the usual special effects, and *"Nellie"* armed, Ken started up and moved to the intersection towards the upward end of the active runway. The car also positioned there, and they waited for the previous act of aerobatics to clear the display area so that they could start their act on time. It transpired that the show was running late. Each time Ken thought the last pass along the crowd line had been made, the aircraft turned back to do more. A quick glance at his watch showed that their take-off time had passed and the minutes seemed to be passing very quickly. Eventually, the offending act cleared but left only about three and a half minutes for Ken. The "villains" in the car also realised the extreme urgency and made a dash to be in front of the crowd line as Ken performed a quick take-off into wind, but with the intention of turning downwind and getting into position for the "combat sequence" without delay.

At about 100 feet, Ken made a downward turn, heading for the display area, which was not beside the active runway. At that moment the engine stopped without the slightest warning. He was too low to attempt a turn, to land into wind, so he could only hope to pull off a successful landing in the rough ground and long grass ahead, at quite a high ground speed due to the wind. He duly flared out, possibly a little high because of the length of the grass and nature of the surface. The moment the wheels touched the ground, or were caught in the undergrowth, a most violent forward somersault occurred, with very dramatic results. In a second or two, the remains of the aircraft were lost to view, and rescuers and ambulances raced to the site of the crash. Before they got there, "007", in his black flying suit, stood up and gave a wave to the crowd and the emergency services. Fortunately, the incident was well recorded by the television cameras.

It was a dramatic mishap and has been featured in the television series *"Great Escapes"*. It was not all bad, however, for it records the "crashworthiness" of the WA-116 design, which protects the pilot even in such a violent situation. After the "prang", Ken had the sad task of loading the wreckage onto his trailer, then driving to catch the overnight boat to Liverpool for home. A quick rebuild was needed as she was booked to fly at the Weston Park Air Display on the 20th July.

Ken promptly set about analysing the fault. Several years after the engine failure in 1969, following the successful speed Record attempt (covered in detail in the next chapter), he was rebuilding the magneto as a routine procedure for the Wallis-McCulloch engine in *"Little Nellie"*; over the years he has made a number of modifications to the converted ex-target plane engine to improve its reliability and longevity. Bearing in mind the failure of the plastic key locating the distributor on the magneto rotor shaft, he decided it would be a wise precaution to additionally locate it by a drop of *"Loctite"* at the metal to plastic joint. He had found this product to be most effective in

191

a number of previous uses. The engine had failed due to a lack of any sparks from the magneto but with the magneto removed, and its cover off, there was no sign of an obvious cause. Removal of the distributor cover revealed the distributor key was still positioning it correctly. He then removed the distributor to investigate the contact-breaker points, inserting a piece of paper between them and then drawing it out. There was then a healthy spark when the magneto turned.

Close inspection revealed that what looked like a very thin flake of semi-transparent plastic had been lodged between the magneto points. Inspection then of the interior of the plastic distributor, where it fitted on the magneto rotor, showed similar very thin plastic flakes: these were hardened *"Loctite"*. One piece of which must have detached in an ideal place to be flung between the contact-breaker points, driven by the cam immediately below the distributor. Ken said his "good idea" had obviously been flawed and he would not get caught like that again. He added that "Loctite", in its various forms, is excellent in many applications but to back up the location of a plastic distributor on a magneto rotor is not one of them! Philosophically, he concluded by saying that *"If one never makes a mistake it is unlikely anyone will make anything"*

"Little Nellie" was soon rebuilt, often using parts of the other WA-116, G-AVDH - the example used for the interior Pinewood Studio shots of Sean Connery "flying". The rebuild was an opportunity to replace some parts, such as the fibre-glass cockpit nacelle. This had suffered damage while being transported in the baggage holds of Boeing 707 aircraft, with other passengers baggage being loaded on top of it in journeys to New York and Sydney, etc. Following the "face-lift, *"Nellie"* was successfully test-flown on the 9th July 1986 and duly performed at the Weston Park Air Display as scheduled.

Ken thought it quite extraordinary that, with rotor blades and "weapons" removed, and main undercarriage legs folded, she could be inserted into the baggage hold of a Boeing 707, especially as the door was very small. He was not convinced, however, that *"Little Nellie"* liked being treated as "accompanied baggage". He recalls that, after they had arrived at the airport in Sydney, he was very worried when he saw the baggage handlers walking all over the baggage with which the autogyro was largely covered in the hold. He was quickly told not to interfere with them though as they might go on strike! *"Nellie"* was soon reassembled for the fifteen displays scheduled in Australia.

Ken believes that the considerable current activity with autogyros in Australia owes much to the displays there by *"Little Nellie"* in 1967/8. At that time, following fatalities with the Bensen DIY "Gyrocopter" design, such aircraft had become banned in that country. *"Little Nellie"* was permitted to fly by their Department of Civil Aviation because she was operating on her U.K. Certificate of Airworthiness, and Ken was duly licensed. Often, after he had done a display, a man would come out of the crowd and introduce himself as the local representative of the D.C.A. Ken thinks that they were mostly surprised to see that the autogyro performed so well and this undoubtedly did much to ease off the previously very negative attitude to this type of aircraft. They now seem to be much used and enjoyed in *"The Land Of Oz"*.

Earlier to all these events Ken had faced a very gruelling experience. On the 9th May 1976, he was due to take off with his fifteen-stone son, David, on his WA-116-T/Mc "mini" two-seater, G-AXAS. This was for him to undertake some photography. Ken feels that he possibly made the mistake of putting some adhesive tape on the leading edges of the propeller to reduce the damage caused by the wheels throwing mole-hills into the air on take-off. This may have slightly reduced the thrust on the quite warm day.

They took off on the grass strip to the South East, at the end of which were some trees possibly affecting the airflow from such wind as there was. Also, there were telephone posts and cables to be overflown. Ken sensed rather marginal climb performance at this high weight so elected to make a Port turn and leave the field downwind. This he says was a stupid mistake (or was it, bearing in mind the other option with the telephone wires?).

Ken explained that, when an autogyro turns, especially as sharply as it was required to in his small field, the "g" forces increase - and rotor rpm also. As he straightened out from the turn, the forward speed had been translated into rotor speed and they flew very slowly but could not maintain height. They were at such a nose-up angle that, when they sank only a foot or two, the first part of the aircraft to strike the ground was a rotor blade of the aft-tilted rotor system.

Bearing in mind that such a blade tip is then travelling at about 330 mph, and that the rotors are quite strong in plan, this sudden stopping of the blade tip will result in an immense acceleration of the rotor head to the Port side. (The rotors turn anti-clockwise when viewed from behind and tilted aft). Suddenly stopping the tip of one blade results in the hub area moving to Port at about 150 mph. Thus, G-AXAS was caused to roll so violently to Port that neither

Ken nor passenger could be induced to roll that fast. Instead, the steel attachment of the passenger's lap strap broke and Ken's 3 inch wide lap strap also broke. In short, the airframe rolled to Port so fast that the occupants could not be accelerated so rapidly; their attachments thus failed.

Ken's son David was a bit bruised and shaken up. Ken was OK but for an almost detached right foot, broken at the ankle. He remembers trying to check that David was all right and only discovering his own injury when trying to walk towards him. At the time of the roll-over, he recalled the feeling of being whirled around on his right foot and the reason was easy to discover. The open-frame aircraft had a foot bar and rudder pedals for control in flight. Behind the fixed foot bar was a nosewheel steering bar on which the feet are placed when taxying on the ground.

As an aside, Ken explained that the nosewheel is steered as though the pilot's feet are on the handlebars of a bicycle. This is the opposite sense to aircraft rudder steering, which is in the "wrong sense", something perpetuated from the early days of flight, with a cable from each end of the rudder bar direct along the side of the aircraft to the rudder horn. Nearly one hundred years ago it should have been recognised this was in "the wrong sense" and the cables could easily have been crossed over between the foot bar and rudder horns.

The nosewheel steering bar had a self-centring spring and at each end of the then straight bar there was an upright bolt rod, with a rubber cushion tube covering it - it was first a piece of thick rubber tube on the bolt. The object of this was to prevent the foot from slipping off the end of the bar when the nosewheel was almost turned at right angles to the keel tube. When the aircraft was whipped into that violent roll, Ken's right foot could not stay on the rudder bar and his leg, at the ankle, contacted the nosewheel steering bar, where it was retained from slipping off by the upright stop at the end of the bar. That was how he came to be whipped around by the right ankle, and the damage was done.

They were both whisked off to the Norfolk & Norwich Hospital and there some doubt was expressed about whether his foot could be re-attached. He was soon in plaster, however, and moving around on crutches, something he had practiced back in 1973 after a road accident. Ken was soon in touch with the Civil Aviation authority medics to see if they would agree to him flying again, even though his leg was in full-length plaster. He did an air-test, flying the Rolls-Royce engine WA-117/R-R, G-AVJV from Shipdham

194

Airfield. All seemed well on the "Fitness to Fly Test" and, after a telephone conversation with both a Mr. Hayley and Dr. Alexander, C.A.A., and Mr. Herman, A.R.B. it was "Satisfactory" and reported to the C.A.A. by letter on the 15th July.

There was a quick return to flying, carrying the "Multi-band Photographic Pack", etc., for such as the UNFAO Seminar at Shenfield, followed by more "007" displays with *"Little Nellie"*. Although he was flying the WA-117 and "Nellie", on serious aerial work and airshows, he had to have his car driven for him. His daughter Vicky took him to fly at *"Metro '76"* at Doncaster 7th August, Bellahouston Park, Glasgow on the 21st and 22nd August, the Shuttleworth Trust in Bedfordshire on 30th August, and *"Metro '76"* at Ingliston, Edinburgh on 4th and 5th September.

Ken then received a call from the Kingsbridge Police, in Devon, late in the afternoon on the 8th September, asking for him to go there with his "Cadaver Search" aircraft G-AVJV to undertake a search for Mrs Pat Allen and her two children in the Salcombe area. Ken drove the car with trailer and arrived at Kingsbridge Police Station at about 0100 hours. That morning he made four flights with the Multi-band photographic system, in collaboration with Plessey Radar. No bodies were detected but there was a suspicion that they might have been dumped at sea by the husband as he had a dinghy. (This story is concluded elsewhere in the book). Ken said that he had to laugh at himself. Having got the aircraft off the trailer, he had to move around using crutches. With the crutches dropped right beside the aircraft he would swing the propeller to start the engine, climb on board and do the flight. Having landed, he had to taxy right up to where his crutches were in order to be mobile again on land.

In retrospect, Ken realised that, had he employed close-fitting shoulder harnesses, rather than lap straps, they would probably have suffered more serious neck injuries. In consequence, and because of the nature of the forces likely to be involved in gyroplane accidents rather than those in fixed-wing aircraft, he is not in favour of full harnesses. Such terrific roll-over forces are not often encountered, however, and therefore he added that it is likely many gyroplane rotors are less strong in plan and would "wrap around" rather than transfer such force to the rotor head at the top of the "mast". Ken said that he would stay with his strong rotors.

In conclusion, Ken said that it was certainly a mistake to attempt that downwind turn at low speed and, maybe, he could have climbed over the telephone wires (there would not have been much room to go under them and over the hedge). Whatever, the result would have been worse.

Sometime in 2005 Ken looked back over his long flying career and logged all of his bail-outs, crashes and forced-landings for me: 7 occurred during wartime operations, plus 1 post-war through engine failure, in the RAF; 13 on autogyros due to McCulloch engine problems, plus 9 other autogyro "hiccups". Ken rounded it up by saying that he *"likes to keep in practice!"*

Following years with few surprises in the air, 2006 delivered a couple of unexpected challenges. Both incidents are covered by Ken in very great detail in his official reports, with photographs and drawings, but I shall include a shorter version here as there is just too much data to copy.

For the first time in 47 years of flying his 18 variants of autogyro, a propeller detached in flight and this was whilst he was attempting 15/25km speed World Records with G-BAHH on 4th February 2006. The cause was the failure of six retaining bolts after the propeller started fretting on its thrust face and then departed. Earlier fretting and bolt failures but with the propeller staying on the hub were covered in his Annual Reports for 1969 and 1974. Ken now believes that the propeller may have swollen having lain in humid conditions prior to fitting and the test flight in October 2005. The retention bolts should have been re-torqued before this later flight following the period under the first compression to combat any shrinkage.

According to the Official Observers/Timekeepers, the speed on the first run near Tibenham was 136mph (thus beating his own World Record) and Ken had not experienced any handling problems. The separation occurred on the second run and Ken observed that in the glide towards the "silent landing" there was no indication of any damage to the rotor system; it was very smooth in flight. He did discover, however, very minor damage to the leading edge of No.1 blade towards the tip. Ken has redesigned the method of attachment and is satisfied that the problem should not occur again.

On the 18th May, Ken was flying his Military XR944, and the site of the mishap was the Playing Field at Robertson Barracks, Swanton Morley. It was a very windy and gusty day but not a problem for Ken as his aircraft had proved virtually impervious to wind in the past, with the 1962 "Pilot's Notes" quoting a conservative "Maximum Surface Wind for Operations" of 43 knots. On this occasion, after an easy take-off and normal flight, an unusual descent started and continued to ground level. The full throttle descent at about 40

196

knots ASI was vertical onto a small goalpost in a violent downdraught but the groundspeed was probably fractionally negative. Ken had no view of the goalpost though doubts anything could have been done to avoid it in any case. Substantial damage would have occurred even if the goalpost had not been struck as the rate of descent was so high - all other aspects were "under control".

Ken later over-flew the site and photographed the area. From this he carried out a scale-model experiment using an electric fan and it revealed that the airflow down the outside of the "V" formation of the trees situated nearby caused a sharp reduction of pressure at its base, adding to the downdraught and causing it to continue closer to the ground. Ken said that he had always visualised air, like water, going over a line of trees or a mountain ridge and tumbling over on the downward side.

XR944 is now completely restored and whilst Ken sustained no damage himself, a new goalpost will likely be needed! I think a lesser man would have been badly shaken by two mishaps in just a few months but then Ken knows his own designs intimately, and their tremendous strength in such situations. He doesn't seem to mind that "his girls" can still keep him on his toes and that he is "still learning". And now for some more of the same!

Three forced-landings but several World Records

Having established that setting World Records involved Official Observers and considerable formal preparation, Ken sought some sponsorship for the first time and went to Shell-Mex and Air-BP, then in association. He was asked what he hoped to achieve so replied that, for starters, he would double the Altitude Records. The obvious place for such an attempt was that of his last RAF posting, the Aeroplane & Armament Experimental Establishment at Boscombe Down, and cooperation was immediately forthcoming.

The 72 hp modified McCulloch target-drone engine had been used in the Bensen and in the Wallis WA-116 autogyro since the latter first flew in 1961. In the mid-sixties, however, an improved piston and cylinder became available, producing a nominal 90hp, so Ken fitted the 90hp version in his prototype G-ARRT.

On the evening of Thursday the 9th May 1968 the aircraft was ready for the Record attempt. It was fitted with an altitude recorder by the French company S.F.I.M.; this employs a spot of light recording on a roll of photographic paper rather than a mechanical lever and scriber. This quite considerable assembly was mounted on the port undercarriage main leg. Ken also had a small oxygen bottle, feeding a face-mask through a plastic economiser bag on his chest. With everything signed, sealed and witnessed he took off confidently on what was a pleasant evening.

During the climb, however, he felt that the engine was not entirely happy and he went to some trouble adjusting the mixture. He steadily gained height but after exceeding 10,000 feet there was a sudden bang, followed by an eerie silence! The inevitable forced landing presented no problems but during the descent he decided to test the oxygen system that he would have turned on only when above 10,000 feet. It was immediately apparent that it was useless as the plastic economiser bag was rigid with the cold. After landing the cause of the failure was immediately apparent. A big-end bearing had failed and a broken connecting rod was protruding from a hole in the crankcase.

Whilst Ken had broken the existing Altitude Records of 7,280 feet set by Dr. Igor Bensen in the USA with a 90hp engine, he did not pursue a claim because he had said he would double the previous Record and was confident that he could do it. He idly wondered if he could also claim an unofficial record for the highest engine failure leading to an autogyro forced landing! That same evening, after tucking away a rather sad G-ARRT at Boscombe Down, he drove the 185 miles to Reymerston Hall and arrived the next morning. Soon afterwards, he set off on the return drive to Boscombe Down with one of his 72hp engines and worked well into the evening of the 10th May substituting it for the damaged engine.

The next day was cloudy but the Record attempt had to be made without delay since the Official Observer was due to return to London in the afternoon. In view of the earlier failure of the unsuitable oxygen equipment Ken decided to make the attempt without an oxygen supply. Air Traffic Control at A&AEE were duly advised and take-off was soon made. At 1,500 feet all sight of the ground was lost and he continued the climb "blind", flying into the known wind for about ten minutes, then downwind for about five minutes in the hope of keeping more or less over the airfield.

He broke out of the top of the cloud at 9,500 feet though there remained a much higher overcast, and G-ARRT continued to climb well as he reached back and re-set the jet adjustment knob mounted on the carburettor. The feat being somewhat more difficult than usual as the altitude and associated cold increased. When over 15,000 feet was showing on the altimeter the climb began to level off and Ken was suffering from the cold and an oxygen shortage. As the objective had been achieved he throttled back for what was going to be an obviously tricky descent in worsening weather conditions.

He trimmed the aircraft for hands-off flight at around 15 knots on entering cloud at a well-throttled descent. Approaching 2,000 feet, Ken became increasingly aware of the possible presence of television masts hidden in the cloud and adjusted speed and descent even more to give a chance of a sighting with some space then for avoiding action. Below 1,000 feet he hoped to see the first glimpse of the ground but it took a while longer before the welcome sight of a golf course came into view. He landed on a deserted fairway adjacent to the clubhouse and, after pulling G-ARRT clear of the course, entered and ordered a double whisky. He then telephoned Boscombe Down to ask the Official Observer if he would kindly bring his Mini van and trailer over to the Marlborough Golf Course to recover the sealed barograph.

After unsealing the Recording Barograph it was apparent that the cold at altitude had reduced the light source until it was only just recording. Fortunately, his first real attempt at Altitude could be properly assessed at A&AEE and his first Federation Aeronautique Internationale Diploma records 5,639 metres (15,220 feet) in Class E3 (Any autogyro) and Class E3a (Autogyros under 500 kgs). With less powerful engine, G-ARRT had more than doubled the previous Records as per his pledge.

Many other commitments, including overseas airshows, delayed the obviously easy 3 km Speed Record attempt until the evening of the 12th May 1969. It was then held by Dr. Bensen at 119.6km/hr (74.3mph). Again, A&AEE, Boscombe Down cooperated and marked off a 3 km course on the long runway, with provisions for the necessary level approaches. After take-off the aircraft seemed to have some high-frequency vibration but, with the Official Observers and Timekeepers in place, there was no time to investigate matters.

An unwelcome 12 knot crosswind degraded the performance of the aircraft so, after completing the four required timed runs over 3kms, Ken landed to wait a while for the wind to drop. He took this opportunity to inspect G-ARRT but there was nothing obviously wrong. With the wind down to 7 knots he made further high-speed runs along the course, then the aircraft shuddered and the engine suddenly stopped. A forced landing was easily made on the runway and Ken exited the cockpit to find smoke coming from the charred and glowing centre of the propeller, on its flange mounting on the crankshaft. In spite of the engine problem and the effect of the crosswind prevailing, 111 mph was recorded. This was an improvement of some 36 mph on the previous 3 km Speed Record.

G-ARRT at Boscombe Down on 12th May 1969 with Harrier XV739, which had just set the London to New York City Centre to City Centre record.

200

On inspection Ken found that the high frequency vibration had resulted from a slightly loose propeller. Excessive torsional vibration of the crankshaft, lacking the "flywheel effect" of the propeller, had caused the key in the plastic distributor of the magneto to shear and stop the engine. The 1,634 cc, four cylinder, two-stroke McCulloch target plane engine, which he had converted for use on his autogyros, placed a high torsional load on the propeller crankshaft flange at the time of the power stroke - two opposite cylinders of the horizontally apposed engine fire together.

The six 5/16 inch D propeller flange retention bolts can fail to positively prevent any torsional movement between the crankshaft propeller flange and the propeller hub. Any movement soon results in the bolt holes in the wooden propeller hub allowing increasing movement, soon leading to total failure. In Ken's "Black Museum" he has six such propeller bolts that have actually broken, though the propeller continued to be turned by the threaded inserts in the flange into which the bolts, on that engine, were screwed. The propeller was pushed towards the flange by its thrust and was additionally retained by the 3/16 inch bolt in the centre of the streamlined spinner behind the propeller hub. That experience had occurred when Ken was exploring the potential of the WA/121/Mc G-BAHH for the 3 kms Speed Record.

In summary, the McCulloch target-plane engine is particularly prone to movement of the propeller on its flange, according to Ken, due to opposite cylinders of the 4-cylinder engine firing together and giving a very sharp torsioned load. As reliance is not guaranteed by the fitting of the six 5/16 inch propeller retaining bolts, an improved frictional key to the wood/metal thrust face has been devised, in which a large area of the thrust face to the flange is in greater frictional contact, and incorporated on the Wallis autogyros.

He next looked at the non-stop distance Record and considered the official Record set by Dr Bensen, of 133.3 kms (83 miles) was hardly worth bothering with. In 1969 he made his first flights in the two-seater WA-116-T/Mc, a minimal machine that soon proved it could lift enough fuel for over 10 hours of flight. Like G-ARRT, however, it was powered by the noisy and not too reliable McCulloch target-plane engine. Ken wanted to set a meaningful Distance Record with an autogyro that could fly long distances for a World Record, and then fly back again, so his Rolls-Royce engine WA-117 Mk2 was considered. It was flying successfully at the time and had obvious long-range potential. By 1972, the 1962-built WA-116/Mc G-ASDY was flying well with a 60hp, two cylinder Franklin aero engine and she became the first WA-117/F.

Ken had purchased two more new Franklin engines and one was installed in his cousin's WA-116, G-ATHL, in place of the McCulloch. On the morning of the 11th September 1972, after about twenty minutes of ground running, Ken decided it was time for an air test. The direction of take-off was to the west/southwest, heading towards the Mile Road for Shipdham by the New Wood. After becoming airborne there was a gradual feeling of power loss but it was not accompanied by any rough running or misfiring. He hoped to gain sufficient height to be able safely to turn back to the field for an emergency landing but it was too late to abort the take-off and telephone cables and trees lining the Mile Road were looming. Suddenly, the engine stopped completely with a violent shudder.

There was no choice for Ken but to attempt a landing on the Mile Road, though there was hardly room to swing the rotor blades in the "tunnel" formed by the trees and cables on the south side of the road and the New Wood on the other. By a miracle there was no traffic on the road and he put down successfully and stopped the rotors as quickly as possible before dragging her to the side of the road. There followed a quick struggle through the hedge and across the field to get the car and trailer to collect the machine before news of the mishap got out.

On inspection he found that the propeller was locked solid with the engine. Any attempt to turn it was merely transmitted to the rubber mountings of the engine. Needless to say, the mysterious failure of this new, F.A.A. Certificated American aero engine was quickly conveyed to the U.K. Agents and the manufacturers. A new exchange engine was promised while arrangements were being made for the failed one to be returned to the U.S. It was then suggested that it would be more sensible for Ken to dismantle the engine and determine the problem himself.

The cause was quickly apparent to Ken once the engine was stripped down. The crankshaft appeared to have overheated at the propeller end and seized, almost "soldering" itself into the big white-metal bearing. The site of the initial overheating was the thrust face of the crankshaft where it pressed upon the crankcase in "pusher" mode. Oil under pressure was fed to the thrust face involved in the tractor ("puller") mode, and a drain back to the crankcase sump bled off any pressure oil before it could reach the pusher thrust face. In the F.A.A. Certification of the engine there was no mention that the Certification only applied to tractor mode. Once discovered it was obvious that it was lucky the same trouble had not showed up with the engine flown in G-ASDY.

With the problem located, and a new set of main bearings and the crankshaft crack-checked and re-polished, it was easy to devise a cure. The drilling to relieve oil pressure before the oil reached the pusher face was blocked off by the insertion of a threaded stud, and an oil way groove in the main bearings leading pressure off to the thrust face was provided.

The propeller end main bearing in the Franklin engine in G-ASDY must have been a little less tight than that in the new engine in G-ATHL. It was lucky it did not also seize. Both engines were duly modified. Because the horizontally opposed two-cylinder arrangement causes large pressure changes in the crankcase, a non-return air valve was incorporated in a breather system above the engine such that negative pressure would be maintained in the crankcase. Also, at that stage, Ken used the crankcase pressure changes to operate the diaphragms of fuel pumps to supply fuel to the carburettor, much in the manner of many two-stroke engines then used in micro-light aircraft.

While all this was going on, Ken was much involved in a research contract with British Aircraft Corporation, plus the usual airshows and aerial work commitments in the U.K. and abroad. The long range Records were placed "on hold" and it was not until 1974 that Ken was able to have sufficient free time to give them serious consideration.

Although he had the 100 hp Rolls-Royce engine WA-117 and the 130hp fully-enclosed WA-120 flying, both with long-range potential, he favoured the 60hp Franklin-powered WA-116 for the long distance Record flights. Rather than improve the streamlining of WA-116/F, G-ASDY, which was serving as a useful workhorse, he decided to use G-ATHM. As 4R-ACK it had been operated by Ray Wijewardene in Ceylon from 1965 to 1969 but when it became Sri Lanka all private flying was banned so he had bought back the machine (named *"Bambara"* by Ray - Ken thinks this was Singalese for Hornet and very apt for the McCulloch engine) under the terms of the original export deal.

The machine had been residing as a "hangar queen" and he felt it was time to give her a face-lift so fitted a larger fuel tank, blending in with the higher cockpit nacelle sides, and installed the new and duly-modified Franklin engine. He also fabricated a long-range tank to fit under the keel tube, using four tinplate containers left over from crop-spraying. This could be jettisoned by the pulling of two retaining pins. Fuel transfer to the internal tank was by the crankcase pressure changes.

By courtesy of RAF Coltishall, Norfolk, a 100 kms triangular course was established with the control towers at RAF Coltishall and RAF West Raynham, plus a road junction near Hardingham, as the turning points. Official Observation and Time Keeping was by RAF Air Traffic and other personnel at the turning points. RAF personnel from Watton manned the Hardingham turning point.

On the morning of 13th July 1974, Ken took off from a piece of the taxiway at RAF Coltishall and started on the long flight around the closed circuit, requiring quite close map reading as there were few major features to follow. As the flight progressed it started to rain and this became increasingly heavy. After six circuits and 5 hours 25 minutes airborne he landed at Reymerston as fuel was running low. A World Record Non-stop Distance in a closed circuit of 670.26 kms (415 miles) was ratified by the F.A.I., together with World Records for 500 and 100 kms Closed Circuit Speed.

This flight had indicated the potential of G-ATHM for a non-stop flight the length of Britain for Straight Line Distance Records so in 1975 he made a special light alloy, long-range, tank with a capacity of 20 Imperial gallons, for mounting on the fittings provided for the previous tank. Fuel transfer to the internal tank was by the same crankcase pressure change system successfully used in 1974 but he added a plastic pipe to the top of the long-range tank leading into the cockpit. His thought was that by blowing into the pipe he might be able to prime the transfer pump if required.

The route chosen for the Straight Line Distance Record was by Lydd, in Kent, to Wick, Caithness. Although the flight would entail a number of diversions, and extra miles, to avoid airports such as Stansted and military airfields and ranges, much of it would be over land. A series of maps were prepared with the course marked, and they were folded and arranged in correct order in the large map compartment provided in the cockpit.

With 15 gallons in the 20 gallons, long-range tank he set off in G-ATHM on the morning of the 22nd September 1975 after everything, including the clockwork recording barograph, was duly sealed and signed by Customs & Excise at Lydd. All went well until he tried to transfer fuel from the long-range tank to the internal tank from which the carburettor was supplied. Checks of the clear plastic pipes showed that no fuel was feeding into the top of the internal tank. As he flew over Lincolnshire he took to blowing hard into the air vent pipe to the long-range tank in the hope of establishing the transfer but without success. He kept trying until the fuel in the internal tank

204

had expired and he made a landing in a stubble field at Upper Burnham Farm near Haxey, east of Doncaster. This did represent a new Straight Line Distance Record but it was nothing like what he had in mind at the time.

After walking to the farmhouse and reporting to the friendly farmer he returned to G-ATHL and removed the long-range tank, transferring fuel from it to the internal tank by means of an empty tin can. He then took off, leaving the long-range tank behind because of its closeness to the ground over the rough stubble, and flew to Doncaster Airport. A kind motorist then gave him a lift to Haxey to retrieve the tank.

On the 23rd September he flew back to Reymerston Hall and after landing selected fuel transfer from the remaining fuel in the long-range tank. It worked perfectly! With this he suspected that the crankcase pressure change system was very sensitive to altitude so he was determined not to be caught out again. He quickly arranged to use a manual air pump, provided for emergency pressure to the main tank in case of any main fuel pump problem, to pressurise the long-range tank. This would necessitate some manual work during the flight but he judged it would probably help to keep him warm.

On Friday the 26th September he flew down to Lydd and booked into a hotel at Romney. The weather was bad on the Saturday and the forecast for the Sunday was also poor. Thinking there was no chance of the flight on the Sunday, he got involved in a wedding party taking place at the hotel and was quite happy to continue the party well into Sunday morning. He was therefore surprised to wake up with the sun lighting up his bedroom at 7 a.m. There was nothing for it but to go to Lydd and see if the flight could be made; it was already quite late in the year for such an attempt.

He again set off on the same route. Fuel transfer was achieved satisfactorily and he was pleased to fly over the forced-landing field at Haxey. It was also very satisfying to put away one map and start on the next as the flight continued up to Scotland. After crossing the Firth of Forth he started to climb to 5,000 feet to clear the Grampian and Cairngorm Mountains. After this it was downhill to Inverness and a turn to starboard for an enjoyable last leg of the flight along the coast to Wick. He landed with ample fuel to spare after 6 hours 25 minutes in the air; he later realised he should have continued beyond Wick and "flopped down" on one of the islands further north. After the appropriate checking of the fuel tank seals and the barograph by Air Traffic Control at Wick Airport, he was glad to be taken to a hotel and enjoy " a hair of the dog" after being slightly "hung over" at the take-off.

A Straight-line Distance Record of 543 miles (874.3 kilometres) was eventually ratified by the F.A.I.; the full distance was nearer 600 miles. There had been a slightly adverse crosswind but his straight-line average speed was 84.6 mph. In addition, Duration Records of 6 hours 25 minutes were established and the Diplomas, signed by HRH Prince Charles now hang with the many others in a ground-floor corridor Ken irreverently calls "Line-Shoot Alley" at Reymerston Hall. The Museum displays copies of all Ken's awards at Flixton and this area we call his "Wall Of Fame". The F.A.I. has ceased awarding Duration Records after Ken since it seems that, as with gliders, it is possible to stay aloft for very long periods in some circumstances and pilots have resorted to drugs to keep them awake.

The flight was truly memorable for Ken and certainly provided an excellent demonstration of the potential of the little aircraft, with a full fuel load. Unfortunately for Ken, Great Britain is too small for him to achieve greater distances and there would be a number of problems in making a straight-line flight in Europe. He had thoughts of a really meaningful flight along the Kalgoorlie/Coolgardie railway line and road in Australia but as a "one-man band" that would have taken a lot of setting-up, and unpopular with Peggy! The return flight was made in appalling weather as he followed the coast from the Forth Bridge, and cloud covered the top of St Abb's Head. *"Bambara"* flew low over the rocks and waves, with seagulls seemingly annoyed at his intrusion into their airspace. After a night at Reymerston Hall, Ken was pleased to fly down to Lydd to collect his car and trailer.

Other activities during the 1970s

Video work started in 1970 and continues to this day using G-AVJV, with the aircraft having been used almost continuously for multi-spectral and multi-band photography. This started with coastal ecology research along the North Norfolk coast and at Dungeness. Later, a refined system was used in connection with Plessey Radar Research that necessitated a Plessey radar altimeter becoming part of the equipment to ensure very accurate height-keeping.

Carrying a British Aerospace Dynamics Linescan Type 213, and a false-colour infra-red camera, leaks were looked for in a 40-mile long pipeline 2.4m (8 feet) underground for Southern Water Authority in 1977. The equipment detected the two test leaks, plus a genuine one! Photography by "narrow-cut infra-red filtration" of a site on Hayling Island, originally described on Ordnance Survey maps as a Roman villa, was able to determine that the remains were of a Roman temple. Television work included aerial shots of the Thames Barge Race off Southend where the lack of rotor downwash was essential to avoid affecting the sails.

Coming back to 1970, a chapter occurred in Ken's life that was to have a profound impact on the reputation of his autogyro and is covered in some detail as a result. The matter still has bad memories for Ken who is usually politely restrained when talking of failures and mistakes by others. He was surprisingly calm when providing the following details in the circumstances, considering that the mistakes made had serious and long-term consequences for the credibility of his aircraft in the hands of others. Having successfully flown examples of his aircraft at the 1962 and 1964 SBAC Farnborough Shows himself, Ken wishes he could have done the same for the 1970 event.

In 1970 it was announced by Airmark, a company based at Storrington in Sussex, that it would commence production of the Wallis WA-117 autogyro with a full Certificate of Airworthiness. Whilst a production ultra-light autogyro was not unusual, one with a full Certificate of Airworthiness certainly was; and it would be expensive. Ken was to work closely with the company, and their design staff, in development work on the production aircraft but continued independently with his own line of development. Ken found the heavier and more powerful Rolls-Royce engine WA-117 much better suited to working roles than the WA-116, then fitted with the very noisy converted target-drone engine.

207

"FLIGHT International" for the 3rd September 1970 carried the headline *'Wallis Goes Commercial'*. Airmark admitted, however, that it was uncertain whether the bulk market was in the private or the commercial sector but saw the export market as the real future and intended to put major effort in establishing an overseas distribution network. Motorway building companies had already shown an interest in the craft and diverse roles, such as for power-line inspection and a spotter for Australian sheep farmers, were being considered for potential sales. Until there was something to see it was intended to maintain interest by public relations schemes, such as showing the Wallis at Harrods, with Ken providing flying demonstrations up and down the country using his own aircraft.

One advantage of the Airmark's location near the south coast was that it attracted ex-Beagle staff into its employ. Initial plans were for one machine a week to be completed by the time of the Paris Air Show of 1971, rising to 100 a year by the end of 1972. Much of the struggle to achieve full certification was likely to be directed towards the choice of engine and the Rolls-Royce Continental 0-200B was then the favourite.

By 1969, Ken's cousin Geoffrey had built himself a copy of the WA-117 but with a slightly wider cockpit to accommodate him. He had then come up against the CAA medics so ended up selling G-AXAR to Airmark to get them started. The company comprised three very pleasant enthusiasts according to Ken and no formal agreements were signed as such.

On the 28th March 1970 Airmark's test pilot (J W C *"Pee Wee"* Judge) first flew the WA-117 G-AVJV. Ken was immediately astonished to witness him taking it up immediately to 130 mph I. A. S., the highest speed to which Ken had told him he had flown in his own testing. He then started testing G-AXAR, which in the early stages had too fine a pitch on the propeller, thus allowing the engine to exceed its nominal rpm limits and restricting maximum speed. Interestingly, he recalls that some of "Pee Wee's" Reports made mention of a rotor vibration setting in at low speeds.

Judge had been available for this work as he had been unemployed at the time and was considered suitable because of some test flying he had done of the WA-116 in the Certificate of Airworthiness work. When employed by Beagle Aircraft Limited in 1961 and 1963 he had accumulated 14 hours 25 minutes over 137 flights. Ken recalls that Judge was meticulous in writing his Reports and a very enthusiastic person but he was too aggressive in his flying of the autogyro in Ken's expert opinion.

208

With the 1970 SBAC Show at Farnborough just ahead, Ken received a call from Airmark concerning an opportunity for the aircraft to be displayed under the Rolls-Royce "banner". He was then told that he could not be the pilot as he would have to go to Germany on the Qualifying Day *"and in any case, when you fly it people think you have an arrangement with God!"*

On his return from the Munster-Telgte Airshow where he had performed with *"Little Nellie"*, Ken drove quickly to Farnborough in time to see Judge's demonstration on G-AXAR but was far from happy with it. Judge told Ken that the rotor vibration at low airspeeds had been getting worse so Ken got permission to test it for himself after the show had closed for the day. A short flight left him horrified that it had been flown in such a state: there had been no check tightening made of the mass balance attachments on the new rotor blades, as would have been normal, and they had become increasingly loose. It was not practical to fix the problem there and then so Ken replaced the rotor blades with those from *"Little Nellie"*. The following day, *"Pee Wee"* expressed great surprise at the smoothness achieved. By the time of the show, one of Ken's four-bladed propellers had also been fitted which gave a much more "top-gear" performance.

Having flown at previous Farnborough Shows, Ken asked to fly on one of the days and did so on the Thursday. Being that he knew the aircraft quite well he was able to give a spirited performance and on landing was soon surrounded by admirers, complimenting the aeroplane's agility and manoeuvrability. Later on Ken could not help but wonder if this had caused *"Pee Wee"* to feel that he needed to show off a little, despite Ken's warning to him against "going over the top". What followed next was to tarnish the reputation of the autogyro and no doubt cause doors of opportunity to close for Ken, although the machine itself was positively not at fault. This was the sad death of *"Pee Wee"* Judge flying the autogyro the next day.

At the time of the crash the aircraft was grossly exceeding the 65 knots I.A.S. (about 75 knots True) laid down for his performance. He was doing some 92 knots at the end of a level run before re-trimming and turning for a hands-off low-speed pass by the President's Tent. At that speed only forward pressure on the stick would keep the aircraft in level flight. The pilot, who had some muscular problems, must have relaxed his forward pressure as he reached for the two trim levers because the aircraft immediately entered a steep climb. The proper reaction to this was to roll the autogyro into a steep turn, keeping positive *"g"* on. Instead, he reverted to a fixed-wing aerobatic response and pushed the stick hard forward up to the stops and thus experienced negative "g". This was established from enlargements taken from the cine film and the position of the streamlined cowl of the rotor head in the different film frames. Fortunately, this irrefutable evidence had been available.

The aircraft then entered a "bunt", literally tumbling forward with the fuselage trying to get ahead of the rotor blades, with rotor stops broken, and the tail being cut off by the rotors. In Ken's opinion, Judge had always been too rough in his handling of the autogyro and one independent witness even described his landings at the show as having been from a "stair-case approach". At the time of the Show, he had only 5 hours 30 minutes over 22 flights on G-AXAR so should not really have been flying it at that time. At the formal Inquest, the Coroner revealed that the post-mortem showed *"Pee Wee"* had cancer of the pancreas with little time left to live. He wanted Ken to know this as he believed it would make him feel a little better about the loss of his friend.

It was not until 1974, after much more formal testing, that the Accident Investigation Branch of the Board of Trade identified pilot error and the design was totally exonerated but by then the harm was done. Ken will always emphasise that flying the autogyro requires sympathetic handling, similar to riding a bike, with a natural "feel" for direction rather than the application of brute force.

As an aside, it is fascinating to record Peggy's claim that Ken was the only person she knew who could fall from a stationary horse. As a great lover of horses herself, it would seem that their interests had some similarity but riding something at sea level and without an engine does not really appeal to Ken. Peggy did venture up on a dual machine on one occasion with him but on landing remarked that the flight had been rather tame - deliberately so by Ken as he knew she was not an over-enthusiastic passenger. Realising she had been over-heard, Peggy vowed never to repeat the venture for fear that he would be tempted to give a full demonstration of the autogyro's agility!

Apart from Farnborough, Wallis autogyros have also had a long association with the Royal Aircraft Establishment at Bedford. The WA-116T two-seater G-AXAS was flown there to determine the type's all-up to empty weight ratio, and in the process established a world all-up-weight to tare weight record for any type of aircraft on the 30th June 1971: a ratio of 3.14 to 1. WA-117 G-AVJV, which underwent stability recording trials there, was later fitted with a Linescan 212 infra-red sensor.

In January 1973, Ken purchased, new, Messerschmitt-Bolkow 209 *"Monsun"* G-AZVA, first flying it after it had been delivered to Shipdham on the 17th. It was hangared there but he did not use it much, though he occasionally enjoyed some aerobatics. Typical flights would be to Shoreham, Leeds-Bradford and Silverstone Racetrack but he found an autogyro much more convenient for day-to-day use. His last flight was around the 9th May 1981 and it then resided in his hangar at Reymerston Hall until acquired by the Hon. John Nivison around 1984, with only around 37 hours "on the clock"; he had it still until last year at Monaco. Ken had earlier been tempted by a second-hand Fieseler *"Storch"* but wanted a spare engine "just in case".

Two Auster A.O.P.9s (G-AZBY/XR246 and G-BGKT/NN441) were stored at Shipdham with wings off and the owner had tried to get them accepted by the CAA for civilian use but met problems along the way. Hangar fees had accrued and ownership forfeited so Ken paid up the dues and towed them to his home. He managed to acquire two spare engines and a spare pair of wings, giving shelter to the lot until around the late '90s when they were sold to the "Auster AOP9 Group" for full restoration to flying condition.

An accident in his motorcar later in 1973 put Ken into the RAF Rehabilitation Centre at Headley Court. Whilst driving his "Mini", he had been hit head-on by a refrigerator lorry approaching on the wrong side of the road. He suffered several injuries including a broken leg and was sent to Headley Court to finish his recovery. He found that a very positive atmosphere existed there, with something of a wartime feel and spirit.

During his stay he received a telephone call from a New Zealand autogyro enthusiast who was in the U.K. and wished to meet up so Ken invited him to the centre. The visitor showed some surprise when Ken met him in the imposing entrance, balancing on crutches. They had coffee and talked while the visitor's slow gaze took in his surroundings but he began to stare when a pair of lady's knickers were spotted hanging from an antler, high on a wall.

The explanation was simple. There had been a typical RAF party a couple of nights beforehand, attended by some female service personnel, including some chaps from the Army who had been injured in Northern Ireland. Before long, a call went out for a pair of knickers to see who could put them highest up the deer's antlers in the hall, and a lady officer happily obliged. Injured inmates then performed feats of ingenuity to win the contest. Finally, to the accompaniment of cheers from the gathering, one patient stood on the shoulders of another, draped the garment over the end of his crutches and hoisted it aloft where it fell over the end of a point. Owing to the height, and later sobriety, the recovery of the knickers was not so easily accomplished and they were left in position for some time afterwards.

On another occasion, Ken received a call from M. L. "Bud" Cohn, then the owner of his Rolls-Royce Special *"The Long Dog"* motor car in the USA, to say that it was to be featured in a *"Whicker's World"* travel programme devoted to automobiles. Ken and colleagues sat down to watch the television with interest and, after a lot of programme time devoted to vehicles with cow horns on radiators and Colt revolvers as door handles, Whicker eventually arrived at Bud Cohn's wonderful collection of classic cars which included all the top-of-the-range types. On spotting the *"The Long Dog"*, Whicker remarked that it looked like an Aldous Beardsley drawing, with the back not looking like a Rolls at all; more a Hollywood studio creation, *"It's a hybrid - an amalgam of everything"*. Bud protested and said that he had received more offers for it than any other vehicle in his collection, and that it handled like a baby carriage. Whicker was then driven around Beverley hills in it. The "put-down" was enthusiastically applauded by fellow inmates and Ken but he was faced with paying for several rounds of drinks in the bar afterwards.

Another promising opportunity presented itself in 1978 when W. Vinten Limited, the makers of aerial reconnaissance cameras, recognised that the autogyro provided a very steady camera platform. They wanted to publicise their new Type 751 Panoramic Reconnaissance Camera in the official programme for the 1978 Farnborough SBAC Show so approached Ken. It would require the camera to be mounted on an autogyro, to be flown along the Thames to continuously record the panoramic views. Helicopters were judged unsuitable owing to vibration. The equipment was mounted on Ken's WA-117 with a Rolls-Royce engine, and two specially-authorised flights were made on the 16th May 1978 with Ken taking off from the playing fields at Woolwich Barracks. Around 180 panoramic transparencies of Central London were taken and these were found to be of incredible quality.

Top: Messerschmitt Bolkow 209 leaving Ken for a new owner.
Bottom: A single panoramic shot of London at 500 feet using a Vinten 751
camera, shown in two sections. *(Photo courtesy W Vinten Ltd.)*

The 1980s

The success of the panoramic views, coupled with other special photography assignments for the company, such as the Tall Ships Race, led to a proposal in 1981 that Vinten develop and market a production autogyro for military or civil roles carrying their equipment. This was timely because of a military interest in the autogyro for use from small fast patrol craft built by Vosper-Thorneycrofts, and also for Post-Attack Airfield Damage Reconnaissance of our NATO airfields. There followed a two-year period in which Vinten could explore the market and make tentative experiments. At the end of this, or earlier, the company had the option then to take up a Production Agreement with Wallis Autogyros with a suitable "up-front" payment. The company first took on a WA-116/F from cousin Geoffrey and commenced to build two V-116 prototypes: G-SCAN and G-VIEW.

In December 1983, there were NATO trials with the "International Long Range Reconnaissance Patrol School" at Altenstadt, situated in the snow-covered Bavarian Alps. Ken had the two-seater WA-122 and two WA-116s there, flying German officers on the former with some of them going solo on the latter from the perimeter track at the snow-covered Kaufbeuren Airfield. This was followed in June 1984 by participation with the same aircraft in the ILRRPS Symposium at the Lake Konstanz Battle Training Area. As a result of the demonstrations, Vinten received a German contract for some 120 aircraft along the lines of the WA-122, possibly for covert SAS-type operations in Eastern Germany, with the first two prototypes having to be shown to meet the Requirement. Unfortunately, the "V-122" designed by Vinten staff bore little resemblance to the WA-122 and was not a success so Ken decided to commence Termination of the Agreement (although it was not finalised until 1989).

The V-122 was first flown less the windscreen and with a pair of Ken's proven rotor blades from Shipdham Airfield on the 6th January 1986: it only just flew. On the 11th, he flew the Vinten V-122 rotor blades on his WA-122 G-BGGW: they flew but were at a greater disk angle than the Wallis blades, probably due to very un-aerodynamic root fittings. Fitted to the V-122 (still without its windscreen) on the 13th January, having built up much speed the aircraft would just lift off, then sank back at full power: that was solo and in about 9 degrees Centigrade.

On the 5th March 1985, a German Helicopter Instructor, a Lt. Col. Uwe Hain,

214

was being converted to autogyros with a view to instructing on the planned Vinten-Wallis military contract to be produced for the ILRRPS role. After brief flights on the WA-122/R-R, two-up at RAF Swanton Morley, and some solo on the rather "Vinten-modified" WA-116/F G-ATHL, he was to be building up some solo time at nearby Shipdham Airfield to qualify for his "gyroplane" licence. He took off for what Ken thought would be some local flying to explore the countryside but, very shortly after this, a car arrived and the driver reported a telephone message from the nearby industrial estate - an aircraft had crashed in a field across the road from them. They rushed to the site of a wrecked G-ATHL but Lt. Col. Hain was completely unharmed. Ken asked him what a German pilot did in such circumstances and he replied *"We fly again"*. Ken quickly went to Reymerston and flew back in WA-116/F G-ASDY, which Hain then flew and enjoyed immensely. After the flight he remarked that it was very powerful but, in fact, it had an engine and air frame identical to G-ATHL. The latter had been much degraded by the "Vinten Changes" plus the additional weight in the wrong places.

As for the crash, Lt. Col. Hain explained that, on take-off, he felt the engine was losing power due to carburettor ice - Ken thought that was quite likely on that particular morning - so thought it best to make a downwind landing on a large grass field ahead. Unfortunately, the "grass" was the first shoots of wheat in a very soft ploughed field on which it was almost impossible to walk. Ken subsequently took an aerial photograph of the site and this was a further example of the "crashworthiness" of the design in giving some protection in such forward somersaults. The places where the mainwheels had first touched the field were clearly visible, as were a total of five such marks as five somersaults occurred before the aircraft came to rest.

WA-122 with F.52 camera in shallow, oblique mode.

Ken was greatly saddened by this missed opportunity for production because he was sure the company did have the capability to build very good autogyros; it also occurred at the time he was gaining for the UK the last remaining World Records flying his WA-116/F/S G-BLIK. During the period of the Agreement, Vinten had also announced separate trials for a remotely piloted version of the WA-116 (G-BKLZ). Ken had flown it in normal form and then through the electrical actuators as would be used when un-manned. These did not give adequate control, as in slow flight and landings so Ken duly reported the need for change.

Ken had previously (in 1969 - and touched upon later) done much work with a view to a remotely piloted autogyro under contract with the British Aircraft Corporation, Guided Weapons Division. Ken feels that Vinten really should have taken notice of the knowledge gained from these very responsibly conducted tests, which were leading to remotely-piloted flight. Logically, the company should have sought his comments on the actuators, until he had flown circuits and landings satisfactorily through them, before adding remote control and ballasting the aircraft.

After the company had experienced a number of problems, one example was finally flown on the 22nd September 1983 from Rattlesden Airstrip in Suffolk, primarily to obtain a photograph of it in the air for advertising purposes. The subsequent press release announced that *'the machine was being developed as an airborne carrier of reconnaissance and sensor equipment for remote or pre-programmed flight, being the only low cost machine available which would carry several hundred kilograms of payload for hours on end'*. An example was taken to Egypt for demonstrating before potential customers but it "pranged" in front of them. Following limited promotion the project was shelved.

Soon after this in 1987, under further MOD contracts, Ken was able to prove, conclusively, the day and night, all-weather capability of the WA-117/R-R equipped with IRLS (Infra-Red Line Scan), with real-time imagery transmission to a ground viewing and recording base. This was in Post Attack Airfield Damage Reconnaissance - Exercise *"Keswick"* - at RAF North Luffenham. Ken obtained the best results of any aircraft in the Exercise so came the closest to meeting the Requirement. As no production autogyro was available, another great opportunity was lost although the Requirement would soon likely have ceased with the end of the "Cold War" just around the corner. There will always be fresh conflicts to deal with, however. IRLS produces a picture made up by a series of images of lines scanned from the horizon on one side of the aircraft, through vertical, to the other side. Ken had first carried out IRLS, in early form, at night in connection with his 1969-72 BAC contract. The equipment was made by Hawker-Siddeley Dynamics at Hatfield. In those days, the infra-red imagery was recorded on photographic film during flight and only processed on landing. This limited the amount of imagery that could be taken in a flight.

In the early (1970) infra-red line-scan images Ken showed me, light areas were warm, and dark represented cold. Thus, where lights were visible in the roof of a building they showed up as emitting heat. Ken added with a chuckle that, at low level, cows were warmer at the rear! Later, as in the Post-Attack Airfield Damage Reconnaissance Exercise *"Keswick"*, the imagery from the Infra-Red Linescan was transmitted in "real time" to a ground viewing and recording base, where it could be studied by the officer in charge of Airfield Damage repair. The WA-117 also carried a vertical aerial camera. A WA-116 fitted with low-light video recording showed promise, and it could also have been equipped for real-time imagery transmission. Originally, the infra-red "eye" had to be cooled in flight by liquid nitrogen. Later, the eye was cooled by air, pressurised at 4,500 psi. Such an air bottle could be readily re-charged, whereas liquid nitrogen has storage problems.

Wallis WA-117 at Royal Aircraft Establishment Farnborough, in front of Cody's Tree - March 1987 - prior to Exercise *"Keswick"*. Carrying Infra-Red Line Scan and real-time imagery transmission to 70mm reconnaissance camera in VLO mode.

Ken was invited to participate in several other military exercises to test the autogyro in battle conditions, such as the Aerial Quick Deployment Exercise *"Green Lanyard"*, with the WA-116 being flown into the STANTA battle training area in Norfolk within a C-130 Hercules aircraft. He was in the company of a 1 tonne truck, a Land Rover and 42 armed Ghurka soldiers of the 5th Infantry Brigade. They took off from Sculthorpe and landed at Watton. Ken then took off from there, operating from the Brigade HG, and landing, for instance, at a forward HQ on the Mundford-Thetford Road between the trees.

On Exercise *"Gryphons Gold"*, held in the same area in November 1983, he flew the WA-116 and WA-122 autogyros (both again being flown at Netheravon) and the first take-off site was a playing field at West Tofts. He then moved to a flinty path where the aircraft could be hidden in the trees a mile or so further north in the Battle Area. Later in the exercise, the HQ was set up at Smokers Hole, near Frog Hill, and he operated from a road there, plus various other roads near "critical points" to which he took senior officers on the WA-122 two-seater.

By then Ken had flown many different aircraft but he was particularly pleased to take control of the Skyship SK-600-01 airship over Bedfordshire on the 2nd August 1990, during a visit arranged by the Royal Aeronautical Society. He recalls that it was difficult not to progress forward in a "corkscrewing" flight path and this worried him but then found that the same was achieved when the Captain regained control so he did not feel too bad.

Top: Ken at the controls of the SK 600-01 airship nearing Cardington.
(Photograph: A W L Nayler, RAeS)
Bottom: The airship when tethered.

219

The lure of the autogyro

'Experiment! Experiment! Flying machines are possible so that a man may sit in the middle of them, turning some device by which artificial wings may beat the Air!' Roger Bacon (1214 - 1294)

Nature probably invented the first autogyro in the creation of the seed from the Sycamore tree but the principle was not understood by mankind until much later. Around 1320, toys with a rotor based upon windmill sails were sent spinning up into the air by pulling upon a cord wound tightly around a stick. This was more than 160 years before Leonardo Da Vinci drew his famous "helicopter" with a helical-screw instead of rotor blades. Even earlier however, in the 4th Century BC, the ancient Chinese were recorded as having a form of "flying top" toy made of feathers that would levitate when rubbed between two hands or by way of string wound around a stick.

Ken certainly has transformed nature's basic design with many innovative features and throughout the many difficult episodes his vision for the autogyro has never diminished. As a result of his development work, he has accumulated a personal fleet of nineteen aircraft at Reymerston Hall. Their practical utility has been amply demonstrated to major aerospace companies, the Home Office, scientific establishments and many other bodies.

The long train of unfulfilled liaisons would surely have crushed a lesser man but, whilst Ken's determination and total commitment to his design have never wavered, his patience must have been sorely tried. When examining all the qualities and issues associated with the modern autogyro it certainly comes across in a very positive way. It has inherent stability, is immune to stalling, flies in any wind condition, is simplicity itself in operation and a successful pilot would require in the region of only 35 hours tuition. All this must surely add up to an advertiser's dream.

For cost-effectiveness Ken's autogyros can do almost any task where the helicopter is too large and expensive to operate. They can operate to an altitude of around 20,000 feet and go undetected from the ground as engine noise can be very low. In addition, the whole machine can be easily loaded onto a lightweight trailer for road transport to a site where it can then be taxied under its own power with the rotor secured and turned on its own length, enabling access to confined areas. Ken has demonstrated autogyros from his fleet more times than he can count but on every occasion the spectators have never failed to be completely enthralled at the now famous "trademark" fast and low pass that has Ken sitting side-saddle on the airframe with arms and legs in the air!

It is worth noting that the airframe of an autogyro has no "lifed" parts apart from the rotor bearing but even that is good for 4,500 hours. The machines are safe in the event of an engine failure and of course "windmill" in operation all the time, which happens to be the "emergency mode" for a helicopter! A comparison therefore with the airflow principles of the helicopter is very illuminating and Ken explains the stability of the autogyro in simple terminology: *"the rotor blades form a shallow cone, with the weight of the machine at the point. In flight there is no downdraught, the air passes up through the rotor which is tilted back to allow this to happen; for example, a paper cone weighted like this will fall in a stable fashion if it is dropped. The blades of a helicopter also form a cone, and the weight is again at the point .... but .... this time the air flows down through the blades. Taking the paper cone model again, it has to be dropped point uppermost with the weight at the top where it is not at all stable".*

In making a comparison between autogyro and helicopter the question of hovering is bound to arise. Whilst the autogyro cannot hover as such, it can maintain height at very low speeds. Ken's first tiny two-seater, flown one-up, can maintain height at about 10 mph until the engine gets hot and loses power. It is possible to pull the forward stick back to zero but this results in a high rate of descent. The aircraft almost asks if you really want to fly like that, with forward stick loads suggesting the nose be dropped a little to regain speed. In practice, nearly all the working roles can be undertaken without hovering and any wind will provide "virtual hover".

The published wind limitation for the certificated WA.116 is 43 knots but Ken regards this to be very conservative because the machine is not wind-limited as such and poor weather operations are governed by the stamina of the pilot, not the efficiency of the autogyro. The altitude achieved by Ken of 18,516 feet was a personal record but would have been higher if he had not become too cold to continue. His summer clothing had been wet with perspiration before take-off and the oxygen system was not functioning properly on the day. He believes that 25,000 feet is possible. He held the World Record for altitude for some thirty years but lost it to Dr Bill Clem in 1998. He lived near Denver, Colorado - "the mile-high city" - so flew with a turbo-charged engine, primarily for take-off performance, whereas Ken's engine was naturally-aspirated.

When it comes to calculating the maximum fuel range for the one-man autogyro, really it is reached at the point the weight and drag prevents it from flying - even at quite high speed on the runway. The WA-116/F/S G-BLIK, with an old technology 2 cylinder 60 hp Franklin aero-engine, has yet to demonstrate its full potential. It has a 20-gallon long-range tank in addition to its internal tank of 13 gallons. In 1988, it took off in 120 yards from Waterbeach Airfield and completed ten laps of a 100 km closed circuit in 7 hours 40 minutes (some 623 miles) but the air miles flown were much greater.

The wind prevailing during the flight was recorded every half hour by nearby RAF Marham. The mean wind at 500 feet, the approximate height of the flight, was 13.9 knots - some 16 mph. This meant that some 122 miles were flown for nothing. The actual total of air miles flown was nearer 745, giving an average speed of about 97 mph. On completing the 1,000 kilometre closed circuit course there was still fuel in the tank for about one and a half hours and the aircraft had been getting faster as the weight reduced. This was the first ever 1,000 km flight by an autogyro in a closed circuit. Ken is sure that G-BLIK could take off with a greater fuel load and that 1,000 miles could be achieved in decent conditions. He had been aloft for 7 hours 40 minutes but this did not qualify for a Duration World Record.

Ken planned a further Record Flight around the same course in 1993, learning from the 1988 flight, but the C.A.A. medics (in Ken's words) *"got difficult"* even though he could easily do 10 minutes on the treadmill at RAF Hospital, Halton; the RAF Group Captain doctor said he had an exceedingly good exercise tolerance. Ken set further Records in 1998 aged 81 and 2002 aged 86.

Ken in G-BAHH ready for his "Time To Climb" Record attempt in 1998.

Closed cockpits and two-seaters

Ken has experimented with a closed cockpit version of the autogyro. He built WA-120 G-AYVO as a long-range model and it first flew in 1971. It has a 73 litre (16 Imp gallon) internal fuel tank and an economical Rolls-Royce 0-240 engine of 97kw (130hp). Heavier than the WA-116, the greater lifting capacity was exploited for specialised photography with a multi-band pack of four Vinten Type 360 cameras operating through narrow-band infiltration. This machine featured in the Science Museum's "Exploration" exhibition from 1976 to 1985, illustrating exploration of the surface of the Earth, and the use of the camera pack demonstrated by the pollution survey of Langstone Harbour conducted by the aircraft.

The benefits of the canopy are lost on Ken, however, because he complains of a loss of "sense of feel" in comparison to the open cockpit versions. He found also a need to read the airspeed indicator when approaching to land, something not required with the open versions. Importantly, in the working roles undertaken by the machines, clear vision is required and this is not possible through a Perspex canopy, let alone with dust or rain settling on it. Over the years he has evolved a windscreen shape that allows viewing the ground without even looking through the screen, or wearing goggles, but provides protection from the air-stream. If coupled with a liquid-cooled engine, with the radiator in the nose, there can be real pilot comfort in quite adverse conditions.

Ken points out that for a similar "purist" reason, the fully enclosed motorcycle has yet to be popular but his standard WA-116 design provides more comfort than the current "open" road machines. It does not mean, of course, that the enclosed version of the autogyro would not appeal to some people and, at one time, he even considered a four-seat cabin. Despite this, he remains convinced that the basic form, with a single seat, is best for the pilot in his operation of equipment whilst the machine maintains its own stable flight.

He firmly believes that the autogyro should gain its spurs in the working role before making a move towards nourishing a likely big market in the "sport and fun flying" niche. Even so, he would still remain greatly concerned should there be attempts to modify the design by a minority of enthusiastic but unqualified new owners. With only one Wallis autogyro outside of Ken's ownership (with Nigel de Ferranti), Ken has steadfastly refused to supply amateur builders with drawings or plans of his aircraft for fear that they would attempt to modify his design and come to grief as a result. He considers the responsibility too great to take chances

Ken has two open-frame two-seater autogyros and the first was G-AXAS, the McCulloch-engine WA-116-T. The experience gained contributed to the design of WA-122 G-BGGW, which is fitted with a 97kw Rolls-Royce engine. It provides more room for the rear occupant and has been a very useful dual-control, pilot conversion trainer. The special low-speed properties of these machines when flown solo, combined with the unimpaired visibility and absence of down-wash, produced ability to tackle other tasks. One was to search near Basingstoke in September 1980 for part of the turbine disc from a McDonnell Douglas F-18 Hornet fighter prototype that had crashed at the SBAC Show nearby at Farnborough. Although this particular search was not successful, on another occasion Ken successfully located a lost bull calf for its grateful owner and mother!

A rather different machine in the stable is the WA-118 Meteorite, G-AVJW, powered by an Italian Meteor-Alfa four-cylinder supercharged radial two-stroke of 89.kw (120 hp), and designed for extreme high altitude capability.

G-AYVO with multi-band camera pack

224

Top: G-AXAS - a minimal two-seater in 1969.
Bottom: G-BGGW with a 130hp Rolls-Royce engine.

More investigation work and film roles

For the detailed search and remote sensing roles, the autogyro has an important advantage over the helicopter in not having any downwash to blow dust into the air, damage crops or frighten cattle. Being always in the "emergency mode" (auto-rotation) of a helicopter and naturally stable, the pilot can also concentrate fully upon the search or equipment operation. The small price paid for these benefits is the need for a short take-off but even shorter landing run, rather than the vertical capability of the helicopter.

In 1969 Ken worked in collaboration with British Aircraft Corporation at Stevenage on a possible military role for a remote-piloted helicopter, required to carry Infra-Red Line Scan. This was a private venture by BAC in the hope of a Ministry of Defence contract and he recalls that this gave him his first opportunity for night-flying with the, then, quite new Hawker Siddeley Dynamics IRLS at the Bovingdon Tank Training Area. A period of flight testing followed and included take-offs and landings in G-AVJV at a playing field by the lights of a car, employing an open-shutter vertical F-24 camera over a strobe-light source on the ground for vibration assessment and analysis, and acoustic recording.

Other testing included recording pitch attitude over a wide speed range, and checking control response and stability. Control input transducers and three-axis rate gyros were fitted, the resulting data being stored on an Admiralty Recorder. The "Concorde" Mobile Acoustics Laboratory was moved to Shipdham Airfield in Norfolk for around five days as part of a series of comprehensive tests and these resulted in a 38-page report. This was able to prove that the WA-117 could not be detected above the ambient noise level of the Norfolk countryside at 3,500 feet vertical, or 3,000 feet horizontal.

Despite excellent results, he believes that the military contract went to Canadair with their "dumb-bell" shaped, un-manned helicopter. An unusual choice, considering that line-scan picture production did not call for a vehicle to have the ability to hover. Although this particular venture did not produce the results he would have liked, his happy relationship with BAC lasted for some three to four years.

In consequence, however, the results of the acoustic report meant that WA-117 G-AVJV was accepted for use in the summer of 1970 for the Loch Ness Investigation Bureau's search for the "monster", with several cameras mounted on the airframe. The procedure followed was to patrol the 24 miles of water at 60 knots, flying at between 4,000 feet and 5,000 feet, when he was able to see just below the loch's surface. The creature managed to go undetected of course but if it had been an insect-eating variety then perhaps the bright colour and size of *"Little Nellie"* might otherwise have been bait to lure *"Big Nessie"* from the depths!

Several of Ken's machines are specifically designed for "remote sensing" operations, carrying Infra-Red, Line-Scan Multi-Spectral cameras, Gamma Ray Spectrometers, etc. His extensive day and night testing of Hawker Siddeley Dynamics Type 212 Infra-Red, Line-Scan photographic equipment during 1970-71 has already been covered. From 1972 Ken undertook extensive aerial photography and survey work on behalf of the Nature Conservancy Board. The varied roles which can be addressed by his autogyros include surveying coastal ecology, detection of hidden objects, leaks in water pipelines, harbour pollution by seaweed, water surface temperatures and detection of military targets.

By early 1975, G-AXAS, G-AVJV and G-ASDY had made 367 flights in an experimental programme carried out by Plessey Radar for the Home Office's Police Scientific Development Branch at Sandridge in Hertfordshire. Carrying a platform, mounting four downward looking multi-spectral cameras, its task was to detect illicit graves by "false colour" photography. Using this equipment, the Sussex Downs were scanned by a Wallis autogyro during the big police hunt for Lord Lucan many years ago, as were parts of the Devon Coast in the search for clues to the disappearance of Mrs Pat Allan of Salcombe on 9th September 1976 and referred to earlier. She went missing with her two children near Kingsbridge in Devon and the police wanted an area of the Hanger Mill Valley and nearby cliffs searched. The task was done using the Plessey multi-band photo pack with nothing being detected during the four flights made. It was thus a positive result.

Interestingly, whilst being escorted to the take-off site by a police car, Ken had to stop to let another vehicle pass in the narrow lane. The driver of the car was John Allen, the husband of the missing woman and a suspect - a woman passenger was said to be his girlfriend. In December 2002 he was convicted of the three murders and jailed as a result of information revealed in a book written by the same woman in 1992, which was investigated by *The Sunday Telegraph*. Allen had faked his own death at Beachy Head in the 1960s to rid himself of his first family and moved north, marrying Patricia in 1968. The fate of Mrs Allen and the children was never discovered.

In 1977, G-ASDY undertook a multi-spectral survey of Langstone Harbour in collaboration with the new Plessey Radar Research Centre but further problems with the Franklin engine taxed his skills. On one flight over the water he noticed a very low fuel pressure being indicated so promptly used the hand pump to pressurise the fuel tank. He managed a safe landing and, on investigating, soon found the cause of the problem. According to Ken, the spring in the *"tatty and rather inadequate crankcase breather valve"* had failed. This adversely affected the crankcase pressure changes operating the fuel pump; it also allowed venting of the lubricating oil. He managed a quick "bodge" on site by using the spring from a *"Biro"* ballpoint pen!

After that incident, he installed mechanically driven fuel pumps on all the Franklin engines with the pump being driven be a flexible connection from the camshaft tachometer connection. He also made titanium reed valves to replace the standard, and obviously marginal, system.

It is worth recording here that another problem was to occur when Franklin introduced, in 1972 under Service Bulletin No 115, a replacement oil pick-up pipe assembly. This incorporated a large perforated plate intended to prevent the oil foaming and surging in the sump, and he duly fitted the new parts. In 1985, however, he was flying G-ASDY for a C.I.D. Police search when he detected fluctuating oil pressure in the gauge so returned home with caution. A strip-down of the oil sump revealed that the perforated "anti-foaming" plate had cracked along a line of perforations and that some of the broken parts had come into contact with the camshaft drive gears.

He checked the other engines and detected cracks in the perforated plates attached to the end of the oil pick-up pipe so they must have been subjected to vibration. The cure was simple. He cut away the plate from the pick-up pipe, refitting the pipe. He then made perforated plates of titanium, the edges of which were folded so that they could be bolted to the sides of the sump. The oil pick-up pipe then passed down through a suitably placed hole in the perforated plate.

Ken also carried out air-to-air filming of radio-controlled aircraft models for the popular television series *"The Pathfinders"*. This series depicted the exploits of the RAF Pathfinder Force of Bomber Command during World War II and was due to be made in 1971. The Aviation Consultant was Group Captain Hamish Mahaddie, who had been a prime figure in the actual force. The operators of helicopters were not keen to undertake filming in the presence of models as they could easily slip out of sight and possibly collide with their tail-rotor, or cause other hazards.

Ken was required to fly with a fixed, forward-looking cine-camera, following a model Lancaster bomber with a 12 feet wingspan when it took off and climbed to around 2,000 feet. It was then possible to shoot a scene with a German pilot's view of the "Lancaster" as it attacked from behind. Hits were recorded before it burst into flames and fell to earth. Such scenes and "beat ups" of the home airfield were all satisfactorily filmed from Ken's minimal, open-framed, two-seat WA-116-T/Mc G-AXAS flown solo.

During 1978 and 1979, he worked on his last film - *"The Martian Chronicles"* - on location in Malta and the Canary Islands. The two-seater G-AXAS was again flown solo and appeared as *"Zeus 3"*, exploring the surface of Mars in the film that portrayed the third manned mission to that planet. The actors Rock Hudson and Bernie Casey starred. Ken carried cameras up to 35mm Panavision for most of the air-to-ground scenes that provided a pilot's point of view, and Ken replaced actors in the film's flying sequences. Filming took place in Malta during October and November 1988, and Lanzarote in February 1989. Ken had got the job at the suggestion of John Stears, Special Effects Supervisor on many Bond films.

A very early big-screen experience for Ken had been a non-starring part in the memorable comedy film *"Those Magnificent Men In Their Flying Machines"* of 1961. (In the singular, perhaps the title of the film aptly sums up Ken!) He received a call in October 1965 from Air Commodore Alan Wheeler who was the Aviation Consultant - he explained that all the replica, old-time aircraft in the film used similar engines so sounded alike. He asked if Ken could make an autogyro "cough and splutter" to provide more appropriate sound effects. Ken replied that they did that for much of the time so would be happy to help.

He took G-ARRT to Booker on the 13th October and made three flights around the sound recorders, adjusting the throttle to the misfiring position. The recordings were duly made and then played back at a slower speed on the soundtrack to be in accord with the early aero-engines. Alan Wheeler had flown autogyros in the RAF during World War II and he asked Ken what it was like to fly the WA-116. Ken duly briefed him and Alan was soon in the air, clearly enjoying himself during the fifteen- minute flight.

The film employed a mix of both original and replica aircraft, and several of these can be seen in the air and on the ground at the Shuttleworth Collection,

Old Warden Aerodrome in Bedfordshire. It is a marvellous place to visit and has many of the surviving aircraft from the pioneering age through to World War II. I am very pleased to be a Life Member of the support society.

A more serious assignment was carried out in 1981 G-ASDY completed a colour stereo-photographic survey of the Broadlands area of Norfolk and Suffolk in three, two-hour flights. The work was for the Institute of Terrestrial Ecology and undertaken with a vertical Vinten Type 360 reconnaissance camera, having a 6 inch lens and automatic exposure control. In 1983 he undertook special aerial photography for the Saudi Arabian Ports Authority in Jeddah and Damman with WA-117/R-R, G-AVJV.

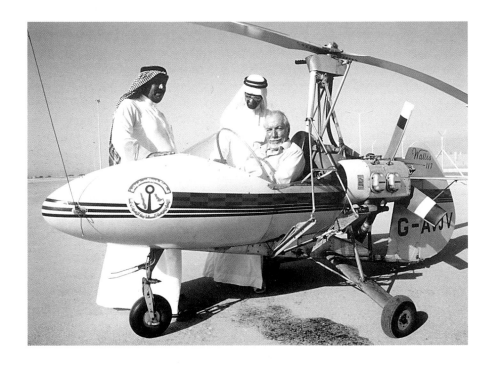

Ken in Saudi Arabia with the Ports Authority

Top: G-AVJV with antenna for lowering beneath the aircraft in flight, linked to a visual display unit in the cockpit, when trailing suspect vehicles.
Bottom: G-AXAS fitted with an experimental electro-statically charged, ultra-low volume crop-spraying system.

Top: WA-122 G-BGGW with long-focus camera fitted; ideal for border surveillance work.
Bottom: With stereo radar for detection of buried objects such as land mines.

Photography – the early years

In view of the numerous photographic assignments, plus work in television and cinema, it is perhaps not surprising to find that Ken has always had a keen interest in photography. Turning back the pages of the family history brings to light that this may have had something to do with the fact that his parents met through a shared interest in photography.

Prior to marriage, Ken's mother was Miss Emily May Barker, a schoolteacher in Cambridge. On one particular day in 1910 she had cause to be very annoyed when all her pupils disobeyed her orders and rushed to the window to watch a Pratts Motor Spirit horse-drawn van pass by, pulling a strange flying machine with folded wings. Emily was a very keen amateur photographer and some time later, at a meeting of the Cambridge & District Photographic Society, the schoolteacher by chance met one Horace Wallis. On learning of his interest in aviation she mentioned the earlier event and discovered he was the culprit, and the cause of the classroom revolt. Despite the circumstances of their first encounter, love obviously blossomed for they married in 1912 and produced young Ken in 1916!

Although an amateur, Ken's mother was a successful and artistic portrait photographer and he can just remember, when quite young, dressing up in all sorts of outfits for her. He also recalls, with a smile, that he often failed to sit still for the obligatory 10 seconds whilst the lens cap was removed, and was scolded on several occasions when the developed plate showed a blurred image. Ken still has many examples of her excellent work. One of these appears within the publication *"The Amateur Photographer & Photography"* for 6 January 1936. It is titled *"Little Pierrot"* and he was then 8 or 9 years of age when posed - he must surely have hoped at the time that it would not be seen by any of his classmates in view of the costume worn.

Many other portraits by her appeared in this publication, and the edition for 11 September 1911 also contained a glowing tribute to her, ending with the following description which is rich in contemporary language: *'An ordinary room (a kitchen), with two windows at right angles to each other, forms her studio. Like many other successful workers, she finds that if one is striving after a pictorial result it is false economy to spare plates. Consequently, each subject receives many exposures before the really satisfactory result is secured. She pays great attention to the drapery of her sitters, endeavouring always to make every part of the picture subordinate to the face. She is a strong advocate of straight photography, and prints mostly in carbon, but confesses that recently the fascination for bromoil has appealed to her'.* She died in 1947.

Artistic ability has passed on to Ken as already mentioned. Ken's father was also a very able sketch artist. Many subjects have interested Ken sufficiently to produce water-colours and sketches, including ships of all types, and even their interiors. Around 1937 Ken designed a large roadside sign for Ely and it was adopted by the Council. It depicts the cathedral with a "Welcome to the City of Ely" message.

The humble camera had not escaped Ken's inventiveness prior to linking them to his autogyro work. In 1942 he acquired parts of an early 35mm camera; it employed 4cm diameter film spools and could feed un-perforated film which gave a larger than standard 35mm format. Rebuilding it with a new outer body, lens and shutter, plus a coupled split-image rangefinder was technically challenging. On completion it proved very useful in the air and on the ground, albeit that he had to accept the intrusion of perforations in the picture from the bulk strips of the early 35 mm film available in those days.

He went on to design a 16mm cine film camera in 1945 with a capacity for over 100 shots through a focal plane shutter providing anything from 1/1000th of a second to time exposures. This was determined entirely by the way in which the release was pressed; the intention was to achieve the maximum film/lens assembly in the minimum size. It was a true "spy" camera and enabled photographs to be taken without setting a shutter speed in the conventional way; it could be worn on a strap on the inside of the wrist or concealed within clothing and activated very easily. It measures no more than 2½ inches long. The definition of photographs taken was (and is) quite stunning, and it can be used with equal confidence for aerial shots of buildings or simply for close-up, table-top work. Ken even used it when a Specialist Armaments Officer in the post-war RAF to record such things as bomb "hang-up" problems in an aircraft's bomb bay.

His role in the RAF at that time usually resulted in research, design and development postings and photography had an important part to play in this work. High-speed cine cameras would record destruction of running jet engines as attempts were made to find the best way to destroy jet bombers. Ken made a special pinhole camera in order to photograph scale models of enemy aeroplanes at different angles and distances. From a graticule included within a photograph, and representing the dispersion of fragments

234

from the warhead of an anti-aircraft weapon, it was a simple process to assess damage at a given range and angle of warhead detonation.

It was not until 1957, whilst in Japan on an exercise with the Strategic Air Command USAF, that he purchased his first modern 35mm camera. His technical expertise in this field was later to be put to very good use in his development of the autogyro for different photographic roles. As early as 1961, the prototype G-ARRT was in use as a photographic platform, sometimes for pure photography and on other occasions for aircraft test recording. Helmet-mounted and fixed 16mm cine cameras were used, backing up strain-gauging and performance trials for certification.

Larger format cameras were his next attraction, starting with the modification of a hand-held ex-Luftwaffe aerial camera using unusual film 8cm wide, with perforation for winding on; the picture format was 7x9cm. Ken adapted it to take a rubber-covered friction roller in place of sprockets for winding on, and manufactured a roller/cutter device for the dark room so that he could reduce the large format aerial film, minus sprocket holes, to the required size. As aerial cameras are set only for infinity, a focusing screw mounting was required for the f2 Schneider Xenon lens. He mounted a 45-degree surface silvered mirror on one of the two capping doors in the camera body which, together with some suitably inserted frosted glass, provided through-the-lens reflex focusing.

Top: an unsuspecting work colleague is captured by Ken's "spy" camera
Bottom: A montage to show the size of the camera and the superb definition
achieved for both a close-up of a coin and an aerial view of Ely Cathedral.

Reproducing the *"Wallbro"* monoplane

In 1973 Ken and his cousin Geoffrey - son of the co-builder of the original aeroplane - decided that the pioneering work undertaken by their fathers deserved to be recalled in a tangible way and set out to build a replica of their *"Wallbro"*. There was a problem, however: no drawings or details existed and he had only contemporary photographs to work from. Using his considerable engineering skills, and knowing the height of his father who was pictured alongside the aeroplane in several shots, he calculated the most likely dimensions, overall configuration, and even the steel tube (1" 20 gauge) used in its construction. The original tube had been supplied by Accles & Pollock and, on making contact, the company readily agreed to produce a quantity for the replica.

A number of other companies were similarly generous in their help and support. Items such as the original lugs made by Chater Lea were no longer available, however, so it was necessary to make about 100 by nickel-bronze brazing pieces of 1 inch internal diameter steel tube. Tootal Fabrics also provided for free a quantity of cotton calico fabric deemed "seconds" which was perfect for the job.

It is interesting to note that about the time the original *"Wallbro"* was under construction, Accles & Pollock was busy building The Seddon Biplane at Oldbury in Worcestershire, a novel aircraft of wholly tubular steel arrangement designed by Lt. J W Seddon R.N. and A G Hackett. Nicknamed *"The Mayfly"*, it was a six-seat, tandem biplane and the world's largest aeroplane at that time. This fantastic structure comprised 2,000 feet of steel tubing arranged as intersecting hoops or geodetics, and was powered by two 65 h.p. N.E.C. engines that drove a pair of Beedle tractor propellers. Unfortunately, it was tested at the Dunstall Park, Wolverhampton, flying ground of the Midland Aero Club late in 1910 but failed completely to emulate its name and was later broken up without having left the ground!

Working with his cousin Geoffrey, the task took some five years to complete and numerous problems had to be solved en route. The choice of engine was largely dictated by the spacing of the frame tubes in the fuselage and as a search for a suitable J.A.P. engine did not produce any leads, Ken turned to a de-rated and converted McCulloch drone engine. It fitted perfectly within the space and was lighter and more powerful than the original so did the job very well. It produced around 60 h.p. consuming 100 octane-plus fuel and only a little of the power was needed, although extra weights had to be added in order to maintain the centre of gravity.

During all this building activity there was one particular heart-stopping moment. Ken received an unexpected telephone call from a cousin living near Exeter to say that she was the daughter of his youngest uncle Garnet. She had spotted that he was booked to display *"Little Nellie"* at The Royal Devon Show and this had caused her to remember a poster advertising the original *"Wallbro"*. She met him at the show - their first meeting - to hand over the document, and returned the following day with some Royal Flying Corps engine manuals that had belonged to his uncle who had served as an engineer in the RFC during World War One.

Some days later, Ken opened one of the manuals and out fell a newspaper clipping from the Cambridge Daily News for 12th May 1910. His initial excitement quickly changed to concern when he saw that it was an expertly written article, providing a mass of technical information about the aeroplane and including such gems as the tube gauge. Once digested, however, he was very relieved to find that he had calculated everything correctly - even to guessing a suitable gauge for the wall thickness of the 1 inch steel tube - so work had not been wasted and the reconstruction could continue as planned. Importantly, he also had answers for those parts still to be made.

The article by the reporter on his visit to see *'the light and graceful machine built at 12 St. Barnabas Road - the first in Cambridge'* went into incredible detail and was an invaluable source for Ken; it even mentioned the width of the wheel hubs and major dimensions to half an inch. Some of the descriptions of the construction employed on the aircraft now make somewhat quaint reading:

'very elegant .... altogether a pretty piece of work .... an ingenious little arrangement'. The report went on to note that *'with the exception of the engine, tractor, magneto and carburetter, the whole of the machine has been built by Mr. Percy Valentine Wallis and Mr. Horace Samuel Wallis of 12 Barnabas-road, Cambridge, two gentlemen well-known in motor cycle racing circles whose successes last year at the Mammoth Show and other motor cycle races in various parts of the country will be remembered.. The engine was tested for a few minutes yesterday and ran splendidly. It proved to be a very easy starter, going off at the first pull of the tractor over compression after the right mixture of gas and air had been found. It very quickly developed a good rate of speed and gave every promise of being capable of*

sending the machine along at a good 40 miles per hour. The power of the engine, although it was never witnessed at full throttle, was evidenced by the way the "Wallbro" tugged and strained at the ropes that held it down to the ground'.

In August 1978, Ken flew the replica *"Wallbro"* Monoplane (G-BFIP c/n WA.1) at RAF Swanton Morley, Norfolk, and the first flight covered about a mile. It achieved an altitude of between 20 to 30 feet and speed of 30 mph. The aircraft later flew on circuits of the airfield and Ken was pleased to note that it had much performance to spare. The original newspaper article in 1910 had concluded that *'the "Wallbro" was a fine piece of work..... with a number of novel ideas'*. A view still held by Ken and many others.

The original aeroplane was clearly ahead of its time in several respects but, sadly, is under-reported in both contemporary and modern journals charting the history of aviation in this country. By building the replica, Ken has therefore ensured that the family's pioneering exploits are now better publicised and also acknowledged - albeit many years after the event. To celebrate the flight, the Stakis Hotel (as it was then called - previously The Ambassador Hotel and now the Hilton) at Norwich Airport opened its new restaurant in November 1989 and named it *"The Wallbro"*.

The aircraft now resides on permanent display at the Norfolk & Suffolk Aviation Museum in Flixton, following many years in the hangar at Shipdham Airfield. Ken made a mock-up of the original, and very rare J.A.P. engine, by fitting silencers of much the same shape as the cylinders of the original on to the McCulloch engine. In 1999 I did manage to track down one of three contemporary J.A.P. engines thought to exist to a company in Wolverhampton - it came to light having been placed on loan and displayed for a time at the Cosford Aerospace Museum nearby - but, unfortunately, it was not possible to acquire it.

Some other members of Ken's family also had links with aviation. His cousin Basil for example - six years his senior who had flown for Imperial Airways prior to World War II. He was an instructor in Rhodesia during the war, and continued flying with Marshall of Cambridge afterwards. His uncle Percy's next son (Bob) flew in the RAFVR but was killed early in World War II at Brize Norton when his Harvard I suffered aileron flutter and both wings came off. The youngest brother (Ken's cousin Geoffrey) - twelve years younger than Ken – had joined the Parachute Regiment after World War II and served in Palestine during the time of the Stern Gang bombing of the King David

Hotel, etc. He had long held a Pilot's Licence until grounded on medical reasons but his son, Nigel, took over and flew both helicopters and fixed wing aircraft. Ken's son and daughters (David, Vicky and Elizabeth) have not followed him into aviation so there is no natural heir to continue his work. Only a commercial contract with a suitably qualified company to build his autogyro design, in line with Ken's direction, will therefore ensure the future of his design and continued development.

The completed *"Wallbro"* Monoplane.

Top: Ken poses next to *"The Wallbro"*.
Bottom: Airborne at RAF Swanton Morley.

241

Achievements and official recognition

It was back in 1968 that Ken's thoughts had first turned to establishing some World Records with the autogyro and since then he has amassed a remarkable collection. To-date, he has been awarded 24 Diplomas in respect of 34 separate World Records set in two classes of autogyro: Class E3 (Any autogyro) and Class 3a (Autogyro under 500 Kilos all up weight) between 1968 and 1998. The complete list of World Records ratified by the Federation Aeronautique Internationale is included as an appendix.

His penultimate World Record - Time-to-Climb to 3,000 metres - was first set on 19th March 1998 flying G-BAHH but he had not actually intended to do this because he was carrying fuel and oxygen equipment for altitude. He had to give up at 18,976 feet because cloud had by then obscured the ground and he was concerned about making a safe descent. Ken was aged 81 at this time and this feat entered the Guinness Book Of Records for being achieved by the oldest pilot to set a World Record in aviation. He had previously appeared in this publication through his speed, altitude and distance records.

Back in 1981 a small but unusual tribute was paid to Ken when he was featured on a philatelic collectors' flown cover. A quantity was taken on board a Gazelle helicopter from RAF Northolt to his home in Norfolk as part of the Royal Air Force Museum's Day of Aero-Philately and Michael Fopp was the employee courier; he is presently Director General of the Royal Air Force Museums. On many occasions Ken has himself flown with aviation postal covers on board to commemorate an event. He also received another unusual tribute when a photograph of him in an autogyro, over-flying the static *"Wallbro"*, was used for the frontispiece of the 1985-6 edition of *Jane's Aircraft* to commemorate the 75th Anniversary of the flight of the historic monoplane.

In September 1998, Ken made an unexpected non-flying return visit to the influential trade show at Farnborough. The SBAC invited him to provide a machine for inclusion in the static display area for historic aircraft that had been featured in past events. Whilst there, Ken was engaged in many discussions with interested visitors to the show but no doubt his thoughts would have wandered back to the tragic event, all those years ago, that had so unfairly tainted the reputation of his design.

By the mid-90s, Ken had received an impressive collection of prestigious awards for his work:

1963 - The Alan Marsh Medal - The Royal Aeronautical Society and The Helicopter Association of GB
1969 - The Segrave Trophy - The Royal Automobile Club and The Royal Aeronautical Society
1973 - The Breguet Trophy - The Aero Club de France and The Royal Aero Club
1975 - The Silver Medal - The Royal Aero Club
1975 - The Rose Trophy - The Helicopter Club of Great Britain
1980 - Honorary Fellowship - Manchester Polytechnic
1982 - The Reginald Mitchell Medal - Stoke on Trent Association of Engineers
1984 - The Rose Trophy - The Helicopter Club of Great Britain
1985 - The Segrave Trophy - The Royal Automobile Club and The Royal Aeronautical Society
1989 - The Salomon Trophy - The Royal Aero Club
1995 - The Rotorcraft Gold Medal - Federation Aeronautique Internationale

It did not stop there, though.

1996. National applause was at last forthcoming and he attended an investiture at Buckingham Palace to be made a Member of the Order of the British Empire for services to aviation. Many people feel that the Honour was long overdue, and that it should have been of much higher status.

1997. This year he received an Honorary Doctorate of Engineering from The University of Birmingham.

1998. During the 1998 European Symposium of the Society of Experimental Test Pilots, HRH Prince Andrew, himself an accomplished Royal Navy helicopter pilot, conferred Honorary Fellowship of the Society upon Ken for Lifetime Achievement as an aeronautical engineer, pioneering the many uses of autogyros.

May 1999. On the 11th he was again honoured and this time it was by The Air League with the Special Award for record-breaking autogyro developments - this was presented to him by HRH Prince Philip at the 90th Anniversary Convention of the Air League held in St. James' Palace.

November 1999. At an Awards' Banquet in Guildhall, in the City of London, Ken was presented with the 1998 Sir Barnes Wallis Medal from the Guild of Air Pilots And Air Navigators by HRH Prince Philip. This was for his exceptional contribution to aviation over more than 50 years - in particular in the design, development and operation of autogyros.

2003. Honorary Ph.D conferred by the Hofstra University, Hempstead, New York - more of this later.

2005. The Pilcher Memorial Lecture Medal awarded by Glasgow University.

2006. Received Honorary Fellowship of the Institute of Transport Administration in October.

This list shows very clearly that there has been steady recognition by aviation, engineering and academic bodies, both here and abroad, for Ken's considerable skills and achievements, plus his major contribution to the science of aviation over many years of dedicated pioneering work in a specialised and difficult field.

A rather different kind of tribute commenced back in 1997 with the Annual Wallis Days, initiated by Rotor Gazette International and now sponsored by the British Rotocraft Association. This unique 2-day event is held in recognition of Ken's pivotal role in the development and popularisation of the autogyro. The weekend attracts many autogyro and light helicopter owners, and enthusiasts, to Shipdham Airfield very near Ken's home. Ken himself "flies in" and provides a short demonstration, then spends much of the time exchanging views and answering questions with those present. Several visits are then organised to his hangar at Reymerston Hall, and the evening usually finds Ken talking for hours to the assembly in the clubhouse.

Ken's fleet of autogyros at Reymerston Hall

244

Top: G-BLIK with World Record diplomas and trophies.
Bottom: Ken beside G-ATHM, the autogyro that made the record-setting flight from Lydd to Wick.

Top: Ken proudly holding The Salomon Trophy
Bottom: Ken having fun!

What of the new millennium?

When I first included this chapter the millennium was young and it was easy to log what Ken was doing, and events, as they occurred. It is now 2007 and I have had to reconsider its purpose and avoid simply copying Ken's diary. I decided to leave the pages devoted to the earlier years but have then been selective. Frankly, I find that Ken is too busy to keep tabs on!

oOo

It is good to report that Ken can still be found demonstrating his beloved autogyros, clocking up over 40 flying hours a year, and often as a result of undertaking specific tasks. A small selection of events follows.

In May 2000 Ken carried the Royal Air Forces' Association Millennium Scroll from his home to RAF Watton for an official handover. Also on board was a postal cover to celebrate the 90th Anniversary of the completion of the original *"Wallbro"* Monoplane. In the July, Ken opened the 28th meeting of the Vintage Gliding Club, with a nine-day long "Vintage Glide 2000" event at Tibenham in Norfolk, and he went on to give a spirited flying display.   He also undertook his almost annual aerial photography exercise for the Norfolk & Suffolk Aviation Museum of their 8-acre site at Flixton, to use in publicity leaflets.

In the June, Ken responded to the Museum's request for aerial photographs of the Bungay/Flixton airfield nearby, to send to USAAF veterans of the resident 446th Bomb Group during World War II, plus detailed shots of the Museum's land for use in support of grant applications to erect a second hangar. Flying G-ASDY, his vertical line, overlap shots in 35mm were superb.

Towards the end of the year, Ken was busily flight-testing a number of his autogyros for the renewal of their Permits to Fly and, very early into the New Year, he spoke to me about the possibility of further World Record attempts but no dates were set. With the demise of organisations such as the Royal Observer Corps, one problem he has experienced is finding acceptable persons to assist on the ground at turning points and suchlike.

The year also saw him accept the role of Honorary President of the Sky Watch Auxiliary Air Service, a Registered Charity. The aims of the organisation are very much in line with an important role Ken's sees for the autogyro: aerial observation. Pilots of light aircraft generally fly quite low so the idea is to get them to keep a lookout and call any incidents into Air Traffic Control for a 999 call then to the Emergency Services. This will hopefully prevent incidents becoming tragedies. Regular air observation patrols now make up the bulk of Air Watch flying and this unique British initiative is the largest voluntary air observation service in Europe. "Eco-light" two-seat micro aircraft are ideally suited for the work as, in addition to their practicality, they are cheap to operate, enabling Sky Watch pilots to fly more, train and expend flying time on patrols on behalf of the community. The aircraft use lead-free car petrol at about 10 litres an hour, compared with 60+ litres an hour "Avgas" leaded petrol of conventional aircraft. They also have a light noise footprint due to silencing and can be flown slowly and unobtrusively.

Ken has always been a fascinating subject for journalists and countless articles have been written about his exploits, plus he has been the subject of several television features and documentaries. His story never seems to end for he is mentioned in the press in one context or another almost weekly. Interest from the media in his flying machines continues to this day and with all ages, as was illustrated by a special report included within BBC1's *"Blue Peter"* young persons' programme on the 17th January 2001.

In January 2002, Ken was invited to attend the 40th Anniversary Luncheon at Pinewood Studios to celebrate forty years of James Bond films. The same month he delivered *"Little Nellie"* to the Bond film set once again but this time for a non-flying sequence. The suggestion was that the aircraft might appear within a scene in the latest film where the new "Q" (John Cleese) examined past equipment issued to James Bond.

January was quite an eventful month for it also produced a letter from the Hofstra University in Hempstead, New York, announcing that the Board of Trustees *'had enthusiastically and unanimously agreed'* to award Ken an Honorary Doctorate; the list of earlier outstanding recipients included George Bush Snr, Gerald Ford and Martin Luther King Jnr.

In February, an episode in the Channel 4 television series *"Salvage Squad"* covered the restoration of an autogyro and Ken was visited at home for an explanation of the type, plus the obligatory flying demonstration. The programme ended with Ken landing at the Duxford airfield of the Imperial War Museum in a two-seater to provide the means for the presenter (Lee

Hurst) to keep his promise to the team that he would take a flight with Ken if their restoration efforts were successful. As Ken landed, Lee promptly beat a very hasty retreat to everyone's amusement.

On September 14th, Ken went to Yorkshire and unveiled an impressive memorial to those who had served on his old station at Catfoss between 1929 and 1963.

On the 16th November, Ken beat his own World Record for Speed Over A Straight 3 km Course (1.9 miles) by achieving 207.7 kph (129 mph); his 1968 Record was for 193.6 kph. The day chosen turned out to be very foggy and on leaving Shipdham Airfield he had some difficulty locating the end of the course at Reymerston. In the circumstances, he did not do as well as he had hoped. We discussed the record in later weeks and Ken was confident that he could easily improve on the speed because he had chosen to fly the 31-year old, one-time altitude record holder WA-121/Mc G-BAHH. She was fitted with 16 feet diameter blades and he had done nothing to optimise the propeller for speed, or to lessen the drag of the undercarriage.

Ken said that he had decided to submit the claim *"simply to keep the flag flying"*. He considered that 200 mph could well be achieved with the dual engine machine he has in the back of his mind. This sounded very exciting and I dared to hope that it was already under construction in his workshop. However, it is really on the "back-burner" whilst other things occupy Ken.

In April 2003, he travelled to New York to attend the special symposium dedicated to the development of the autogyro, organised by the Hofstra University at Hempstead. He gave the keynote address before receiving an Honorary Ph.D in recognition of his contribution to the science of aviation. Ken's host during his stay, Dr Bruce H Charnov, undertook considerable research into the work of autogyro pioneers around the world for the event and has now published a book under the title *"From Autogiro To Gyroplane"* (ISBN 1567205038). This is a welcome addition to a somewhat sparsely occupied shelf on the subject in most bookcases.

In the summers of 2003 and 2004 I asked Ken to take aerial photographs of the Museum site, both prior to building work commencing on re-erecting a 1937 Boulton & Paul hangar - previously built by this local company on the site of the old Ipswich Airport - and following completion of the project. This he duly did and, for speed, dropped the finished film to us attached to a small parachute. This turned out to have been used in the Bond film *"You*

Only Live Twice" to carry aerial mines by *"Little Nellie"*, for dropping upon the SPECTRE helicopters. Needless to say, it was promptly accessioned into the collection at Flixton and placed on display!

May 2004 saw us both attending the Waddington Air Show weekend on the official stand of the British Rotorcraft Association where Ken had little time to rest. A constant stream of people queued to take his photograph, shake his hand, ask for his autograph, or buy a copy of the book, a signed Corgi die-cast model of *"Little Nellie"* or a personalised tee-shirt.

In the August he was invited to attend the Rolls-Royce Centenary event at Duxford Airfield so took along WA-117 G-AVJV, which has a Rolls-Royce engine. Interestingly, Ken had also attended the 50th and 75th Anniversary events and chuckled at remembering the former of the two. It had been held in Kensington Gardens, London, and his "self-built" Rolls-Royce *"The Long Dog"* won a trophy prize in the Silver Ghost & New Phantom section much to his surprise and pleasure.

Near the end of August there was the annual Wallis Days weekend fly-in event at Shipdham, which saw most attendees visit his hangar collection at Reymerston Hall. In September Ken, as our President, was at the annual Royal Observer Corps "At Home" Day event at Flixton, and *"Little Nellie"* was with him. Around 1,000 people attended and enjoyed numerous flypasts and a concert by a "big band", plus chatting with Ken. In November, Ken opened the week-long military history experience *"Anglia At Arms"* at Ecotech in Swaffham and made the closing speech.

2005 followed a very similar pattern but in the April we both attended the London Air Show at Earls Court where *Wallis Autogyros* had its own stand. The three days were tiring for us all in view of the constant stream of visitors, with most wishing to buy copies of this book and models of *"Little Nellie"*, speak to Ken or have their photograph taken with him. Ken is simply a magnet on these occasions and is treated by all ages with great reverence, respect, and even affection. It is something to behold in this day and age but I am sure his warm personality has much to do with it.

Ken was very pleased to have on the stand a half-scale, flying model of the *"Wallbro"*. This fine reproduction had been made by father and son Norman and Bob Brett of Nacton, following careful examination of Ken's replica at Flixton. Towards the end of the year, Ken went to Glasgow University to deliver the Pilcher Memorial Lecture, held in commemoration of aviator

Percy Pilcher (1867-1899), and was presented with the Pilcher Memorial Lecture Medal.

2006 started with Ken's wall calendar in his study already very busy with events; some being annual commitments but also with many new venues. On April 22, the Museum at Flixton held a special celebration for members and friends for Ken's 90th Birthday, and to commemorate the beginning of his 30th year as President. I think that Ken will choose to remember one and forget the other! A superb portrait of Ken, with many of the aircraft he has flown as a background, was painted in oils by John Constable Reeve (Museum Vice President) and presented on the day. A large cake was baked by member Jill Blythe with Ken reproduced in the icing. I was pleased to give a talk on Ken's early life, and some filming was undertaken by Diamond Eye Productions for inclusion in a planned DVD documentary on Ken's life.

Ken also celebrated his birthday in another way by taking his 90-year old friend Tony Cooper for a flight in G-BGGW. Tony was a Spitfire pilot in No.64 Squadron during World War II and lives at Oulton Broad, Norfolk. Ken summed up the day by saying *"You are as old as you feel. I intend to make a date to do this with Tony in 10 years time!"* Birthday celebrations continued with bellringers in his parish church, St. Peter's, ringing a quarter-peal dedicated to him. Ken was Patron of Reymerston Ringers millennium appeal to restore and re-hang five bells, and add a new treble.

Ken is often asked to participate in functions connected with James Bond films and one such event was the *"Bond Girls Are For Ever"* at Pinewood on the 2nd July. Ken willingly puts *"Little Nellie"* on display, signs autographs and rattles the collecting tins on these occasions. That week also saw him providing several flypasts locally, guiding parties of visitors around his hangar, and giving two talks. One being at Howden in Yorkshire celebrating the 70th Anniversary of the Wellington bomber. Ken said he was pleased to relate some of his flying experiences and say how grateful he was to Barnes Wallis, and the "Wimpy", for his continued existence, thanks to the wonderful geodetic structure employed.

On the 23rd July, Ken received a telephone call from RAF Marham, asking him to be outside his home between 13.55 and 14.00 as someone wanted to fly over and take a photograph. He was surprised and thrilled to see a Canberra escorted by Jaguar fighters perform a flypast in salute before they returned to Marham to end the last official flight of the Canberra - a truly wonderful aircraft with which Ken had a very close association.

Ken often appears on television for one reason or another and a new series on aviation and aviators featured him just before Christmas. The series was called *MARTIN SHAW - AVIATORS*, narrated by Stearman-owner/pilot and popular actor Martin Shaw. The opening episode included an interview with Ken and a look around his hangar. Shaw clearly found both Ken and his spirited demonstration of the autogyro quite remarkable. When the trademark "hands/feet off" flypast was performed he summed up the day with the words: *"just incredible!"* The series was shown on Discovery Realtime but is likely to reach other channels in due course.

The theme running throughout the episodes is the gradual rebuild of Shaw's beloved Stearman biplane following a catastrophic crash with another pilot at the controls. The work was undertaken by "friends-of-Flixton" Paul Bennett and Bob Sage who are based at Tibenham. The next episode featured another "Flixton friend" in Maurice Hammond and his aircraft, particularly the Mustang.

On the 10th December, Ken performed the unusual task of turning the first sod for the site of a state-of-the-art technology centre on the edge of Norwich. The launch of the centre at Thorpe St Andrew School promotes it to technology specialist status. Future pupils in North Norfolk schools will be able to design something on computer and send it to the centre, and video conferencing will enable them to watch the concept turn into a prototype which will then be sent back to them. Ken was the obvious choice in their minds as he is renowned for his engineering and inventing skills, and he also agreed to be Patron of the project. A leaflet about the project states *"These are qualities we hope to inspire in our students. We have no better role model as Patron"*.

I later discovered that Ken had similarly cut the first turf for the Norfolk Centre for Engineering Excellence at Hethel a year or two earlier and had forgotten to tell me. All in a day's work for Ken and just a small sample of the many and varied events that fill his very full life - when not providing tours of his hangar collection and building autogyros of course.

2007 so far has seen Ken very active with a busy calendar building, and being unselfish as ever with his time. He was sad to lose a friend and contemporary in Alex Henshaw - Supermarine's renowned test pilot. Ken had been out to lunch in Newmarket on the 16th February and noted that, whilst in good health himself, Alex seemed troubled about his pet dog. Alex passed away in his sleep a few days later aged 94.

Ken has been showered with honours and awards by national institutions and academic bodies both here and abroad; he is also greatly revered by a large proportion of the thinking general public in this country and overseas. Letters to me use expressions such as *"a True British Hero; a National Treasure"*. It would seem to this author, therefore, that whilst much of the U.K. population recognises his worth, role-model qualities and many international achievements, he might have been held in higher esteem by those responsible for authorising awards under the State honours' system if he had (mis)spent his youth by kicking a ball around the streets of Ely and joined a football club. Perhaps a large donation to a political party might also have clinched it!

Proper recognition for Ken's wartime flying exploits, and important post-war work whilst serving in the Royal Air Force, is now perhaps beyond appropriate recognition but there is still time to rectify the lamentable omission of a commensurate State honour for his distinguished service to this country. I take every opportunity that arises to pursue this and have not given up hope.

In view of the story so far, it would be disappointing for Ken's revolutionary autogyro designs to be found languishing in our museum in years to come, rather than under active manufacture and in the air where they belong. Preferably for Ken this would be in performing scientific and military tasks, certainly to begin with, rather than be considered solely for fun-flying or sport. Sadly, only *"Little Nellie"* has enjoyed mass production - by model-makers Airfix and Corgi; the latter as part of issues such as *The Definitive James Bond Collection*, with all the other models being cars. Unfortunately, and despite Ken pointing out the errors, all Corgi models are made without the all-important compression struts, and have reversed rotor blades.

Recognition of his aircraft for full commercial production is still Ken's dream and, for someone so determined, who knows what he will go on to accomplish during this millennium. Certainly, there has been renewed interest and some interesting approaches in recent times so a possible fifth edition of this book might have something to record on this. Ken's fertile mind and exceptional skills have combined to create a man of considerable achievement in two centuries - truly he is an engineer and aviator "extraord...in...(the!)...aire".

Top: Ken's usual pitch next to my Hunter FGA.9, with an admiring crowd.
Bottom: Together at Flixton - my Canberra T.4 to the left.

Top: Giving a lift to friend Tony Cooper in April 2006
Bottom: Arriving at Shipdham Airfield for the start of Wallis Days 2006.
Both courtesy of *Eastern Daily Press*.

A good portrait of Ken taken in his study during April 2002 for my "Pilot Biography" feature in the July edition of *Aeroplane (Ian Frimston/Fuji Lab)*

Ken with friend and fellow test pilot, the late Alex Henshaw MBE FRAeS, taken around 2004. Alexander Adolphus Dumfries Henshaw died in 2007 aged 94. *(Photo:Val Leggett)*

World Records

Date	Record Set	Performance	Type	Location
11.05.68	Altitude	4,639 metres	WA-116	Boscombe Down
12.05.69	Speed over 3 kilometres	179 km/hr	WA-116	Boscombe Down
13.07.74	Distance in closed circuit without landing	670.3 km	WA-116	RAF Coltishall
13.07.74	Speed over 500 kilometres closed circuit	126 km/hr	WA-116	RAF Coltishall
13.07.74	Speed over 100 kilometres closed circuit	130.7 km/hr	WA-116	RAF Coltishall
28.09.75	Non-stop distance in straight line	874.3 km	WA-116	Lydd - Wick
28.09.75	Duration+	6 hr 25 min	WA-116	Lydd - Wick
20.07.82	Altitude	5,644 metres	WA-121	Boscombe Down
14.08.84	Speed over 15 kilometres*	189.6 km/hr	WA-116	RAF Wyton
17.04.85	Speed over 100 kilometres closed circuit*	190.4 km/hr	WA-116	Waterbeach Airfield
18.09.86	Speed over 3 kilometres	193.6 km/hr	WA-116	RAF Marham
05.08.88	Speed over 1,000 kilometres closed circuit*	130.8 km/hr	WA-116	Waterbeach Airfield
05.08.88	Speed over 500 kilometres closed circuit*	134 km/hr	WA-116	Waterbeach Airfield
05.08.88	Distance in closed circuit*	1,003 km	WA-116	Waterbeach Airfield
06.12.90	Time to climb to 3,000 metres	8 min 8 sec	WA-121	RAF Swanton Morley
19.03.98	Time to Climb to 3,000 metres*	7 min 20 secs	WA-121	Shipdham Airfield
16.11.02	Speed over 3 kilometers*	207.7 km/hr	WA-121	Shipdham Airfield

These seventeen World Records count double because they were set in both Class E3 (Any autogyro) and Class 3a (Autogyro under 500 kilos all up weight). A total of 24 individual World Record Diplomas have been awarded to Ken by the FAI.

* Ken still holds these absolute World Records in both Classes of autogyro.

+ Although Ken no longer holds this Record, it could have been increased to 7 hours 50 minutes following the 1,000 km Closed Circuit Record (total time - not just on the circuit) but it seems that the F.A.I. no longer recognises such Duration Records, for reasons mentioned earlier in the text.

The Non-Stop Straight Line Distance Record is now held by Ken's Aussie friend Andy Keech who lives in Washington D.C. Andy now also holds the Altitude Record with a Rotax 914 turbo-charged engine of 120hp. Ken is pleased to comment that he has still flown further and faster!

Bibliography:

The Book of Westland Aircraft (A. H. Lukins) Harborough Publishing

British Flight Testing - Martlesham Heath 1920 - 1939 (Tim Mason)
Putnams
British Research and Development Aircraft (Ray Sturtivant)
Haynes Publishing Group
The Great Racers (Terry Gwynn-Jones) Guild Publishing

Helicopters And Autogiros (Charles Gablehouse) Fredk. Muller Ltd.

****

Suggested web sites to visit:

www.kenwallisautogyro.com.

www.aviationmuseum.net.

Aerial view of Flixton taken by Ken in 2004.

260